Under a Bad Sign

UNDER A BAD SIGN

Criminal Self-Representation in African American Popular Culture

JONATHAN MUNBY

The University of Chicago Press CHICAGO AND LONDON

JONATHAN MUNBY is senior lecturer in American studies and film studies at the University of Lancaster in England and a fellow of the W. E. B. Du Bois Institute for African and African American Research at Harvard University. He is the author of *Public Enemies, Public Heroes: Screening the Gangster from "Little Caesar" to "Touch of Evil,"* published by the University of Chicago Press.

The University of Chicago Press, Chicago 60637
The University of Chicago Press, Ltd., London

Printed in the United States of America

20 19 18 17 16 15 14 13 12 11   1 2 3 4 5

ISBN-13: 978-0-226-55035-0 (cloth)
ISBN-10: 0-226-55035-4 (cloth)
ISBN-13: 978-0-226-55036-7 (paper)
ISBN-10: 0-226-55036-2 (paper)

Library of Congress Cataloging-in-Publication Data

Munby, Jonathan.
Under a bad sign: criminal self-representation in African American popular culture / Jonathan Munby.
p. cm.
ISBN-13: 978-0-226-55035-0 (cloth: alk. paper)
ISBN-10: 0-226-55035-4 (cloth: alk. paper)
ISBN-13: 978-0-226-55036-7 (pbk.: alk. paper)
ISBN-10: 0-226-55036-2 (pbk.: alk. paper) 1. African Americans in popular culture. 2. African American arts. 3. Crime in popular culture—United States. 4. Popular culture—United States. I. Title.
E185.M898 2011
973'.0496073—dc22   2010048788

⊗ This paper meets the requirements of ANSI/NISO Z39.48-1992 (Permanence of Paper).

Contents

Acknowledgments

Many people have contributed to the completion of this book. Its inception can be traced to a seminar that Lary May and Paula Rabinowitz asked me to deliver on hip hop's gangsta culture toward the end of my graduate studies in the American studies program at the University of Minnesota. The media hype and moral panic surrounding gangsta culture in the early 1990s bore an uncanny resemblance to the troublesome reception of Hollywood's white ethnic gangsters in the 1930s, the subject of my research at the time. The chance to discuss the gangster/gangsta relation also fueled the development of an undergraduate course on African American popular culture. So I have the American studies faculty and fellow graduates in Scott Hall, as well as the students on the consequent course, to thank for setting me on the road to writing *Under a Bad Sign*. A particular shout-out has to go to John Wright, who insisted I dig up Claude McKay's *Harlem: Negro Metropolis* in the rare books section of Wilson Library to see how deep the provenance and complex the relationship was between black denizens of the American city and their gangster culture heroes.

Since then, various people have enabled me to think through and present the many aspects of an interdisciplinary and multimedia project. Dan Flory and Eithne Quinn, fellow researchers in issues of race and criminal representation in American popular culture, have been truly generous in sharing their ideas. Csaba Toth and George Lipsitz have never stopped cajoling and encouraging me from across the Atlantic, and I thank them for supporting me through sponsoring guest lecturing and research visits to the United States. I thank James and Yoshi Marshall for being wonderful hosts on my research visits to Los Angeles—and Ms. Lillian Allen, hundred-year-old Hill District beautician and community organizer, who, having attended my Pittsburgh lecture on race film moviegoing in the 1930s and 1940s, strengthened my faith in the project by telling me that I had "told it as it really was."

In the UK, Michael Heale and Richard King have never hesitated in providing institutional backing for the project. Douglas Tallack and Liam Kennedy, through the "Three Cities" conferences co-hosted by the Universities of Nottingham and Birmingham's American studies programs, provided vital venues for the first formal articulation of ideas central to the book—I thank them in particular for making it possible to meet Carlo Rotella, who told me I had to read the novels of Julian Mayfield if I wanted to further explore the culture of the numbers racket in Harlem. I thank Mark Jancovich, Peter Stanfield, Mark Glancy, Scott Lucas, and Winfried Pauleit for inviting me to present papers related to this book at their respective institutions—and for being such supportive colleagues. My African American Popular Culture students at Lancaster University have all contributed—I hope they can see something of their own ideas in the book. Thanks go to Nick Gebhardt, Patrick Hagopian, Max Haymes, and Tim Hickman—fellow Americanists at Lancaster—all of whom have influenced my work directly through team teaching and research seminar discussion, as well as through informal quotidian banter and the sharing of anecdotes, news, and references over matters relevant to my research. Equally, I have benefitted immeasurably from the irreverent intellectual companionship and support of Fred Botting, Mick Dillon, Paul Fletcher, Richard Rushton, and Scott Wilson—all of whom have helped me laugh, chill out, and think mo' better thoughts.

In the final stages, William L. Van Deburg and George Lipsitz provided great feedback on the manuscript, and my editorial team at the University of Chicago Press was exemplary in supporting me. Erin DeWitt and Tim McGovern handled my myriad minor queries with friendly efficiency, and Dawn Hall did a splendid copyedit. Over the entirety of the project, Doug Mitchell has proved to be the paragon of patience—thanks for hanging in there.

Some parts of this book are based on previously published material: A shorter version of chapter 2 appeared as "The Underworld Films of Oscar Micheaux and Ralph Cooper: Toward a Genealogy of the Black Screen Gangster," in *Mob Culture: Hidden Histories of the American Gangster Film*, ed. Lee Grieveson, Esther Sonnet, and Peter Stanfield (New Brunswick, NJ: Rutgers University Press, 2005), 263–80; part of chapter

4 appeared as "Signifyin' Cinema: Rudy Ray Moore and the Quality of Badness," *Journal for Cultural Research* 11, no.3 (2007): 203–19; and part of chapter 5 appeared as "From Gangsta to Gangster: The Hood Film's Criminal Allegiance with Hollywood," in *The New Film History: Sources, Methods, Approaches*, ed. James Chapman, Mark Glancy, and Sue Harper (New York: Palgrave, 2007), 166–79. I thank the editors and all those involved in reading and providing valuable critical feedback on these earlier drafts.

Primary research for this book was conducted at the New York Public Library Schomburg Center for Research on Black Culture; the Library of Congress Motion Picture and Television Reading Room, Washington, DC; and the Academy of Motion Picture Arts and Sciences Margaret Herrick Library, Los Angeles. Research at these various institutions in the United States was aided by support from Lancaster University's Faculty of Arts and Humanities and Faculty of Social Science research funds. The project also received the generous and invaluable support of an Arts and Humanities Research Council (AHRC) Research Leave Award. In addition, I am grateful to the W. E. B. Du Bois Institute for African and African American Research, Harvard University, for awarding me a Sheila Biddle Ford Foundation fellowship, which greatly aided in the final revision of this book.

I can only apologize if I have forgotten anyone. Given the support I have enjoyed, it should be clear that any failings and shortcomings in the book are entirely mine.

As with all large projects, they have their ups and downs—and some folks have had to put up with the downs more than others. Alexander and Hannah Munby have humored my low-budget film and arcane music proclivities in the battle to control the DVD and CD players. Love and greatest thanks go them and to Karen Juers-Munby, who has always been there for me.

INTRODUCTION

Trickster Badness and the Fight against Subordination in African American Vernacular Culture

"Cruel Stack O'Lee"

Police officers, how can it be
You can arrest everybody but
Cruel Stack O'Lee
That bad man!
O, Cruel Stack O'Lee!

Mississippi John Hurt's 1928 blues song "Stack O'Lee" tells us that African American folklore's most infamous "badman" is so bad that even the police steer clear of him. Hurt's version of this tale was sung in the context of a society ruled by Jim Crow laws designed to support a system of racial segregation that also made black people subordinate to white in the American South.[1] As Cecil Brown surmises, in such a world "there was probably no place ... where a white policeman was afraid of arresting, shooting, or killing a black man."[2]

The singular ability of the mythological black badman to remain immune to white power, however, depended on his ruthlessly violent treatment of members of his own community. The story goes that Stack O'Lee (who also goes by other variants, such as Stagolee and Stagger Lee) shot and killed Billy Lyons in a dispute over a five-dollar hat, rejecting Billy's pleas for clemency as a married man with two children to care for. When bad old Stagolee is finally arraigned, executed, and sent to hell, his capacity for evil means that he outranks Satan himself:

> When de devil wife see Stack comin' she got up in a quirl,
> "Here come dat bad nigger an' he's jus' from de udder worl'."

All de devil' little chillun went sc'amblin' up de wall,
Say, "Catch him, pappa, befo' he kill us all."
Stack he tol' de devil, "Come on, le's have a lil fun,
You stick me wid yo' pitchfork an' I'll shoot you wid my 41."
Stagolee say, "Now, now, Mister Devil, ef me an' you gonna have
 some fun,
You play de cornet, Black Betty beat de drum."
Stagolee took de pitchfork an' he laid it on de shelf
"Stand back, Tom Devil, I'm gonna rule Hell by myself."[3]

Stagolee's success is predicated on being a bully who can bully the bullies, a man who can take on the devil but who is also a sociopath among his own people. While the terms of this ur-type's heroism are paradoxical and seemingly counterproductive, they continue to structure African American cultural production.

African Americans have made probably the biggest impact on American (and global) culture in the realm of mass culture. Frequently, however, mass entertainment success for African Americans has depended on pandering to white racist visions of black identity. The costs involved in ministering to a distorted white mirror have had to be weighed against the benefits involved in gaining access to the realm of mass representation. This book focuses specifically on the stakes involved in the choices black popular cultural producers have made in perpetuating *criminal* visions of themselves and their community. In so doing this book charts the history of a significant form of self-conscious black "minstrelsy" from the mythological badmen of African American folklore to the "gangsta" rappers of today.

The rise to popularity of hip hop culture and rap music—especially gangsta rap—has raised awkward questions about the need of the disenfranchised to be complicit with their oppressors as a prerequisite to success. Most conspicuously, gangsta rappers have profited from the self-conscious marketing of stereotypes that equate black male youth with ghetto life and violent criminality. My project examines the complex history of African Americans' own controversial and seemingly counterproductive investment in criminal self-representations of black identity across popular American media (in music, fiction, film, and television) and over the last century. In the process I shall be asking what role such self-representation, or "*noir* by noirs" to borrow a phrase from Manthia Diawara, has played in the ongoing struggle to breach the limits of essentialist and binary racial categories in the construction of black cultural identity.[4]

Overall this book provides a historical genealogy that connects the discourse on the more controversial elements of black hip hop culture at the turn of this century to the first quest by black folk to be recognized as modern rather than being associated stereotypically with the plantation South, at the beginning of the last century. The book shows how and why black popular cultural producers of music, fiction, film, and television have consistently mobilized African American badman imagery against the grain in their attempt to meet, negotiate, and counter the problems of a society built on racialized hierarchies.

In the course of writing this book, the people of the United States have elected an African American as president for the first time. While such a historical breakthrough might signal the beginning of the end for Stagolee, Barack Obama's journey to the White House was something predicated on a road made possible by hellion dreams. Over thirty years ago, George Clinton, the funk maestro of the appropriately named Parliament, described a future that seemed to be the stuff of drug-induced fantasy, America-as-"Chocolate City" (CC):

Uh, what's happening CC?
They still call it the White House
But that's a temporary condition, too.
Can you dig it, CC?
. . .
Chocolate city
Are you with me out there?

And when they come to march on ya
Tell 'em to make sure they got their James Brown pass
And don't be surprised if Ali is in the White House
Reverend Ike, Secretary of the Treasure
Richard Pryor, Minister of Education
Stevie Wonder, Secretary of FINE arts
And Miss Aretha Franklin, the First Lady
Are you out there, CC?
A chocolate city is no dream.[5]

SIGNIFICANCE OF STUDY

With the exception, perhaps, of literary criticism that has attended to the way blues musical themes and structures have been integral to black literature, existing scholarship has tended to study significant aspects of African American culture separately. Seminal work has been done on the black literary tradition, popular music, and cinema. Yet there is surprisingly little work that attempts to discuss these various media together, as a cultural ensemble. Furthermore, most studies of African American propagation of seemingly counterproductive self-images have been fueled by the topicality of the issue, the moral panics surrounding gangsta rap being a prime example. It is rare to find work that has a developed understanding of how contemporary criminal self-images produced by black Americans are part of a rich legacy of race rebellion. Vital work on badman folklore and the role of oral tradition in culture building has been conducted by scholars such as Roger D. Abrahams, Alan Dundes, Lawrence Levine, Bruce Jackson, and John W. Roberts. Such studies need connecting to other arenas and other historical moments of African American self-representation.[6] Recently, Jerry H. Bryant has shown how the folkloric badman has influenced concepts of violence in African American literature, setting an example for those of us interested in tracing the import of such criminal tropes and figures beyond their oral form and origins.[7] Perhaps most provocatively, Abdul JanMohamed, in his compelling study of Richard Wright's writing, makes a case for the resistant and emancipative political potential of the redeployment of violence and death (of suicide and murder) in the context of a culture subjected since slavery to the constant threat of death.[8]

Accordingly, I take my cue from scholars who have initiated forays into cross-media analysis, on the one hand, and those who have made more extensive historical links between the choices that black popular cultural producers make today and their forebears, on the other. The former approach is exemplified in Houston A. Baker Jr.'s examination of the relationship of the blues to African American literature, and S. Craig Watkins's analysis of recent black cinema's relationship to other arenas of black audiovisual expression.[9] The latter approach is demonstrated by Robin D. G. Kelley's initial linking of gangsta rap to a long tradition of badman signifying, and William L. Van Deburg's broad analysis of the significance of African American popular culture heroes from sports, film, crime fiction, and music in sustaining hopes for a better day coming during the 1960s and 1970s.[10] His subsequent study of African American villainy provides invaluable insight into the antebellum construction of the black badman as part of a nation-building process by a prejudicial white ownership class and its attempted subversion by disenfranchised blacks. This idea of a double investment from both sides of the color line during the forging of ideas about citizenship and nation in the early republic is used primarily to underscore the contradictory power of the gangsta in contemporary America.[11]

As much as this work draws attention to how slavery fostered the conditions for violent social banditry on the part of the fettered (exemplified most sensationally by Nat Turner), other studies have highlighted how the folkloric black badman came to full prominence only in the postbellum era, precisely as a means to mediate not so much fear of the black man per se but the fear of black freedom. If the postbellum black badman seemed complicit with white resentments under Reconstruction, he was also a violent figure of identification for those who felt, in turn, betrayed by the capitulation of Reconstruction to the culture of Jim Crow. As George Rawick highlights, the postbellum period was one of increased hostility and division between whites and blacks defined in part by the struggle for and against ways to continue the subordination of African Americans consequent on the formal abolition of slavery.[12] And in one of the pioneering treatments of folkloric outlawry in black culture, Lawrence Levine argues: "The creation of these kinds of heroes required the growth of a more pronounced Western orientation, the decline of the sacred universe, and the growth of the individualist ethos among black Americans. All of these developments accompanied freedom."[13]

My study fills in and elaborates on this work by giving more concerted attention to the way different periods of the twentieth century are related in their use and abuse of the black badman across a wider range of interrelated media. In bringing together elements normally kept separate by disciplinary boundaries and by the lack of an extended historical perspective, *Under a Bad Sign*'s engagement with the long history or genealogy of black criminal self-representation in American popular culture across various media contributes to this new trajectory.

Adopting an interdisciplinary and multimedia approach allows us to examine the cross-fertilizing of different forms and registers of black popular expression while examining the relationship between these forms and those of the dominant culture. Moreover, this book, in providing a more extended historical frame, shows how past and present struggles bear a strategic resemblance to each other. Understanding the provenance of today's postindustrial, media-hijacking image of the African American outlaw or gangsta helps overcome historical amnesia about how such self-representation is part of a rich and long-established vernacular response to being "othered" in white America.

Engaging the history of African Americans' own investment in badman representation is necessarily dirty work. The issue is not reducible to the imposition of stereotype by a dominant group over a subordinate one. The appropriation and proliferation of a violent and criminal self-image by African Americans has everything to do with wresting the badman's meaning from the enemy. The often-close correspondence between the environment of the badman fable and real lived conditions for lower-class African Americans only complicates matters. A convenient confusion of culture for behavior services the interests of those who would blame the iniquity of African American impoverishment on the black poor themselves. Yet as I hope to illustrate here, the badman as a cultural construct constitutes an ingenious way to speak truth to power.

Any examination of the badman type will necessarily raise important questions about the politically oppositional value of popular cultural expression in the ongoing black quest for full enfranchisement in the United States. Doing such work involves overcoming prejudices as one confronts the problem of disciplinary boundaries, on the one hand, and residual understandings about what is fit for academic study, on the other. As Todd Boyd puts it so clearly:

> Why have I never read an intense study of the films of Rudy Ray Moore, the novels of Iceberg Slim and Donald Goines, the music of Tyrone Davies, etc.? Why? Because they do not fit in so easily with what we consider acceptable, and because they are works of the lower class that have never transcended the work of folk culture in which they exist. In addition, their politics are a huge stumbling block in light of the resulting contradictions.[14]

Well, I hope that this book goes some way toward remedying such exclusions (especially in terms of Rudy Ray Moore and Donald Goines).

THEORETICAL STAKES

My approach is sensitive to the distinct modes of analysis associated with discrete modes of communication. I highlight, however, the limits of existing models and paradigms of popular cultural analysis and race representation—especially in cases where the maintenance of certain boundaries tends to affirm the ontology of blackness and whiteness in the process. To this extent, my approach is indirectly responsible to questions raised about (the use and abuse of) race within critical and cultural theory about the academic reification and sequestration of black studies.

Critical race theory and whiteness studies have attended to the way the racial contract guarantees white privilege while keeping its benefactors blind to their own complicity in a racialized system. Scholars such as Derrick Bell, Homi Bhabha, Richard Dyer, Paul Gilroy, David Theo Goldberg, George Lipsitz, Charles W. Mills, and David Roediger have shown that raising white consciousness (or naming whiteness) is a vital part of the struggle to redress the injustices visited on people of color not only in the United States but also globally.[15]

Black feminist scholars such as Hazel Carby, bell hooks, and Michelle Wallace have led the way in attacking the limits of essentialist race thinking—seeing racial subjectivity as something both abrogated and reinforced in its relationship to gender.[16] Recently, scholars such as Victor Anderson, Michael Eric Dyson, Kenneth Mostern, Ross Posnock, and Mark Reid have all addressed the way the impasse of essentialist race thinking has structured and defined the philosophical reflection of seminal African American intellectuals and political leaders.[17]

As such black studies has increasingly come to bear an awkward relationship to this kind of critical engagement with racism. Ironically, in a political climate increasingly hostile to affirmative action, calls for something that breaches racial ontology or breaks down essentialist identity politics may undermine the very rationale that has until recently guaranteed the existence of institutional space for nonwhite academics—and for the study of black culture per se. The very ground and language of civil rights and black advancement is at stake. And hip hop's most commercially successful forms (gangsta and "Mack" rap, for example) have only muddied the water. Objections to or skepticism about the resistant character of black popular culture seem increasingly justified in a mass-media world that has co-opted African American talents to service conspicuously capitalist and patriarchal ideologies.

Yet any understanding of the power of black popular culture to resist or transform dominant ideologies has to first analyze the relationship of African Americans to masks constructed by white racism. The body of theory that comes closest to this aspect of my work is that concerning minstrelsy. Work on minstrelsy has concentrated primarily on *white* appropriations and constructions of black masks (Susan Gubar, W. T. Lhamon Jr., Eric Lott, and Michael Rogin, for example).[18] Minstrelsy is seen rightly as a contradictory act of white racist colonization. In contradistinction, my work examines what is at stake in the comparatively underexamined area of African American investment in and apparent complicity with such an imposed notion of blackness. Clearly, such self-representations attest to the hegemonic power of white racism in determining black identity. Yet while I am indebted to the work of Frantz Fanon in this regard, I shall be attending to the *counter*hegemonic possibility of criminal self-representation that resides in how it plays with the designated subordinate position of blackness in the field of cultural relations.[19] Most particularly I shall concentrate on the way criminal self-representation pressures a "*productive* ambivalence" (to borrow a phrase from Homi Bhabha) *within* the logic of colonial discourse.[20]

As JanMohamed articulates in his analysis of the contingent terms of freedom at the heart of Richard Wright's writing, it is imperative that we attend to the political logic behind choices that otherwise appear inchoate, insane, and irrational. In Wright's oeuvre, violence and recourse to actual-death (through suicide and/or taking the life of another) is understood as a negation of the social death of slavery and Jim Crow—a way to resist perfect subjugation by the master. In the context of a "life" determined by the constant threat and fear of death, "freedom" is redefined as "seizing the capacity to actualize [one's] death away from its monopolistic control by the master."[21]

Under the aegis of white racism, the ordinary character of the black life-world is one where one is unavoidably guilty—"guilty of blackness." It is not surprising, then, that the criminal milieu (or noir predicament) is one that has held special attraction for African Americans as a prescient space to dramatize and expose not only the contingencies of white power but also the power to resist. As such, my approach engages the "ill-logic" of criminal self-representation on the part of black popular cultural producers as a form of strategic essentialism in the battle to counter one's psychological, social, and economic determination through race and to sustain the possibility of a postracist world.

OVERVIEW

Criminal self-representation in African American popular culture has taken different forms and has a long and complex history (which can be dated at least to 1895, the putative date of origin for the Stagolee saga[22]). Today's gangsta rappers are very much part of a rich vernacular tradition of "toasting" and "signifying" (verbal sparring) about badmen and tricksters that can be traced back to stories of slaves outwitting their masters. The more famous toasts about Stagolee, the Signifying Monkey, and Shine need to be examined as vital responses to forms of subordination not only for their historical value (as the origins of an enduring tradition) but also for their critical-theoretical significance with regard to the struggle against racism. The badman-pimp-hustler-trickster demands to be known as something other than "other"—and yet does this through seeming conformity to a white racist stereotype about black male behavior and priapic prowess. Moreover, these stories demand complicity between teller and tale. For the value that inheres in these stories lies as much in their style and quality of telling as in their content. The "toast" is only as good (or bad) as its teller; the badman's story demands a dynamically "baad" performance from its narrator. Audiences and rivals engage and respond to the teller's performance, fueling escalation in derogatory braggadocio.

As a figure of ambivalent value to the community that both venerates and fears him, the badman-pimp-hustler-trickster of black folklore clearly violates the doctrine of racial uplift that is meant to pave the way to equality. He is antithetical to that which the leaders of the struggle against racial subordination have required and invoked to legitimate their cause: the idea of a unified and virtuous black community. He claims a name (possession of a reputation) through the disrespecting of other's names (bragging and besting others through superior insult exchanges—leading more often than not to murder).

In exploring the ambivalent value of the black badman figure, this book raises questions about the attribution of moral and political purpose to impoverished forms of cultural production. In the process it rejects the easy syllogism that low-budget fare equals poor culture symptomatic of counterproductive politics. Given its ludic (or disruptively playful) relationship to essentialism and appearance, criminal self-representation in African American popular culture necessarily runs the gamut of encounters with the problem of racial ontology, identity politics, "blackulinity," and minstrelsy. Although the book is organized chronologically, it remains sensitive to the "ill-logic" of its subject matter.

Chapter 1 ("Original Gangsta Culture: Fortune Economy and the Criminal Mediation of Black Entry into Modernity") examines how and why one of the most definitive features of black Harlem in the 1920s and 1930s was the numbers racket (or policy). The heyday of the Harlem Renaissance was also the golden age of the black gangster. These modern urban Stagolees operated as numbers racketeers or policy bankers, as dealers in black fortune. It was one's fortune (good or bad) to have been born black in white America. One needed fortune in order to make it (to acquire a fortune). And black gangster enterprise held powerful significance among African Americans as an emulative modern cultural practice. The numbers racket constituted a simulation of corporate organization and principle. One of the few areas of enterprise owned and controlled by blacks, policy was structured like big business, with salesmen (runners) answerable to middle management (collectors), who in turn reported to the boss (banker). And the winning numbers were calculated from Wall Street Clearing House records. Thus while investment in the policy racket by players and gangsters alike may have been driven by economic exclusion from (and frustration with) the surrounding skyscraper world, participation in numbers speculation was also seen as a way to demonstrate involvement in a modern form of organization—a way to show off a modern competence—a way to pass.

The practice of playing numbers was bound up with other notions of fortune. So-called conjure men and women (black voodoo shamans), as well as Christian cultists and spiritualist organizations, all found a calling in offering black Manhattan a way to exploit and remedy the lottery of capitalist practice. Denial of life chances (materially and culturally) among the black community could be redressed through increased and more intense investment in fortune-telling (conjuring) and the policy game. Gaming and conjuring went hand in hand as a core Harlemite characteristic. As an urban modernizing space made complicated by the misfortune of white racism, Harlem came to be ruled by what might be called a ludic underworld economy; that is, an economy ruled by play, gaming, and apparently useless activity—a jocular or burlesquing mirror to the "legitimate" world. And the most important agents of this ludic underworld were the numbers bankers, the so-called kings and queens of Harlem who were in many ways the original gangstas.

This chapter connects folklorist insights about the "ill-logic" of the black badman in relation to the struggle against racial subordination to the space and time of the city. In the process it engages the legacy of Gunnar Myrdal's pathological conception of the Negro as "problem" and "distorted development . . . of the general American culture" in the field of sociology.[23] The primary materials for this chapter are drawn from various contemporaneous sources: the surprisingly neglected work about the black underworld and cults by Claude McKay, *Harlem: Negro Metropolis*, and Arthur Huff Fauset, *Black Gods of the Negro Metropolis*; the first major socioeconomic studies of the urban black belt by St. Clair Drake and Horace R. Cayton, *Black Metropolis: A Study of Negro Life in a Northern City*, and Gunnar Myrdal, *An American Dilemma: The Negro Problem and American Democracy*; the Harlem novels *The Walls of Jericho* (1928) and *The Conjure Man Dies* (1932) by Rudolph Fisher (whose undervalued status in the black literary canon will be a point of significance here); and the gangster and policy dream blues of Bumble Bee Slim and William Bunch, who adopted the moniker of "Peetie Wheatstraw"—a folkloric black badman who was "the devil's son-in-law."

Chapter 2 ("Sin City Cinema: The Underworld Race Films of Oscar Micheaux and Ralph Cooper") takes the "ill-logic" of black criminal self-representation a step further—into the realm and era of the talking race film. The awkward symbiosis between white overworld and black underworld that features in the previous chapter is given further refinement in a discussion of talking films made for a segregated black audience during the 1930s and 1940s. Not only did these films primarily focus on the urban experience, but they also adopted many of the tropes and conventions associated with the Hollywood gangster film.

In discussing why this was so, the chapter focuses on the asymmetrical economic relationship between Hollywood and race films (especially once sound was introduced). The screen projection of black experience was framed by the problem of working from within a visual and narrative economy that from its very birth (*Birth of a Nation* [1915]) was dependent on the consolidation of either/or conceptions of race and identity that dated back to the first minstrel shows. White cinema staged blackness predominantly in a subordinate position within its diegesis—as sideshow (the space of entertaining diversions that offered temporary "time out" from the center of dramatic attention, which was the white world). On the rare occasion that Hollywood made a commitment to a fuller portrayal of black experience, this too was screened to preserve an ontological distinction between black and white. All-color cast films offer a classic example. Most set the scene of blackness in a premodern Old South. Black actors continued to be cast in servile roles—as spiritual-singing, God-fearing, plantation workers. In such cases blackness signified a lost prelapsarian America set to the nostalgic sound of lamentation songs. Thus even where Hollywood put a black world center stage, this was inevitably encoded as something that had passed before the time and space of the modern (of cinema itself). Given such constraints, I argue that the underworld milieu constituted the best way for black filmmakers to renegotiate the place and time of blackness on the (white) screen.

The key protagonists in this challenge to white cinema were Oscar Micheaux (who had a hegemonic influence on the style and content of race films) and Ralph Cooper, the original black screen gangster. Looking at both these race film figures illuminates how far the race film industry bore a contradictory relationship to Hollywood (especially the mainstream screen's representation of African Americans). That is, the discussion is about more than just the content and themes of the race film per se—but is also about the way these were overdetermined by the economics of white racism in the entertainment industry.

In such a context the issue of minstrelsy as it operates in screen representations is germane. Micheaux was very much a self-styled race man, whereas Cooper had a less reverend and prognostic notion of racial advancement and the role black films should play in this. Yet in spite of these differences, as African Americans involved in the making of popular films, both Micheaux and Cooper had a common investment in the image and context of the black underworld. Why did they gravitate to criminal self-representation? Clearly, given their pronounced differences, Micheaux and Cooper would not have had altogether similar goals (bar profit) in the making of black underworld films. Micheaux believed that popular film could be morally edifying and an instrument of pedagogical force in the advancement of the race. Cooper limited his motivations to the provision of entertainment to black folk that put blacks in roles denied them on the white screen. In spite of these differences, as filmmakers who happened to be black, both Cooper and Micheaux necessarily had to engage the limits of a prevailing white racist visual economy.

Micheaux has been accused of supporting the very system of racial ontology that he was trying to combat so conspicuously. He often appeared to "color-cast" the relative moral value of his characters (lighter skin tones signifying higher moral value, the darkest tones signifying moral lassitude). I argue that Micheaux's color coding is far more complex than this—and that his films constitute vital examples of what might be called a black film aesthetic. Key to this aesthetic is the problem of making the space and function of black performance fit the prescriptions of a narrative economy committed to moral edification. Most obviously, the space of the Harlem underworld offered Micheaux a way to address the predicaments confronting urbanizing black folk as well as providing the full range of moral types. Yet there is clearly a tension between his desire to communicate moral lessons and the fact that the best way to draw an audience was to showcase the best of black entertainment talent. This talent (musicians, dancers, singers, stand-up comedians) was drawn from the (under)world of the Harlem nightclub. And Micheaux struggled to integrate this revue world into his moral frame narratives. The seamed montage or diegetically discontinuous character of many of his talking pictures was only compounded by his lack of access to the investment and technology afforded white filmmakers.

Ralph Cooper could also be accused of reinforcing prejudices about black folk as innately criminal. While cultivation of the black gangster image provided exciting entertainment fare and drew good audiences, such self-representation, it would seem, would have done nothing to counteract white racist views of black folk. However, Cooper's very gravitation to the gangster cycle/genre points to an alternative evaluation of his cinematic efforts. A fairer reading would see his imitations of Hollywood films such as *Public Enemy* (1930), *Little Caesar* (1931), and *Scarface* (1932), as entirely consistent with the need to subvert and challenge the way Hollywood organized and policed American identity around racialized categories. As I have argued elsewhere, the early 1930s Hollywood gangster film was all about the contradictions of a social order predicated on a system of ethnic exclusion. The mainstream gangster film dramatized the Italian- and Irish American quest for cultural acceptance against the grain of White Anglo-Saxon Protestant hegemony.[24] Given this, it is not entirely surprising that black filmmakers would have recognized in the gangster film a way to stage their own desires and grievances. Gravitation to the underworld as the preferred setting for the talking race film was only reinforced by the need to find an optimal form through which the realities of life in the black belts of big-city America could be addressed.

In analyzing the cultural work, talking race films performed in the name of undermining ontological notions of race (including the prejudicial assumption that black folk could not master the technologies of mass representation), the conclusions this chapter reaches about the talking race film extend insights by Stuart Hall and James Snead on the problem of "naming" black popular cultural expression "black."[25] The talking race film did not oppose white racism from a space and through a language separate from the dominant culture. The adaptation of tropes and conventions associated with the Hollywood gangster film allowed black filmmakers to articulate their world to the larger one in a common (modern) language that did not acquiesce to the established ordering of white over black. As such this body of black underworld films needs to be understood as having more than sociological value—for their "realness" clearly connects to "reelness," the development of a criminal aesthetic that sought to redress the racialized connotation of black on white screens.

Chapter 3 ("Hustlers in the House of Literature: Julian Mayfield, Chester Himes, and the Black Literary Ghetto") shifts focus onto the production of urban literature consequent on the demise of the race film in the late 1940s. Issues of prejudice would be commandeered by Hollywood sporadically in the form of "passing" melodramas (such as *Pinky* [1949], *Lost Boundaries* [1949], *Imitation of Life* [1959], *I Passed for White* [1960], and *Black Like Me* [1964]) as the mainstream screen struggled to find inoffensive means to representing an increasingly hostile period of civil rights activism. In the end it delegated almost the entire representational burden onto Sidney Poitier, the icon of and martyr to the "cinema of integration."

While the uppity Stagolee was denied the limelight on-screen, he was kept alive by black writing. African American writers—in the light (or darkness) of Langston Hughes's criticism in 1940 of the failure of the Harlem Renaissance—found themselves consumed by the impossibility of the choice facing them as representatives of the race.[26] And the production of literary noir by noirs was the result. As hustlers in the house of literature, Malcolm X, Julian Mayfield, and Chester Himes dramatized the way ethical ambiguity and ambivalence continued to haunt and define what made black literature and the black predicament "black." The metaphor of the hoodlum world serviced a need to both represent the real lived conditions of black folk in the period and to critique the way aesthetic categories continued to buttress racial ontology.

Malcolm X's self-staging as an "ex-"hoodlum-thief-pimp in *The Autobiography of Malcolm X* (1965) is of seminal importance in black writing—in our rethinking of the value of criminal aesthetics and "ill-logics." As Mostern so perspicaciously highlights, the *Autobiography* enlists the trust of its readers by conflating gangster with activist identity, precisely because the former is needed to authenticate the latter as trustworthy.[27] The "ghetto" credentials of Malcolm's criminal self-representation sanctioned the production of an unapologetic hard-core urban black experience faction that viewed the street and prison as an organic form of schooling, embodied most graphically in the work of Robert Beck and Donald Goines. But before the advent of this uncompromisingly explicit black experience literature, other African American writers were also testing the limits of prevailing literary standards and proscriptions for good black literature.

Analyzing the overlooked work and lives of Julian Mayfield and Chester Himes sheds new light on the crises confronting the more canonized members of the black literati of the 1940s and 1950s (especially Wright and Ralph Ellison). As writers committed to more popular forms, Mayfield and Himes drew attention to the problem of literary aspiration, even as they paid a price for doing so. What makes the criminal aesthetic "criminal" in the writing under review is that it disorganizes the high/low distinction on which not only cultural taste but also racial hierarchy is built under the regime of bourgeois aesthetics. Much has been written about the problematic reception of and status accorded to Richard Wright's work in this regard (most excitingly by Houston Baker and JanMohamed[28]). Yet the status of "artist manqué" probably applies even more to writers such as Chester Himes and Julian Mayfield—both of whom made a self-conscious effort to produce what might be classified as an "*écriture* manqué" (or "bLack" literature). Mayfield agonized over an appropriate way to write the black predicament. He opted to situate two of his three novels (*The Hit* [1957] and *The Long Night* [1958]) within the Harlem ghetto and orient its action around the game of numbers. Having worked through the possibilities of such urban writing, Mayfield took to militant political activism, a choice that led to his eventual flight to Ghana, where he would work as an aide to President Nkrumah as part of the first postcolonial independent regime in sub-Saharan Africa.

Himes, from a more embittered position of self-imposed exile in Europe, chose to deliver his critique of black possibility in white America through a series of detective, or "domestic," novels (again set in Harlem) written from the late 1950s to the late 1960s. Much like Rudolph Fisher, then, their work is deeply informed by the problem of form and the costs of making blackness legible in a world dominated by white aesthetic categories. And again, like Fisher, these writers as a consequence of their aesthetic choices ran the risk of being forgotten or undervalued.

Even for a writer such as Chester Himes, who had long championed the crime novel as a productive way to express the impossible choices confronting black folk in white America, the end of the 1960s constituted a political (and literary) nadir. In *Blind Man with a Pistol* (1969), Himes plays out the endgame of ghetto-centric self-representation. This novel reveals the way the myth of black community has been exploited by black political charlatans and disabuses black folk of their dream of full, integrated citizenship. In Himes's deterministic world, the very (masculine) individualism required to provide ego-fulfillment and defy the co-opting powers of white power is revealed to be simultaneously merciless, amoral, and without direction. Disaffected parody about black political possibility would seem to be all that is left. Even the foreword to *Blind Man with a Pistol* (one that quotes "A Harlem Intellectual") frames the narrative of race advancement in dispassionate and dysfunctional terms: "Motherfucking right, it's confusing; it's a gas, baby, you dig."[29] And by the end of the novel we are left with the impression that all that is left is abject acquiescence to the law of the jungle (rebellion disintegrates into riot) and the perpetuation of self-delusion about both power and resistance.

This is an impression that seems compounded when these writers' work is set against the heroic action and rhetoric of the civil rights struggle. Yet the unfinished anti-institutional character of ghettocentric writing keeps its readers alive to the contradiction of integration. Necessarily, this chapter sidelines the grand narrative of the period's civil rights struggle in order to make available those unresolved and apparently more ephemeral street stories that refuse the politics/ideology of closure. It concentrates on popular literary production as something consistent with this move to decenter the dominant understanding of the period and its cultural meaning for black America.

Chapter 4 ("From *Up Tight!* to *Dolemite*: The Changing Politics of Baadasssss Cinema") follows up on Mayfield's and Himes's road to exile, examining how and why badman trickster transmogrification defined the black popular cultural response to the disappointments of post–civil rights America in the late 1960s and 1970s. Such a development appeared to work against the grain of previous transformations of black selves made by perhaps the most public masters of the "toast," Cassius Clay (the "Louisville Lip") in becoming Muhammad Ali, and Malcolm Little (Detroit Red) in becoming first Malcolm X, and then El-Hajj Malik El-Shabazz. These figures shape-shifted from more ambivalent and hellion identities to more fixed (separatist) political ones in a climate of growing Black Nationalism. Separatism necessarily disputed the validity of integrationist politics—but in doing so confirmed a determinist vision of black possibility in white America.

In 1968 both Julian Mayfield and blacklisted filmmaker Jules Dassin attempted an American comeback by colluding on a film about the political direction of the civil rights movement. *Up Tight!* was based on John Ford's film, *The Informer* (1935), which was itself a screen adaptation of Liam O'Flaherty's novel about an IRA foot soldier who betrayed his comrades by naming names to the British authorities. Aside from the allusion to the era of the Red Scare (of "naming names" American style), which had led to Dassin's exile, the film attempted to depict the impasse that has resulted from a split between integrationists and separatists consequent on the assassination of Martin Luther King. Mayfield co-wrote the screenplay and starred as the informer, Tank. The film failed at the box office, perhaps as a consequence of its bleak outlook on political progression.

The same did not apply to the first screen adaptation of Chester Himes's detective fiction, *Cotton Comes to Harlem*, in 1970. Himes's absurdist vision had finally found its time and audience. Perhaps his outlook matched changes in self-understanding by those at the vanguard of funk (most notably George Clinton and Sly Stone—the reincarnation of Stagger Lee according to Greil Marcus[30]) whose music signaled the rise of a more creative and positive engagement with the apparent end of integrationist dreams. Funk music's "on the one" rhythm countered the closed and commoditized framework that dominated much of popular music production. The shift of the bass guitar from supporting instrument to star worked in tandem with increasingly irreverent sartorial display to unsettle the look and sound of mainstream black performance. Significantly, Motown, the most recognized black-owned business in the United States, got the funk—with stalwarts Marvin Gaye and Stevie Wonder demanding and producing music more militant in both sound and meaning.

This chapter, then, examines how the earnest features of the criminal aesthetic in the 1950s and 1960s were self-consciously commoditized, exploited, and even inverted—in the form of "blaxploitation" in the 1970s. Trickster shifts in musical and literary expression are related in particular to blaxploitation cinema. The "fly" "Mack-daddy" protagonists of the cycle's defining films, such as *Super Fly* (1972) and *The Mack* (1978), seem entirely servile to the amoral economy's logic of self-exploitation in the name of money and kudos. Yet they provide a camp and slavish imitation of the most ruthless aspects not of the black, but of the legitimate world—the world of "the Man." *Super Fly* and *The Mack* more or less bookend the era of blaxploitation cinema—and in many ways they encapsulate the particular way this cycle of films, in exploiting the cross-racial meanings of the underworld trope, both repeated and developed the stratagems of the talking race film.

While some blaxploitation underworld films clearly copied mainstream formulas, most provided something distinctive. Like the talking race film, the impoverished production context often influenced (delimited) the style and marketing of this era's black filmmaking. It made economic sense to adopt tested formulas (the gangster) that could be located in contemporary settings—and which could incorporate topical themes germane to the black community. And as with the talking race film, a critical component in some of the blaxploitation cycle's more successful films was the music. *Super Fly*, for example, was sold on the basis of Curtis Mayfield's funk soundtrack. Even a film such as *Black Caesar* (a barely disguised reworking of *Scarface* that also sought to capitalize on the success of *The Godfather* in promotional taglines) employed the talent of James Brown in providing a funky black beat to what was otherwise rather generic fare. There was even room for a degree of generic experiment and fusion—something exemplified in *J.D.'s Revenge* (1976). Centering on a trickster motif in which a long-dead gangster's demon spirit takes possession of a likable young man, this film combined voodoo and gangster tropes to stamp itself as something that "belonged" to a world of African American self-representation. And these various innovations were epitomized in films made by blaxploitation's most idiosyncratic figure, Rudy Ray Moore.

Moore guerrilla-financed his films through the sale of his "party records" that featured famous street "toasts." In a manner not too far removed from that of Oscar Micheaux, Moore's films often suffer from (or enjoy) a lack of narrative continuity and coherence. While this can be partly attributed to the problems of working with a low budget, it is also clear that Moore was invested far more in the performative possibilities cinema held for African American self-representation. Significantly, Moore staged and screened himself as a latter-day reincarnation of two of the "baddest" badmen in street toasting folklore, Dolemite and Peetie Wheatstraw (eponymous heroes of his most successful films). In Moore's hands the deterministic and predictable logic of the gangster plot takes a pat backseat to the "ill-logic" of an African American storytelling pattern. *Dolemite*'s plot, for example, is a cartoonlike chaos. The story of a "Mack-daddy" nightclub entertainer's fight (with the help of his all-girl army of kung fu killers) against crooked cops and the notorious gangster Mr. Big is really an elaborate ruse designed to service situations where the major protagonist can recite badman toasts. Such innovative inversions move the criminal aesthetic out of the world of social realism (or the derivative gangster form) and reconnect criminal self-representation with the world of the trickster. In this way Moore presaged much of what would become "gangsta," while also emulating the adoption of hellion identity by earlier black entertainers—most obviously, 1930s gangster-bluesman William Bunch, a.k.a. "Peetie Wheatstraw."

Chapter 5 ("Keeping It Reel: From Goines to Gangsta") covers how the funky turns that characterized black film and music of the 1970s period worked alongside gravitation to more grotesque representations of "the street" in black popular fiction and presaged the emergence of gangsta culture. Donald Goines and Robert Beck (who published under the pseudonym of Iceberg Slim, and who lent his "Ice" moniker to a generation of gangsta rappers) are the supreme cases in point and feature as a central part of this chapter, as is Holloway House, the independent publishing company devoted to delivering black experience fiction and biography to a lower-class (and often imprisoned) African American readership.

This chapter examines the way gangsta culture became symbolically central to American popular culture in the late 1980s and early 1990s—in spite of the fact that its producers declared themselves as representatives of the social periphery. The moral panic associated with two of gangsta culture's originals Ice-T and N.W.A. (Niggaz With Attitude) and the first cycle of ghetto-centric "hood" films (often starring gangsta rappers) that launched hip hop cinema (*Boyz N the Hood* [1991], *New Jack City* [1991], *Juice* [1992], *Menace II Society* [1993]) is redolent of the stink created around the first talking gangster films. The self-conscious "sampling" of the Hollywood gangster by gangstas needs fuller explication in this regard.

Much like the race film and blaxploitation cinema that preceded it, hip hop cinema's gangster/gangsta relationship allies the African American struggle over representation in the late 1980s and early 1990s with the struggles of non-Anglo-Saxon Protestant white immigrants in the early twentieth century. And again, much like the previous moments in black film, the Hollywood gangster references are overt and often doubled (as in the case of a gangsta rapper choosing to name himself "Scarface"—or in raps and hip hop movie scenes that pay homage to James Cagney).

In the late 1980s and early 1990s, however, such deliberate semiotic alignment of black self-representation with established gangster conventions and tropes proved troubling on a scale that far exceeded any previous reaction to African American criminal self-representation. The gangsta, it seems, finally realized the potential of previous criminal self-representations to disturb the outside/inside organization of black/white relations. Nick Tosches asks, "Is the pose of many contemporary rap groups not dissimilar in essence to that of the black coon acts of the past?"[31] The answer depends on how one interprets the politics of the coon show. I maintain that the gangsta image is not the same kind of minstrel show. The gangsta constitutes a significant shift in the way "blackface" fits into the general symbolic economy. As Ice Cube pronounces: "It's the *American* way cos I'm a G.A.N.G.S.T.A" (my emphasis).[32]

In making a case for the transformational grammar of the gangsta, then, we need to acknowledge that like the gangster, he commits his major offense in embodying the most ruthless and dysfunctional aspects of what passes as *legitimate*. On film and music video, gangstas put dominant cultural values into relief. On display is an all-consuming amoral conspicuous materialism embodied in money, cars, possession of women—all of which can only be guaranteed through violence and relentlessly homophobic and misogynist behavior. Tricia Rose's forceful critique of the debilitating impact on hip hop of the commercial promotion of the "gangsta-pimp-ho trinity"[33] notwithstanding, the identity at stake is not so much that desired and adopted by (disenfranchised) black men per se, but that which is central to the American Dream. As Michael Eric Dyson puts it, "Gangsta rap's greatest 'sin' may be that it tells the truth about practices and beliefs that rappers hold in common with the mainstream and with black elites."[34] That white youth have been drawn to gangsta culture as its biggest consumers has only heightened anxieties about such "diss"-identification. What is to be feared is the way gangsta culture reveals rather than conceals the less palatable features of the mainstream rather than the margin. This is the gangster/gangsta's productive ambivalence whose provenance dates back to both Stagolee and Cagney as original "Public Enemies."

Significantly, there are remarkable parallels between the way the 1930s Hollywood gangster and hip hop's gangsta were received. Both were greeted by moral panics whose rhetoric of moral condemnation masked the ethnocentric and racist basis of the fear surrounding the gangster/gangsta. The lack of a historical appreciation for the interconnections between gangster and gangsta (both as representations that share a common language across the color line and as objects that shared similarly hostile receptions by guardians of the moral and cultural standard) has truncated the debate about gangsta culture. As such this chapter seeks to better define the significance of gangsta rap's cultural violations and infractions by paying proper attention to the deliberate way this part of hip hop culture "samples" a dissonant past. Not only does this do justice to the way gangsta culture "remembers" its progenitors (both within and outside a distinctively African American tradition of self-representation), but it also does justice to the way rap has inverted strategies of expropriation and stealing that have always dogged the black contribution to American popular culture.

And it is in the spirit of sampling that I acknowledge blues artist Albert King as the inspiration behind the title of this book:

Born under a bad sign,
I been down since I began to crawl,
If it wasn't for bad luck,
I wouldn't have no luck at all.

The title track of King's eponymous 1967 Stax Records blues album, *Born under a Bad Sign*, was drawn from an old blues refrain. The pathos and aporia inherent to the song's articulation of the bluesman's fortune as misfortune is typical of a tricksterlike capacity to turn disadvantage into something generative, to make good on the bad.

PRIMARY MATERIALS

This book is the culmination of primary research in the areas of black crime fiction (from the work of Rudolph Fisher to Donald Goines), black crime films (race films of the 1930s and 1940s, blaxploitation of the late 1960s and early 1970s, hood films of the 1990s), and the badman music tradition ("toasts," blues, and rap). Major parts of this research were conducted at the New York Public Library's Schomburg Center for Research in Black Culture; the Motion Picture Broadcasting and Recorded Sound Division of the Library of Congress, Washington, DC; and the Margaret Herrick Library, Academy of Motion Picture Arts and Sciences, Los Angeles.

1 Fortune Economy and the Criminal Mediation of Black Entry into Urban Modernity

Original Gangsta Culture

In 1940 one of the scions of the Harlem Renaissance, Claude McKay, reflected:

> Playing numbers is the most flourishing clandestine industry in Harlem. It is the first and foremost of the rackets and the oldest. Exciting the masses' imagination to easy "hits" by the placement of tiny stakes with glittering quick returns, it squeezes Harlem in its powerful grip. To the Negro operators it is not so enormously profitable today as it was in its halcyon period, when its foundations were laid and spread with impunity, not fearing white competitors and the action of the law. At that time the operators ("kings" and "queens" as they were called) each had a turnover of a quarter of a million dollars yearly. . . . Through all the changes Harlemites have played the game increasingly and apparently will as long as Harlem exists. Numbers is a people's game, a community pastime in which old and young, literate and illiterate, the neediest folk and the well-to-do all participate. Harlemites seem altogether lacking in comprehension of the moral attitude of the white world toward its beloved racket.[1]

Understanding the role of the numbers, or "policy," racket in black Harlem life in the 1920s and 1930s is complicated by the African American's self-knowledge of him/herself as excluded from the legitimate (white) world. The 1920s and 1930s Harlem underworld as it was represented in the period's black popular fiction and music, on the black independent screen (the subject of the next chapter), and in the form of numbers speculation on the part of Harlemites themselves, constituted not simply an ironic emulation of white capitalist mythology (of going legit). The black urban underworld (both imagined and real) was a means to overcoming the interrelated problems of economic and cultural marginalization on the basis of racial discrimination.

The self-staging of black entry into modernity was necessarily criminal. The new urban black community found itself sequestered and denied equal access to metropolitan opportunities. In the city within the city, an alternative economy evolved that mixed gambling and superstition. A syncretic system, or "fortune economy," that fused business acumen and magic was born out of the frustrated ambition to be recognized as urbane and enterprising citizens. Looking forward and outward (at a future modern self-image and at Wall Street from the wrong side) was serviced through recourse to putatively "backward" practices associated with both southern and African roots culture as a means to overcoming exclusion and disadvantage. As Maurice Dancer, correspondent for the premier African American newspaper, the *Pittsburgh Courier*, observed on December 16, 1933, the interrelationship between gambling and faith was a conspicuous and defining characteristic of Harlem:

> Gambling is the human urge to get something for nothing, or a lot for little ... in Harlem nearly everybody gambles ... the big gamble is policy—a word applied to the ordinary game of "numbers." ... Harlem is a community of high-lights and low-lights—of the advanced thinking Negro, the college graduate who goes quietly about his business—of domestic workers who travel downtown to cook and clean each day, returning to Harlem at night to care for their children and cheap dance-halls and poolrooms.... And every day the police records give evidence that Harlem is also a community of credulous people, in whom lurk all the superstitious beliefs of darkest Africa, with its voodooism and black magic.

The disparaging view of how black folk's credulity made them open to criminal deception probably corresponded with an African American bourgeois perspective that strove to distance itself from a premodern identity. White observers were both perplexed and concerned about the pervasiveness of the so-called black arts in Harlem. A *New York Herald Tribune* piece on October 16, 1927, declared: "Although there are many races to whom witchcraft is real, such as the Sicilians, who have among them persons reputed to have the evil eye, the colored population suffers most from the alleged witches of New York." The article sees charm vending and the flourishing of witchcraft in Harlem as a kind of extortion "racket" run by spurious "herb doctors," "fakirs," and "voodoo witches" capitalizing on the gullibility of their patrons. These intelligent "necromancers" are seen to originate mainly in the Deep South or West Indies—and it is proclaimed that "a deplorable feature of the situation is that educated persons are willing to take enormous sums from the wage earners for worthless drugs and charms."[2]

While such observations certainly identified the exploitative side of Harlem's fortune economy, they also betray a lack of understanding about the context in which people would make themselves "victims" of such charlatanry. As McKay highlights, Harlem's hoi polloi live in a world where white and bourgeois moral judgment is inappropriate. The *New York Herald Tribune* article inadvertently provides answers to how and why the proclivity for lottery and witchcraft remains unabated despite the chicanery of necromancers. A list of herbal remedies is provided, each of which is designed to protect an individual against local instances of bad luck or ill health. "High John," "Adam and Eve," and "John the Conqueror" are best in fending off evil, while "love philters," also known as "Keep 'Em Powders," are sold to those trying to keep their lovers faithful. As idiosyncratic as these potions appear, their consumption reflects the understandable concerns of a segregated and oppressed community for good health, family stability, and financial security—a collective desire for a better fortune in the widest sense.

In a sense, then, the confused view on gambling and voodoo as popular Harlem cultural practices plays out the contradictions definitive of the higher artistic engagements associated with the Harlem Renaissance. The writers and artists in this movement dramatized the problem of reconciling modern desires with folkloric traditions; of demonstrating mastery of white aesthetic codes, on the one hand, while trying to retain a distinctively black heritage, on the other. Given that this first black arts movement depended in large part on appealing to white patrons, it also ran the additional risk of confirming rather than dismantling stereotypes—especially when it came to primitivist expression. The appeal of this particular notion of "black" in the context of urban-industrial transformation lay in it appearing as an exotic antidote to the ailments of overcivilization. Yet this aesthetic construction of black culture ran counter to the more modern possibilities the city held out for African Americans.

For migrating black Americans in the 1920s, coming to New York constituted arrival at the heart of the United States' most dynamic metropolis. New York offered a chance for a black American to be something other than an ex-slave. A heady mix of propagandistic and anecdotal appeals by northern African Americans (through intellectual-literary vehicles such as *Crisis* and word-of-mouth dissemination by the retinue of black Pullman porters who manned the trains) were sent down South proclaiming the move North as a chance for self-advancement and full and proper integration. New York was sold and perceived as a destination of choice for the black community. Unlike the original black arrival on the North American continent as slaves and bonded laborers, the migration to the northern city was a product of manumission. That the freedom to engage in wage labor and exercise a degree of self-determination was a promise deferred and frustrated through the imposition of Jim Crow segregationist policies in the South only increased the mythic appeal of the North as a place of salvation. As LeRoi Jones highlighted in *Blues People*, going to the northern city constituted a vital opportunity for the black community to "begin again" as "would-be Americans" with a chance "to make the American dream work, if it were going to."[3] And of all the urban destinations, it was Harlem that held the most powerful place in the black imagination.

Here in Harlem was gathering a mixed black community, not simply of removed southerners but of long-established northern blacks and West Indians. The mixed cultural heritage of these diverse groups enabled a cross-fertilization of traditions and a rich engagement with the terms and prospect of African American transformation, economically, politically, and culturally. Variously imagined as "home" (*Home to Harlem*, Claude McKay), "heaven" (*Nigger Heaven*, Carl Van Vechten), "city of refuge" and "promised land" (Rudolph Fisher), Harlem's site in the midst of Manhattan placed its black denizens in a dynamically contradictory relationship to the wider white culture and its priorities. An urban version of Jim Crow continued to delimit black opportunity in all major American cities, and New York was no exception. White racist real estate practices and mortgage redlining dictated that black folk were forced to live in segregated areas, while similarly prejudicial employment practices also set severe limits on the kind of work black Americans could expect and in which they could succeed.

These problems notwithstanding, the Harlem of the decade and a half following World War I was celebrated in its day as a place of African American rebirth—and it is also canonically remembered as such. Harlem in the 1920s was a gathering point for a growing class of black intellectuals, artists, and activists who fueled the growth of organized black political movements, most notably the National Association for the Advancement of Colored People (NAACP), with W. E. B. Du Bois at its helm and *Crisis* as its official mouthpiece; the United Negro Improvement Association (UNIA), led by the charismatic Marcus Garvey; and the National Urban League, with *Opportunity* as its journal, edited by Charles S. Johnson. Self-styled New Negroes proudly proclaimed black America's political and cultural arrival and demanded that the wider society take note of its black membership and finally deliver on promises of equal rights and representation. This belated flowering of black-led organization and movement prospered until the Wall Street crash of 1929—and wilted with the onset of the Great Depression. As a rare and prodigious moment of coordinated black assertion, especially in the arts, the Harlem Renaissance has assumed its rightful place as a key object of study, not only within the field of black studies but also U.S. history and culture more generally.

Most critical attention has been devoted to the analysis of the Harlem Renaissance and its internal contradictions, especially as a Janus-faced cultural movement putatively compromised by white patronage, on the one hand, and an essentialist notion of "Negritude," on the other. The contemporaneous antagonisms within the African American intellectual and artistic community illuminate the complex richness as well as the problems involved in the generation of an adequate black self-image at the time. Ideas of roots in "Africa" and "the folk" were pitted against ideas about a more urbane and cosmopolitan identity. The tension between a desire to assert a sense of black independence and autonomy and the desire to appeal across the color line was at the heart of the movement.

In the context of quite polarizing ideas, to focus on popular and folkloric cultural practice risked an array of criticisms. One could be accused of feeding a counterproductive exotic primitivist image. Behind the mask of a campaign to celebrate a non-Western notion of identity and tradition was the problem of white reception and the ironic further separation of black from white at a time when the New Negro was seeking full equality and acceptance as an American regardless of racial difference. Du Bois, for example, was to become increasingly dissatisfied with the way Harlem Renaissance writers and artists perpetuated strong differences between "high" European tradition and what he regarded as a retrogressive notion of black folk.

Central to this problem was the popularity of a white author's controversial vision of Harlem. Through the story of a relationship between two young African Americans (a demure librarian and aspiring writer) tragically compromised by racism, Carl Van Vechten's *Nigger Heaven* (1926) introduced readers to a comprehensive Harlem world of jazz clubs, speakeasies, numbers racketeers, coffee-drinking intellectuals debating racism, and elites arguing over art. While some black artists and intellectuals appreciated Van Vechten's work as heralding new possibilities for black writing, others were outraged by the book's promulgation of depraved stereotypes. Du Bois took the lead in castigating Van Vechten in a review for *Crisis*: "To him there are no depths.... It is the surface mud he slops about in.... Life to him is just one damned orgy after another, with hate, hurt, gin and sadism."[4] While Du Bois could attribute some of Van Vechten's sins to the fact that he was a Caucasian looking in on black Harlem, McKay had no such alibi. How could a black writer produce work that seemed to follow the misguided path of *Nigger Heaven*? Du Bois would pronounce that "*Home to Harlem* ... for the most part nauseates me, and after the dirtier parts of its filth I feel distinctly like taking a bath." He went on to suggest that McKay had "set out to cater for the prurient demand on the part of white folk."[5] In his lambasting of Van Vechten and McKay, Du Bois expressed his fear that these writers promoted a new form of minstrelsy that pandered to white fantasies of African Americans as exotic "others" undermining efforts to conjoin metropolitan African Americans with progressive (revolutionary) political crusades at home and abroad.

On different political terms, George Schuyler, an avowed proponent of assimilation, wrote a famous polemic against "a great renaissance of Negro art" for *The Nation* in June 1926. Titled "The Negro-Art Hokum," the essay argued: "Negro art 'made in America' is as non-existent as the widely advertised profundity of Cal Coolidge.... Negro art there has been, is and will be among the numerous black nations of Africa; but to suggest the possibility of any such development among the ten million colored people of this nation is self-evident foolishness."[6] Schuyler is particularly sensitive to the fact that any reinforcement of racial difference in America risked sanctioning white supremacist notions of racial hierarchy that naturalized black as inferior to white:

> Because a few writers with a paucity of themes have seized upon imbecilities of the Negro rustics and clowns and palmed them off as authentic and characteristic Aframerican behavior, the common notion that the black American is so "different" from his white neighbor has gained currency. The mere mention of the word "Negro" conjures up in the average white American's mind a composite stereotype of Bert

> Williams, Aunt Jemima, Uncle Tom, Jack Johnson, Florian Slappey, and the variant monstrosities scrawled by the cartoonists.[7]

According to Schuyler, black artists in America would do well to imitate their brethren in other nations by contributing to rather than deviating from the "national norm" and make the issue of color "incidental." Otherwise the African American artist helped to legitimate a core "Negrophobist" premise: "that the blackamoor is inferior and fundamentally different" because that premise depends on "the postulate that he must needs be peculiar; and when he attempts to portray life through the medium of art, it must of necessity be a peculiar art."[8]

An immediate response to Schuyler's scathing rejection came from Langston Hughes in the following week's edition of *The Nation*. In "The Negro Artist and the Racial Mountain," Hughes put forward a compelling counterargument. The particular history of African Americans should not be jettisoned because it fed an inferiority complex. Rather, black artists were responsible for turning a history of disadvantage into something generative. A distinctive black aesthetic could overcome shame and give dignity to such a past when honed from the creative responses to the deracinating and sequestering experiences of removal from Africa, slavery, and Jim Crow:

> Let the blare of Negro jazz bands and the bellowing voice of Bessie Smith singing the Blues penetrate the closed ears of the colored near-intellectuals until they listen and perhaps understand. Let Paul Robeson singing "Water Boy" and Rudolph Fisher writing about the streets of Harlem ... cause the smug Negro middle class to turn from their white, respectable, ordinary books and papers to catch a glimmer of their own beauty.[9]

While Hughes set himself up in an antagonistic relation to Schuyler in advancing a notion of black pride, he did so in order to show how cultural practices tied to a racially distinct experience could be part of a modern and modernizing world. He continually emphasized how drawing on black expressive traditions brings something *new* into being. His championing of jazz in particular is significant as a form that looks backward and forward simultaneously.

The fact that black success was signaled through an engagement with and creative innovation within the sanctioned "high" cultural arenas of orchestrated music, painting, dance, theater, and literature has tended to obfuscate the other ways in which 1920s and 1930s Harlem constituted a black means of mediating entry into modernity. While members of Harlem's literati such as Langston Hughes, Jean Toomer, Zora Neale Hurston, and McKay turned toward vernacular forms and traditions for inspiration, they transformed these into modernist works of art. While the Harlem Renaissance's deliberate appeal to an Arnoldian notion of culture and cultural production was politically prescient as a means to countering white racist understandings of black as inferior, the intellectual valorization of 1920s and 1930s Harlem as a site of aesthetic rebirth has delimited the study and understanding of its popular cultural practices in quite rigid and problematic ways. Street and folk customs have been accorded a relegated status as material for either aesthetic bowdlerization or moral uplift. Indeed, in the case of the development of urban sociology, most seminally in the work of Gunnar Myrdal, the quotidian practices of the black lower class have been held up as evidence of that community's pathological condition.

As Henry Louis Gates Jr. points out:

> What *does* seem curious about the Harlem Renaissance is that its creation occurred precisely as Harlem was turning into the great American slum. The death rate in Harlem was 42 per cent higher than in other parts of the city. The infant mortality rate in 1928 was twice as high in Harlem as it was in the rest of New York.... The unemployment rate, according the Adam Clayton Powell Jr., was 50 per cent. There was no way to romanticize these conditions.[10]

While Gates sees a contradiction between the harsh socioeconomic realities of Harlem and the work and aims of the first black arts movement, his observation does not invite us to look more closely at the culture of the black urban poor on terms that would counter pathological interpretation. And this seems indicative of the way the Harlem Renaissance has been positioned as a romantic movement, capable of turning the uglier prosaic features of a history of disenfranchisement and the squalor of a new urban world into something sublime or transcendent. The legacy of this framing and conceptualization has been a problematic prioritization of who is worth remembering as central to the movement and what works by those remembered are worth canonizing. As a corrective, and to help resuscitate a repressed understanding of what it meant in the early twentieth century to be both black and metropolitan, this chapter is devoted in part to looking at a forgotten Harlem Renaissance author, Rudolph Fisher, and an overlooked work, *Harlem: A Negro Metropolis*, by a celebrated writer, Claude McKay.

FORTUNE ECONOMY: RUDOLPH FISHER'S LITERARY ILLOGICS

Until recently very little attention has been given to Rudolph Fisher—a significant figure in black literary circles in the late 1920s and early 1930s (who as we can see from Hughes's contention in the excerpt above ranked alongside Paul Robeson and Bessie Smith as a vital representative of "new" black possibilities at the time). Fisher died young and consequently, perhaps, his full literary potential was not realized. Yet at the time of his death at the age of thirty-seven in 1934, he had already written fifteen short stories, two novels, a number of journalistic articles, and had made strides as a roentgenologist (which tragically also led to him developing intestinal cancer as a result of exposure to X-ray radiation). Very much a "renaissance man," Fisher was well-known and admired in his day as one of the most talented New Negroes. Accounting for his surprising absence from the record since, Maria Balshaw explains that "the lack of a collection of his stories before his death meant that for a long period his stories were unavailable to anyone but those willing to trawl through the archives of the magazines which originally published his work."[11] The consequence of such difficulty in locating his shorter work and the indifference to his novels going out of print has meant that Fisher has been left out of the history of the Harlem Renaissance. The work of John McCluskey Jr. in assembling Fisher's short stories for the first time as a collection in the late 1980s has helped to remedy this problem—sparking interest in republishing both of his novels in the 1990s.[12]

Stephen F. Soitos describes Fisher as the writer who set "new standards for applying detective story conventions to African American concerns."[13] As a writer who, according to Arna Bontemps, "gave us pictures of ordinary workaday blacks who were largely neglected by other Renaissance writers," Fisher worked both with and against the grain of his New Negro peers.[14] In providing a rich view of Harlem's class structure and in experimenting with a popular form, detective fiction, he would be difficult to categorize—something that probably contributed to his subsequent neglect by those charged with anthologizing the Renaissance canon. We now place Fisher as part of a tradition in black detective fiction, as "a key antecedent to those later writers like Chester Himes and Ishmael Reed who deal with key Fisher themes of crime, detection, the black inner city and popular culture."[15]

Fisher's two novels represent related but different approaches to African American urbanity. *The Walls of Jericho* (1928) reads like a roman à clef playing out the key dichotomies of 1920s Harlem. The "dicties" (members of Harlem's social elite) rub up against the "rats" (lower class) in a story that satirizes white patronage of African American causes and the color prejudice internal to the black community itself. Issues of skin tone and language interweave, as the bowdlerized and arch language of the "fay" "dickty" striver clashes with the fecund slang and "bump-the-bump" dance moves of the "eight-ball" "jiver" "rat." A series of social vignettes is held together by two stories. A romance develops between Shine (a dark-skinned removal man) and Linda (a beautiful "Sheba" and "kitchen mechanic" [maid])—both of whom are employed by a black lawyer, Merrit, who can "pass" for Caucasian and sets out to break Manhattan's racist segregation practices by moving into a white neighborhood. Two jester-cum-chorus figures, Bubber and Jinx, surface at various moments, providing comic relief in espousing folkloric wisdom from the wings on events center stage in pure "Harlemese" street talk (Fisher is kind enough to provide a glossary of "contemporary Harlemese" at the end of the novel).

The Walls of Jericho could be described as an exercise in Harlem sociology from an insider perspective—one that refuses to be co-opted to the rationale of an objective and external scientific gaze (which is itself subject to parody in the form of Miss Cramp—a prejudicial white onlooker and patron of the Harlem scene). Fisher is keen to deal with the mediating force of language and cultural difference in everyday Harlem life through the discourse of Harlemites themselves. The consequent intermixing of high and low cultural practices poses questions about what kind of literary production is adequate to African American urbanity. And such questions receive their most sustained philosophical interrogation in Fisher's second novel, *The Conjure Man Dies* (1932).

Subtitled *A Mystery Tale of Dark Harlem*, *The Conjure Man Dies* features a clash between scientific rationality and African spiritualism. Frimbo, the conjurer "psychist," is an African king involved in fortune-telling and the purveying of various elixirs to Harlemites wishing to improve their luck. At the outset of the novel, Frimbo is discovered dead by Bubber Brown and Jinx Jenkins (the clowns from *Walls of Jericho*) at his conjure table in his apartment above Samuel Crouch's mortuary. Bubber dashes across the street to fetch Dr. Archer. Spatially, the world of the psychist faces that of the physician—the houses of fortune-telling and medical science on different sides of the same street. This configuration is further complicated by the location of the first scene of investigation, the undertaker's parlor. Here Dr. Archer examines the body and confirms that Frimbo is dead. Yet in a further twist, while Archer and his friend Detective Perry Dart (the only black Harlem policeman with a rank above patrolman) are searching for clues in Frimbo's apartment, the corpse disappears. In his struggle to solve the crime, Archer provides an unwitting premonition when he muses: "Some day I'm going to write a murder mystery ... that will baffle and astound the world. The murderer will turn out to be the most likely suspect."[16] Shortly afterward Frimbo dramatically reappears, returned from the dead. The site of embalming transforms into one of regeneration. A philosophical duel evolves between the undead African conjure man and the physician and the reasoning sleuth. The skills of Western medical science and deductive logic are pitted against Frimbo's more mysterious powers of divination in the mutual quest to find out who killed Frimbo.

This seemingly illogical premise is played out against the backdrop of Frimbo's clients and possible enemies, all of whom are involved in some form of fortune economy or are seeking solace in superstition. It emerges that Frimbo has a particular gift in being able to predict number combinations and has been winning big from a major policy racketeer, Si Brandon—something that has put his runner, Spider Webb, under suspicion. That we later discover Frimbo's gift to be quite scientific (he has been able to work out lucky numbers through a complex mathematical formula) does nothing to dispel the way Fisher opens up Harlem as a place where issues of occult divination and scientific rationality cannot be polarized. Indeed, the simplistic opposition of Western logic and African spiritualism is subject to deconstruction very early in the novel.

In their initial investigation of the murder scene, Archer and Dart come across Frimbo's study. To the declaration, "This man was no ordinary fakir," Archer draws attention to Frimbo's framed Harvard bachelor's degree certificate. Such documentation of Frimbo's provenance clearly questions the easy syllogism that *fakir* equals *faker*. In the process the basis of deductive procedure is also put into doubt. Archer browses the bookshelf, noting titles concerned with determinism, such as Tankard's *Determinism and Fatalism: A Critical Contrast*, Bostwick's *The Concept of Inevitability*, Preem's *Cause and Effect*, Dessault's *The Science of History*, and Fairclough's *The Philosophical Basis of Destiny* (16–17). Confronted by the limits of his own either/or logic, Archer later articulates his sense of confusion over Frimbo: "a student of philosophy and a sorcerer. There's something wrong with that picture" (93). The book titles betray an apposite obsession for both scientist and conjurer with the problem of deterministic logic.

The difference between Frimbo and the doctor-detective duo is that he is capable of inhabiting the worlds of science and superstition simultaneously. In an unreflecting manner Dart pronounces on the "Africanness" of N'Gana Frimbo's name: "This sounds definitely African to me. Lots of them have that 'N' in their names. The 'Frimbo' suggests it too—mumbo—jumbo—sambo." To which Archer adds in a more contemplative manner, "Limbo" (16). That Fisher calls his doctor and detective protagonists Archer and Dart is clearly part of this name game. The unidirectional (and connected) connotation of the words *archer* and *dart* betrays a single-minded and unquestioning commitment to the principles of medical diagnosis and scientific reasoning (including the blindness on Dart's part to the import of his own name). Dart's metonymic linking of "Frimbo" to "mumbo—jumbo—sambo" exposes the degree to which apparently objective explication is highly pejorative. Archer arrests this tendency with the interjection "limbo" because unlike Dart he is prepared to question the certainties of deductive procedure. Before Frimbo "done done a Lazarus" (102), as Bubber Brown puts it, Archer is already ill at ease, stating, "I've a very uncomfortable feeling that something is wrong. . . . I mean something in the way we've been reasoning. It's so easy to ignore the obvious" (95).

Indeed, the relationship between Archer and Frimbo is itself determined by conversations about reason. Frimbo pronounces that "our very faith in reason is a kind of mysticism" (128). His ability to state "a mystic paradox in terms of level reason" (103) is integral to a rhetorical game designed in part to throw the doctor and detective off course. We find out that he has resorted to a degree of dissembling in order to carry out a vital African burial duty. To protect Frimbo from possible assault by enemies, his servant had been posing as the conjure man. Mistaken for Frimbo, the servant and fellow tribe member had been killed. As his king and brethren, Frimbo was obliged to carry out a cremation within three days of the homicide in order to guarantee the man's afterlife. For this ritual to take place, the corpse had to be protected from police procurement and lengthy autopsy. While such logic may explain the dead man's disappearance and resurrection, it does not undermine or explain Frimbo's commitment to mystical custom. In this sense Fisher reinforces a mystical paradox even as he shows the conjure man to be a man of considerable reason.

Archer's discomfort with Frimbo's Africanness encourages him to diagnose the conjure man's behavior as abnormal. When Frimbo describes the "rite of the gonad" to him, for example, he rationalizes its strangeness as the product of individual psychological delusion rather than a valid cultural practice. To Frimbo, testicular extract is a form of "germplasm" that preserves "the unbroken heritage of the past." The jars of sex glands in his study contain

> the only vital matter which goes back in a continuous line to the remotest origins of the organism. It is therefore the only matter which brings into the present every influence which the past has imprinted upon life. It is the epitome of the past. He who can learn its use can be a master of his past. And he who can master his past, that man is free. (159)

Archer reduces such ideas to paranoid desires to counter determinism whose side effect in this case would lead to Frimbo becoming addicted and "oversexed" (172).[17]

To Frimbo, however, law and lore are not to be bifurcated. The world of the conjurer is one where it is possible that "a gentleman . . . turns out to be one of the suspects in his own murder case" (125). And in such a world, the rational can be exposed to its own contradictions. As he describes to Archer:

> You are working with a common assumption that any creature who is alive cannot have been dead. This is pure assumption. If a body which has presented all the aspects of death, resumes the functions of life, we explain the whole thing away merely by saying, "He was not dead." We thus repudiate all our own criteria of death. (108)

Frimbo's primary challenge is to overcome determinism—something that for the most part seems to be a quite arcane metaphysical indulgence. Archer, however, diagnoses Frimbo as suffering from paranoid delusions of grandeur, the consequence of his feeling the victim of racial prejudice. Frimbo had told him that his skin color had made it difficult to get into college in America. Dart interjects, stating, "Where's the delusion in that?" (152). Using pure deductive reason, Archer dismisses any argument made on the basis of racism:

> The delusion in that is that plenty of students the same color, but with more satisfactory formal preparation, have no such difficulty. Also that plenty the same color with unsatisfactory preparation don't draw the same conclusion. And also that plenty without his generous inheritance of pigment and with unsatisfactory preparation have the same difficulty and don't draw the same conclusion. (152–53)

In spite of Dart's further objection ("Call it a delusion if you want to . . ."), Archer then concludes that one delusion necessarily demands a compensatory further delusion, summarizing Frimbo's logic as follows: "Well, since I'm so persecuted, I must be a great guy" (153).

Archer's confidence in his own methods is challenged, however, in a critical exchange with Frimbo over the very value of deductive reason in a world where the illogical force of racism holds sway. On the occasion of this meeting, Archer states, "I had really intended to discuss the mystery of this assault . . . ," to which Frimbo responds:

> Mystery? That is no mystery. It is a problem in logic, and perfectly calculable . . . genuine mystery is incalculable. . . . The profoundest mysteries are those things which we blandly accept without question. See. You are almost white. I am almost black. Find out why and you will have solved a mystery.
>
> . . . what on earth does it matter who killed Frimbo, except to Frimbo? . . . The rest of the world would do better to concern itself with why Frimbo was black. (136)

The solving of the crime is a distraction or red herring (as is the diagnostic rationale used toward this end). The genuine mystery is the problem of the color line. Fisher thus confronts the logic informing Western metaphysics with the absurdity of race prejudice. In doing so, that which appears irrational and delusional (the rite of the gonad, masquerade, conjuring, fortune-telling, gambling) can no longer be dismissed as such. The witch doctor's quest to conquer the odds can be read not so much as a pathological response to white racism but as an apposite means to self-determination. In pitting Dr. Archer, MD, against conjure man Frimbo, the question Fisher leaves us with is this: exactly what kind of a doctor makes sense in providing remedies for the ills of a racially segregated urban ghetto?

DIVINING NUMBERS/THE BUSINESS OF NUMBERS: CLAUDE MCKAY'S POETIC SOCIOLOGY

As Fisher outlines, the trafficking in obeah and voodoo was connected to policy speculation in Harlem. Fisher's questions about how and why conjuring might have a place in a modern black urban environment addressed the intricate dependency of gambling and divination. In *Conjure Man Dies*, our access to the street world of pool halls, blackjack, numbers running, addiction, and infidelity is provided by Bubber Brown—himself a marginal figure to the major center of narrative interest—Frimbo, and Archer. Brown takes us out of the rarefied atmosphere of the drawing room and into the more fecund parts of Harlem, running errands on behalf of the doctor and detective. As he trawls through bars, pool halls, and nightclubs, we see an array of types at "work," gambling, drinking, singing, dancing, and running numbers. The relation between this space of speculation and play and the metaphysical debate between MD and witch doctor is indirect—something left for readers to infer or deduce from Frimbo's vocation. While *Conjure Man Dies* provides only glimpses of the wider social world that framed Harlemites' passion for both playing numbers and investing in occult prognostication, Claude McKay set out to provide a fuller picture.

In *Harlem: Negro Metropolis*, McKay connects the world of occultists to that of the policy racket. The more ancient customs of the one are connected to the more modern practice of numbers playing. As he notes, "The innumerable cults, mystic chapels and occult shops which abound in Harlem are explainable only by tracing back to the original African roots. For Africa remains the continent of magic."[18] Yet it is precisely "magic" that enables business:

> A few of the prominent occultists are known in the wider field of the community's life.... The most interesting of all perhaps is Madam Fu Futtam, the last wife of Sufi Abdul Hamid, the former labor agitator and cult leader.... Very industrious in the art of clairvoyance, she has published a series of dream books with interpretive numbers which have made a fortune for her. (79)

In a subsequent chapter, "The Business of Numbers," he goes on to describe the peculiar appeal of this kind of speculation to the inner-city black community. A small penny bet on a three number combination (gig) promised a disproportionate reward of six dollars. An auxiliary industry of number diviners and fortune-tellers held consultations and/or produced dream books that enabled players to translate private and public events into number sequences. Perhaps most importantly, the policy business was seen to be a community enterprise whose bosses (numbers bankers known as "kings" and "queens") were often black like their customers. Although illegal and having to operate from behind legitimate fronts (such as realty offices, barbershops, cigar and candy stores), policy was a structured hierarchical organization of bankers, controllers, collectors, and runners. And the determination of the "hit" or lucky number was dependent on Wall Street Clearing House records. In this sense, not only did numbers represent and demonstrate black organizational business acumen, but it also offered its clients (as quasi-shareholders) a chance to emulate the speculative practices of the white world from which they were excluded.

McKay's particular attention to the figure of Casper Holstein provides vivid insight into the way numbers defied white prejudice. The white epithet for policy was "nigger pool" or "nigger pennies," indicative of the contempt held for a system of gambling that appeared to have no high rollers and seemed to reflect the inferior status of black economic behavior. Such outward appearances, however, hid a different reality: "The white world never imagined that the pennies of Harlem's humble folk were creating fortunes of thousands of dollars and 'kings' and 'queens' in Harlem" (102). And one of these kings was Casper Holstein.

Unlike some of the other major number bankers (the so-called big six) in Harlem, Holstein "never flashed his prosperity in the flashy big-shot-of Harlem way. . . . He dressed quietly, like a dignified broker" (105). He used the front of being a realtor and was known as a top philanthropist. As McKay describes, Holstein was "persona grata among Harlem's elite ... he gave pecuniary assistance to struggling and aspiring writers and artists," and he funded literary prizes through his collaboration with *Opportunity*, the Urban League's monthly journal (which gave him column space to voice his grievances against the U.S. government's maltreatment of his birthplace, the former Danish Virgin Islands) (102).[19] Such philanthropy from a "Talented Tenth gangster"[20] exposed a crucial relationship between the flowering of the first black arts movement and the skills of African American economic entrepreneurship; both were born out of creative responses to racial exclusion at the very heart of the nation's supposedly most cosmopolitan city. Just as artists wrestled with the pitfalls of trying to meet mainstream standards while articulating something distinctively black, the African American financier fought to build economic structures that emulated those of legitimate white barons.

On September 21, 1928, Holstein was kidnapped by four white hoodlums who demanded a ransom of $50,000. The incident made front-page news. Its shock value had everything to do with the way it drew white attention to something they could never imagine. In the first instance the very idea that a black American could be ransomed for such a huge amount of money was astounding. The event overturned prejudicial concepts of policy as well; "nigger pennies" were clearly supporting a business system more complex and ingenious than the white imagination had presumed:

> Holstein's kidnapping flashed the searchlight on a Harlem underworld, different from the drab ugly tenements nauseating with odors of fried pork chops and rot-gut gin. This was an underworld comparable within its dimensions to the dazzling dynamic underworld of the whites, a world in which the shrewd enterprising members of the Negro minority chiseled out a way to social superiority by exploitation of the potentialities of their own people.[21]

With the police hot on the trail, Holstein was released on the fourth day of his capture. Perhaps wary of drawing further attention to his enterprise, he remained evasive about what had happened. According to McKay, Holstein's decision not to reveal the identity of his captors had less to do with honoring conditions for his release than obeying a gangster code of never squealing.[22]

The consequences of the case did have negative consequences for Holstein. In advertising the scale of business to be done in Harlem, white gangsters tried to muscle in on what was otherwise one of the few industries run predominantly by black entrepreneurs. The key offender was Dutch Schultz, who went to war with the black bankers, forcing them to acquiesce to white mob control. Initial resistance by African American policy bosses Bumpy Johnson and Stephanie "Queenie" St. Clair gave way to an asymmetrical deal in which the mob allowed St. Clair to run a minor operation and Bumpy Johnson was given responsibility in managing the black collectors and runners.[23] Schultz had been forced to realize that his operation would not work without an African American face. As McKay outlines, when the white mob initially took control, the black controllers, collectors, and runners went on strike. And to compound matters the players, in an act of solidarity, also boycotted the policy wheel. Collectively, black Harlemites demonstrated passive resistance to the violent intrusion of white mobsters into something they valued as belonging to their community.[24]

In spite of its rich insight into the life-world of Harlem in the 1920s and 1930s, McKay's *Harlem: Negro Metropolis* has been largely overlooked as a source of information on the significance of Harlem. As a collection of essays published in 1940, the work appeared after the show was over, as it were, tinged with nostalgia for the heyday of Harlem. It did not sell well and proved to be McKay's last book. Although it did not succeed in its day, this reflective study was written by one of the movement's most celebrated figures, and as such it remains puzzling as to why this work, unlike James Weldon Johnson's *Black Manhattan* (1930), for example, has remained confined to rare books collections of academic libraries.[25] As the contemporaneous success and subsequent influence of Langston Hughes's *The Big Sea*, published in the same year (1940), suggests, the time was right for a summary or hindsight account of the Harlem Renaissance. Hughes's autobiographical work provided an insider account of the ambitions and flaws of the movement, chronicling his growing dissatisfaction with the way the Harlem Renaissance distanced art from political struggle.

Intriguingly, Hughes and McKay had been traveling in opposite ideological directions. Hughes's increased political radicalization had led to him visiting the Soviet Union in 1934. In that same year McKay returned to Harlem following twelve years of overseas sojourns in the Soviet Union (in 1923 he delivered an address to the Fourth Congress of the Communist International), France, Spain, and North Africa. McKay's experiences had led to a rejection of communism and a turn to Catholicism (he converted in 1944). Hughes's account of "When the Negro Was in Vogue" (the title of the section on the Harlem Renaissance in *The Big Sea*) was framed by a political journey that by 1940 had led him to a putatively balanced centrist position. He enjoyed the authority of a seemingly objective reflection authenticated by firsthand experience. While McKay could claim that his observations were firsthand, it is clear that *Harlem: Negro Metropolis* reflects his own rejection of the logical secular world of political causes for the apparently illogical one of cultism, faith, and superstition. Although the work represented an apparent turn to a sociological essayistic account of black Manhattan's significance, its overwhelming focus on the ludic aspects of Harlem life probably made it awkward to categorize.

As sociology manqué, *Harlem: Negro Metropolis* lacked the full and comprehensive empirical rigor that characterized St. Clair Drake and Horace R. Cayton's seminal *Black Metropolis: A Study of Negro Life in a Northern City*, which would appear in 1945. Nor is it a driven historical corrective to the gloss that the cultural achievements of New York's black community hid, such as Gilbert Osofsky's *Harlem: The Making of a Ghetto* (a timely and rigorous study of segregationist real estate practice and its consequences), which covers the period 1890 to 1930 and was written in the climate of 1960s urban race rebellions. By contrast, McKay's work is permeated by poetic allusion and structured by apparently quite subjective predilections for charismatic cultists, occultists, and politicians (who become difficult to distinguish from one another)—giving most space to the less salubrious aspects of Harlem's "business" practices (policy racket, beauty business, mystic realty ventures). Compounding matters was the fact that McKay's reputation and legacy as the militant race-conscious poet laureate of the Harlem Renaissance undermined acceptance of his shift to social anthropology.

Nathan Huggins's authoritative overview, *Harlem Renaissance* (1971), only makes very brief reference to *Harlem: Negro Metropolis* as providing evidence for a more balanced view of McKay as not simply novelist or militant poet but as "consummate essayist."[26] While this is an important qualification, one could argue that in making such an assertion Huggins runs the danger of polarizing the fictional and essayistic aesthetic and thus missing the point about the liminal status of McKay's sociological gaze. What is interesting about *Harlem: Negro Metropolis* is its awkward status—what I would like to call *poetic sociology*. Symptomatically, Gilbert Osofsky refers to McKay's work as "primarily a popular history of Harlem in the 1930s."[27] While a poetic sociology sounds like a contradiction in terms and might seem to be a spurious basis for advancing larger claims about what has gone missing in accounting for Harlem's significance in black history, I would argue that McKay's study is invaluable because of its sensitivity to the generative rather than pathological character of everyday Harlem life—in its aversion to the very dualities that construct sociology (rationality/empiricism) in contradistinction to the sacred and superstition. To this extent it is not difficult to connect *Harlem: Negro Metropolis* to issues central to Fisher's *Conjure Man Dies* when it comes to exploring the black inner city.

Perhaps the biggest obstacle to a better appreciation of *Harlem: Negro Metropolis* was the flurry of major sociological tracts that superseded it. Not only did Drake and Cayton's landmark study of black urban experience establish extraordinary standards for fieldwork in this area shortly after McKay's effort, but also national attention became dominated by the work of the Swedish economist Gunnar Myrdal. Appointed by the Carnegie Corporation to direct a project devoted to the study of the Negro in the United States in 1938, Myrdal would go on to publish *An American Dilemma: The Negro Problem and Modern Democracy* in 1944. Myrdal's framing of the sociology devoted to the modern black experience as the "Negro Problem," while driven by an admirable quest to substantiate and redress the iniquity of white racism, perpetuated a pathological view of the African American community. The work's influence forced Richard Wright into introducing Drake and Cayton's book accordingly:

> The hour is too late to argue if there *is* a Negro problem or not. Riots have swept the nation and more riots are pending. This book assumes that the Negro's present position in the United States results from the oppression of Negroes by white people, that the Negro's conduct, his personality, his culture, his entire life flow naturally out of the conditions imposed upon him by white America. To that extent this book supplements and endorses the conclusions arrived at by Gunnar Myrdal in his *American Dilemma.*[28]

Myrdal provides a view of black experience that is deeply determined by institutional racism. While he accentuated this environmental argument to counter notions of racial difference grounded in biology, Myrdal provided a disparaging view of African American attempts to challenge such discrimination. The community is seen to be wide open to exploitation by its own charlatans. Black business is portrayed not as an example of entrepreneurial guile against the odds but as the exploitative result of a segregated market. Ordinary denizens of the black ghetto are seen to be passive dupes and victims. Equally, his view of churchgoing and other faith practices is skeptical. The recourse to the supernatural is indicative of how the desire to change things was politically defused:

> The instability of the Negro family, the inadequacy of educational facilities for Negroes, the emotionalism in the Negro church, the insufficiency and unwholesomeness of Negro recreational activity, the plethora of Negro sociable organizations, the narrowness of interests of the average Negro, the provincialism of his political speculation, the high Negro crime rate, the cultivation of the arts to the neglect of other fields, superstition, personality difficulties, and other characteristic traits are mainly forms of social pathology which, for the most part, are created by the caste pressures.[29]

In his chapter "The Negro Church," he would surmise:

> Potentially, the Negro church is undoubtedly a power institution. It has the masses organized and, if the church bodies decided to do so, they could line up the Negroes behind a program. Actually, the Negro church is, on the whole, passive in the field of intercaste power relations. It generally provides meeting halls and encourages church members to attend when other organizations want to influence the Negroes. But viewed as an instrument of collective action to improve the Negroes' position in American society, the church has been relatively inef-

ficient and uninfluential ... in the North it has only occasionally been a strong force for social action.[30]

The political expediency of Myrdal's desire to make social research a force for policy transformation notwithstanding (and indeed his work made a difference in animating civil rights legislation in *Brown v. Board of Education*), the legacy of this view of blacks and black community as the pathological products of white racism tends to denigrate the history of common cultural practice in urban black communities. Myrdal would pronounce: "In practically all its divergences, American Negro culture is not something independent of general American culture. It is a distorted development, or a pathological condition, of the general American culture."[31]

As Roderick Ferguson has argued, approaching the black community in this way means that "African Americans enter Myrdal's framework as the antithesis of heteronormative American identity, and thus, as the antithesis of Enlightenment rationality."[32] Myrdal attends to the excessive emotionalism, "other-worldly," and overly demonstrative character of black religious ritual and the putative instability and disorganization of the black family as evidence of the pathological costs of excluding African Americans from the same rights as whites. What goes unquestioned here is the hegemonic insistence on the rightness of the epistemologies this kind of sociology assumed would open up African American identity and experience to study and understanding. Drawing on James Baldwin's engagement with the pathological force of sociology in *Notes of a Native Son* (1955), Ferguson adumbrates that the investment in "rational reflection ostensibly to record" sponsors the construction of African American culture "as the site of irrationality."[33]

Against the grain of this paradigm, African American observers provided a more dispassionate view of such putatively pathological practices. In the same year (1944) that *American Dilemma* pronounced pejorative judgment on black religion, one of the first African Americans to earn a PhD in anthropology, Arthur Huff Fauset, published *Black Gods of the Metropolis: Negro Religious Cults of the Urban North*. Fauset's study of the plethora of church and spiritual movements in the black belts of the United States' northern cities highlighted how these held the potential to become the bases for political agitation. Drake and Cayton also provided a more generative understanding of the role of the church and its congregation. In the first instance they highlight the degree of criticism that is directed toward the church (as a kind of racket) by everyday urban black folk, revealing a far from passive community. At another level they also reinforce Fauset's prognosis that the church is a critical space for the development of an uncompromised black leadership:

> The Negro church is largely free of white control. Negro preachers have the greatest "freedom" of any Race Leaders. Politicians must fit themselves into machine politics. Most "civic" leaders are dependent on white philanthropy. Most of Bronzeville's preachers are answerable to no one except their congregations. They can say what they please about current affairs and race relations. . . . Because they are so largely free of the political and economic controls of the white community, Bronzeville expects them to be *real* Race Men. Preachers are subjected to continuous community criticism, and to retain the allegiance of their followers they are forced to concern themselves with a wide range of secular activities—political action, protest against discrimination, advice on securing jobs and legal aid, and the encouragement of Negro business enterprises.[34]

Black Gods of the Metropolis has a content list and approach not dissimilar to McKay's, indicative of a shared understanding of how and why apparently spurious behavioral indulgences matter in ways conventional approaches cannot understand. The contents page of *Harlem: Negro Metropolis* is as follows:

Harlem Vista
The Negro Quarter Grows Up
God in Harlem: Father Divine, 1935 A.D.F.D.
The Occultists
The Cultists
Harlem Businessman
The Business of Numbers
The Business of Amusements
Harlem Politician
Marcus Aurelius Garvey
Sufi Abdul Hamid and Organized Labor

This list has much in common with Fauset's:

I Negro Cults in the Urban North
II Mt. Sinai Holy Church of America, Inc.
III United House of Prayer for All People (Bishop Grace)

IV Church of God (Black Jews)
V Moorish Science Temple of America
VI Father Divine Peace Mission Movement
VII Comparative Study
VIII Why Cults Attract
IX The Cult as a Functional Institution
X The Negro and His Religion

To Fauset and McKay, following cults and sects, playing numbers, are not so much symptomatic of pathological traits as evidence of organized creative practice and response to living with the bad sign of blackness in white America. Where James Weldon Johnson saw charlatans duping the idiot lower social strata, and Myrdal saw irrationality, McKay and Fauset see something different, certainly not to be decried. Alongside McKay, Drake and Cayton, through their interviews with legitimate businesspeople (such as a bartender, tavern owner, street food peddler, and coal man) also saw policy and cultism combining to form an alternative economy—evidence of rational business organization (to counter a pathological view) supporting a more legal economy against the odds.[35]

Indeed, Drake and Cayton corroborate McKay's view of the policy king as a community patron and race leader. They make the salient point that for a community "denied full participation in the economic life of Chicago . . . every attack on South Side gambling [is] interpreted as an attack on The Race."[36] In their identification of the cult aspects of policy, Drake and Cayton avoid promoting a denigrating view of both spiritualists and players. Policy "has a hold on it devotees which is stronger than the concrete gains from an occasional winning would warrant. . . . Just any number will not do for a 'gig.' People want 'hot' numbers. Numbers and combinations of numbers derived from 'lucky' situations are much more powerful."[37] And perhaps the most important source of lucky numbers is one's dreams. The key means to translating dreams and significant personal experiences and public occurrences into number combinations was the "dream book." Numbers divination is a subsidiary business that taps into a community's desire for their dreams to be realized. Drake and Cayton do not describe this as a parasitic relationship.

It would take until the 1960s and the establishment of folklore studies as a full-fledged discipline for the insights of McKay, Drake, and Cayton into an economy of fortune to be supported. George J. McCall's "Symbiosis: The Case of Hoodoo and the Numbers Racket" was published in 1963 and then reprinted a decade later in a seminal folklorist collection edited by Alan Dundes, *Mother Wit from the Laughing Barrel: Readings in the Interpretation of Black Folklore*.[38] McKay's work on policy would finally be treated as an authoritative account in the mid-1990s by Rufus Schatzberg in *African American Organized Crime: A Social History*.[39] Significantly, however, it was a blues historian who was first to pursue the interlinking of luck and money as a key feature of urban black experience.

CODA: POLICY BLUES

Paul Oliver's seminal *Blues Fell This Morning*, dedicated to "meaning in the blues," was first published in 1960.[40] Linked to Drake and Cayton in also being endorsed by a foreword from Richard Wright, Oliver chronicled the predominant concerns associated with blues music. Two central chapters, titled "The Jinx Is on Me" and "Let the Deal Go Down," concern the interlinking of superstition and gambling. Here we find that the fortune economy is not limited to the practices of seeking counsel from conjurers and playing numbers but extends to themes at the heart of popular music. African Americans seeking release from everyday troubles and frustrations found themselves being entertained by musical performances that represented their core obsessions. In the red-light areas of the black inner city, at house rent parties, bars, and on record, blues musicians reworked the old blues refrain, "If it weren't for my bad luck, I'd have no luck at all."

The blues artist who perhaps best encapsulated dealing with living under a bad sign was Peetie Wheatstraw: The Devil's Son-in-Law. Born William Bunch, he adopted the moniker of a folkloric badman shortly after establishing himself as a major blues musician in East St. Louis in the late 1920s. A rural childhood in Tennessee and Arkansas gave way to a peripatetic hobo existence before taking up residence in East St. Louis on Third Street, which ran through the center of the city's vice district (known also as the Valley) in 1929.[41] In this journey from the country to the city, Peetie Wheatstraw updated older folkloric traditions for urban consumption. William Barlow notes that the self-styled "Devil's Son-in-Law" "began to build his public image as a streetwise, self-confident, jive-talking blues rebel. His signature piece, 'The Peetie Wheatstraw Stomp,' was a boisterous bit of self-aggrandizement that aligned him with the supernatural forces of the Christian underworld."[42] Performing in venues at the heart of East St. Louis's prostitution and gambling zone, he would declare in his "Peetie Wheatstraw Stomp," "I am Peetie Wheatstraw, the High Sheriff of Hell," possessed of hellion powers to "come into your town" and make "the women and men clown."[43] He merged spiritual and secular underworlds, freely exploiting clichés about outlawry and organized crime in songs such as "Machine Gun Blues" and "Gangster Blues," where he declares:

Last night buddy, I caught you kissing my wife.
Don't you know I'm going to take your life.
I got the gangster blues. (x3)
Boys, I am feeling mean.

I'm going to take you for an easy ride.
Drop you off on the river side.

I'm gonna bind your mouth so you can't talk.
Tie your feet so you can't walk.

You can start your screaming, but must give in.
I'm gonna tear you to pieces, and put you back again.

Put up your hands and reach for the sky.
Gonna let you down before you can bat an eye.

I'm gonna bury you out on the lone prairie.
Because I know you're (biting) on me.[44]

Wheatstraw's badman character connected urges for revenge and redress of personal wrongs to a range of pressing black urban working-class issues, such as urban renewal ("Third Street's Going Down"—a lament to the gentrification of the "Valley," the tearing down of brothels, bars, and gambling houses), factory work ("Chicago Mill Blues"—a song in which opportunity to work is recast as an opportunity for sexual conquest), relief jobs for the Works Progress Administration ("Working on the Project"—in which the payday is too far away and your woman spends it all anyway), and unemployment ("304 Blues"—receiving a 304 slip meant the WPA had made you redundant, which to Wheatstraw was a blessing in disguise). As Barlow emphasizes: "Sex, work, play—whatever the subject, the persona of Peetie Wheatstraw opposed bourgeois attitudes and social practices. He was a self-indulgent anti-hero and a fun-loving raconteur—a braggart and a sage."[45]

In the context of the Depression and its attendant socioeconomic immiseration, Wheatstraw's music proved immensely popular in its day. As Elijah Wald highlights, Wheatstraw's recording output of 161 songs between 1930 and 1941 was bettered by only four other blues artists: Tampa Red, Big Bill Broonzy, Lonnie Johnson, and Bumble Bee Slim (Amos Easton).[46] In the reconstruction of blues history, however, Wheatstraw has been overlooked, primarily in favor of Robert Johnson, as the primary badman blues artist.[47] Yet as Wald adumbrates, not only was Johnson relatively unsuccessful in the 1930s, but it also seems clear that one of his prime inspirations was Peetie Wheatstraw. Wheatstraw's laid-back vocal style, with his falsetto "oooh well, well" refrains, are elements that Johnson emulated. Additionally, Johnson went on to cover many Wheatstraw songs as well as duplicating the idea that he had entered into a satanic compact.[48]

Wheatstraw's repertoire included songs that dealt with policy, such as "Numbers Blues" and "Cut Out Blues," where he advocates giving up playing policy:

> I'm gon' cut out playing policy because my numbers just won't fall. (x2)
> Somebody's put a jinx on me, oooh, well, and I can't have no luck at all.[49]

In this he shared an ironic view of gambling and the policy wheel with other notable blues artists of the era, such as Blind Blake and Bumble Bee Slim.

In "Playing Policy Blues" (1930), Blind Blake declares, "Numbers, numbers 'bout to drive me mad.... Thinkin' about the money that I should have had," and places faith in a dream that "the woman I loved was dead." If he had interpreted his dream correctly, he should have played the "Dead Row." Instead he opts to play 3, 6, 9—which, of course, fails to hit. "I acted the fool and played on 3, 6, 9.... Lost my money and that girl of mine.... I played on Clearing-House, couldn't make the grade." Out of pocket and miserable, he seeks sexual gratification with a girlfriend: "I begged my baby to let me in her door.... Wanted to put my 25, 50, 75 in her 7, 17, 24."[50]

Certain numerical sequences—most notably 3, 6, 9 and 15, 60, 75—were valued for their scatological and sexual significances (3, 6, 9 being the number assigned to feces; 15, 60, 75 called "Big Dick"). Clearly, Blind Blake plays with common knowledge of what specific gigs signify in a humorous exercise of double entendre. The popularity of gigs with fecund associations testifies further to the way policy, as an unlicensed imitation of stock market speculation, attempts a kind of alchemy on behalf of the dispossessed, turning dirt into gold.[51]

Bumble Bee Slim sees policy as a "racket" that is "awful hard to beat."

His "Policy Dream Blues" features a verbal sparring match in which a numbers "writer" persuades him to play a gig recommended by one of the most popular policy dream books, "Red Devil." The gig, 4, 11, 44, is one of the most well-known combinations, the ultimate "lucky" number as it stands for the policy office and lottery itself. Bumble Bee Slim is skeptical especially as the writer himself is betting on a different gig based on his dream last night. Yet having "promised to leave that policy alone," he plays his last dime and ends up broke in the county jail. Six months later, he encounters the writer again, who on this occasion takes Bumble Bee Slim's bad luck to be a good sign, stating that he will play his name as a result. An inversion of fortune is taken once again to be a portentously positive sign:

> I said, "Your policy racket is a cryin' shame."
> He said, "Just for that, mister, I'm gonna play your name.
>
> The polic' draw is good, buddy. But your name is the best.
> It (signed) up last night in the east and west."
>
> I said, "Go on, Mr. Writer! That jig ain't comin' out."
> He said, "You'd better get on it. I know what I'm talkin' about."[52]

Such art attends to popular cultural activity and production not as evidence of the pathological condition but as a form of inventive, creative, and self-actualizing improvising enterprise within and against highly proscribed limits. Such songs inverted the problem of fortune through the blues artist's trickster wit. Peetie Wheatstraw, Blind Blake, and Bumble Bee Slim find in the ill fortune of their community their own calling as singer-sages committed to an underworld ethos. For Wheatstraw, that this calling was so bound up with his invocation of Satan made his brand of "devil's music" particularly conspicuous—and his demise a form of ludicrous fulfillment of bad sign destiny. Forget the afterlife, it was this present world that mattered he shouted in "Bring Me Flowers While I'm Living":

> Don't bring me flowers after I'm dead, a dead man sure can't smell.
> And if I don't go to heaven, oooh, well, well, I don't sure need no
> flowers in hell.[53]

Having recorded this and the equally tragically apt "Hearse Man Blues" in Chicago in November 1941, Wheatstraw returned to St. Louis only to be killed in a car crash on the twenty-first of December—his birthday. Putatively, spurned on by early morning celebratory drinking, Wheatstraw had challenged a friend to push a Buick to the limit, a joyride that ended with the vehicle crashing into a standing freight train one block from his home in East St. Louis.[54]

As insider observers of their communities, Fisher, McKay, and Wheatstraw developed modes of representation that refuted pathological characterization of the emerging black urban experience. Attention to the "ill-logic" informing the terms of African American modernity did not mean confirming an abject understanding of black as "problem." Indeed, Fisher's critique of deductive reason, McKay's investment in cults and lottery, and Wheatstraw's mobilization of badman folklore to address Depression realities, pointed in exactly the opposite direction, toward the perversity of normative whiteness. And nowhere would this be made more obvious than in the history of the underworld race film.

2 The Underworld Race Films of Oscar Micheaux and Ralph Cooper

Sin City Cinema

To talk of black American commercial cinema is to talk about a highly truncated legacy of false dawns in the struggle against white racist representation on the big screen. Moreover, the few moments where a discernibly black commercial cinema has appeared seem to have depended on the manufacture and perpetuation of criminal stereotypes for their economic viability. The furor surrounding the 1990s cycle of hood films starring members of the gangsta rap fraternity highlighted an apparent contradiction at the heart of any attempt on the part of black popular culture producers to gain entry and access to the mass market. *Boyz N the Hood* (1991), *New Jack City* (1991), and *Juice* (1992) drew media attention as films that provided tough and controversial views of inner-city black experience. Deploying the talents of gangsta rap stars Ice Cube, Ice-T, and Tupac Shakur, respectively, these films consolidated the hood cycle's style—blending contemporaneous explicit street realism with long-established conventions and tropes associated with the Hollywood gangster. However much participants in this kind of cinema defended it as a candid indictment of white racism ("keeping it real," in gangsta argot), the films remained open to accusations of being complicit with white racist visions of black male youth as indolent and violent. In the process, stewards of both black and white morality placed a peculiar burden on black film—as a form of entertainment with a particular mission: racial uplift.

Yet the previous moments in which a discernibly black commercial cinema appeared have also been marked as "criminal." The so-called blaxploitation cycle of the late 1960s and 1970s indulged self-consciously in exaggerated criminal self-representations, telling stories of gangster "Caesars" and pimping "Macks" who, although they occasionally had the chance to "kick whitey's ass," bore a highly ambivalent relationship to the mission of racial uplift. Continuity between these cycles has drawn a degree of critical attention recently. Work by Michael Eric Dyson, Robin D. G. Kelley, William L. Van Deburg, and Eithne Quinn has identified how this kind of self-representation is part of an enduring and misunderstood lore of the badman in African American culture.[1]

The moment, however, that such criminal self-representation first appeared on the big screen—in the form of the 1930s talking "race film" as shaped by two of its key proponents, Oscar Micheaux and Ralph Cooper—has gone relatively unnoticed until very recently.[2] Paula J. Massood's *Black City Cinema* stands out as the first sustained attempt to examine continuities of screen representation—concentrating as it does on the metonymic relationship between African American film and city film (as the conjoining of the terms "black," "city," and "cinema"). As she puts it, "Black films . . . are political acts in which the city becomes the symbol of—sometimes the synecdoche for—African American political life."[3]

The silent cinema of Oscar Micheaux has received extensive scholastic treatment in recent years. Micheaux pioneered the making and exhibition of films made for segregated black audiences—and, as Ron Green (foremost of Micheaux scholars) has adumbrated, his career more or less spanned the entirety of the history of the race film, 1919–48.[4] The indubitable influence of Micheaux has encouraged a vision of race film as a separate cinema (and has certainly encouraged an auteurist approach to his own career). The tendency to treat the race film as a cinema apart has been fueled by mutually reinforcing forces: the status of the business as something conducted outside the major studios, the fact that these films were dedicated to a segregated audience, and the desire on the part of scholars to define this cinema's significance against the dominant white cinema.

Although the race film was not a one-man show, its conditions of production, distribution, and exhibition necessarily involved "independent" economic behavior. Like other filmmaking concerns operating outside the major studios, the race-film business did not enjoy control of distribution and exhibition of its wares. Through the ownership of theaters and the practice of block booking, major studios maintained monopolistic control of distribution and exhibition of their products.[5] In such a context, a filmmaker like Micheaux was forced to make his films on the cheap and try to recover investments through road showing his films (a practice that bypassed the distributor either by taking a film directly to an exhibitor and booking the picture on a percentage basis, or leasing the theater for a temporary period). Road showing came to exist alongside the more pervasive practice of selling films on the states' rights market—a system responsible for distribution of products in various territories for a fee or a percentage of box office income—and for a limited time.[6]

Race films were even more clearly separate from most other parts of the movie industry to the extent that they were "all-Negro"/"all-Colored" cast films directed at a segregated movie audience. African Americans invariably experienced such entertainment separated from whites either in terms of time or in terms of space. The race film was often a staple of "midnight rambles," the time at which black folk were allowed to enter otherwise whites-only cinemas. In more mixed houses black audiences were constrained to so-called nigger heaven, seating in the upper tiers or "Gods." Within such segregated space, race films put black actors into roles mainstream cinema denied them and dramatized aspects of the black experience that were given no representation on the white screen. Yet race films *were* bound up with Hollywood to the extent that they adopted many of the generic frameworks (especially once sound arrived) that defined the dominant cinema. The prime reason for the race film's apparent acquiescence to the dominant cinematic style was the advent of sound and the consequences of the Wall Street crash in 1929. Sound brought with it additional costs that could only be relieved through standardization. Much like Hollywood's product, race films were presold on the basis of generic categories that were familiar and popular with black audiences in order to help guarantee investors a financial return. Such consolidation was only exacerbated by the onset of the Great Depression, which placed additional pressures on the business of getting audiences to spend their decreasing dollars on recreational pursuits.

Race-film criticism has given less attention to the more "standardized" talking products of the business than to its more idiosyncratic silent era products. Perhaps this is because these more generic efforts hold out less interest for those seeking to uncover a distinctively black cinema aesthetic. Many of these talking race films are categorically less easy to separate from the mainstream and thus less easy to accord a (positive) value when it comes to discussions of the relationship underlying race, racism, and commercial American cinema. Equally, for those trying to retain a degree of independence from Hollywood conventions, sound's compounding of the difficulty of making films on such low budgets could lead to discontinuous and dissonant montage. Micheaux seems to have been open to both failings once he moved from silent to talking pictures. To some his "jumbly-fumbly manner of directing" worsened.[7] Thomas Cripps lamented that one of Micheaux's earliest talking pictures, *Ten Minutes to Live* (1932), "typified the shoestring race movie, with its tangled racial theme, spare sets, snippets of vaudeville padding, and jagged continuity patched together with subtitles."[8] Sharing Cripps's despondency, African American film theorist Mark Reid argues further that sound spelled the end of black autonomy: "It is absurd ... for film historians and critics to call Micheaux's post-1931 films 'Black independent cinema,' for these films herald the start of two decades of Black-directed, white-financed, low-budget, commercial films made outside of Hollywood."[9]

The particular story of Micheaux's declining ability to remain truly independent once sound arrived (which forced him into league with white financiers) has also reinforced an impression that the silent era held out more possibilities for the development of a distinctive black cinematic aesthetic and politics. For example, Henry T. Sampson asserts that these talking race films,

> although technically superior in many respects to earlier black film productions, followed the typical Hollywood movie genre so popular in the late 1930s. Westerns, gangster, and comedy films were made using all-black casts. Unlike the black features of the previous decades, they made no serious attempt to treat the unique aspects of the black experience in America.[10]

Furthermore, according to Cripps, economic impoverishment and increased dependence on white money encouraged not only the "mirroring" of Hollywood but also revealed how far the race film could not "match ... Hollywood competence." Under such conditions the history of black versions of staple genres became one of "progressively weaker imitations."[11] Such negative accounts of standardization are understandable in the context of the struggle for African Americans to gain visibility on their own terms.

Taking a less pejorative stance, Jane Gaines intimates that sound worked against Micheaux's intention to make the race film a vehicle for "betterment." Betterment was one aspect of uplift or improvement of the race.[12] Micheaux's attraction to narratives that dramatized the elevation of the downtrodden and celebrated the fight of the bourgeois moral *few* to save the lower-class *many* from turpitude seems to have been compromised by the advent of the talking picture: "The economics of sound recording . . . need to be factored into the evaluation of Micheaux's aesthetic, since his low-budget use of the expensive new technology undermined his message in the sound years."[13] Dedicated as it is to uncovering the complexity and richness of silent era race films, Gaines's work does not explore the consequences of sound's undermining of Micheaux's agenda. In arguing that the introduction of sound can be understood as generative rather than debilitating, I shall elaborate on Cedric Robinson's rejoinder to "Cripps's contention that the wave of Black films beginning in the late 1930s were all low-budget 'mirror reversals' of the mainstream movie industry."[14] The shift to sound needs to be read against the grain of those who maintain too simplistically that talking race films are diminished works compared to their silent forebears.

To some extent the valorization of the aesthetic freedom of silent film against the straw man of standardization/commercialization is allied with the search for an ontologically "black" cinema. Yet critical observers as varied as Stuart Hall, James Snead, and Gaines have argued that looking for an essentially black cinema risks blinding us to the value of black cultural production that takes place within the limits of a white racist political and visual economy—blinds us to that which seeks to transform things from within the field of cultural relations.[15] That is, it conveniently obviates any need to deal with the more compromising world of crossover influences. And such a pejorative view of generic similitude has contributed to the forgetting of key race-film figures who excelled in more standardized products—especially Ralph Cooper, the original black screen gangster.

Although the transition to sound certainly exacerbated the race film's generic streamlining (contemporaneous African American press reviews often lamented that talking race films constituted a poor man's version of the Hollywood experience), what should interest us, instead, is what forms became favored within this process of apparent standardization during the 1930s. These putatively impoverished emulations of the dominant cinema proved to be significant venues for the showcasing of black revue talent in an age of decline for live black entertainment. Sound synchronization may have been expensive, but it opened up cinema's possibilities for African Americans, especially in terms of music and dance. And any attempt to evaluate the significance of the talking race film needs to acknowledge that, in this kind of cinema, investment in the delivery of performance and spectacle took priority over obligations to narrative continuity. In this context I will argue that it made particular sense for race-film producers to adopt the tropes and conventions of the Hollywood gangster film—and that a proper reading of why should lead us to different conclusions about the aesthetic and political consequences of the talking race film's apparent standardization.

The mass-screen projection of black experience was framed by the problem of working within a visual and narrative economy that from its very birth depended on the consolidation of either/or conceptions of race and identity dating back to the first minstrel shows. Film criticism often equates the birth of American narrative cinema with D. W. Griffith's *Birth of a Nation* (1915). That this birth seemed dependent on the consolidation of Old South stereotypes associated with blackness on the white screen left a peculiar and debilitating legacy for African Americans. *Birth of a Nation* set the scene in its epic portrayal of the troubled period of post–Civil War reconstruction in the Deep South. Under threat from newly emancipated slaves, white virtue is defended heroically by the Ku Klux Klan. The white racist tenets of *Birth of a Nation* maintained that emancipation was an unnatural state for African Americans. A stock vision of good and bad black screen types was consolidated. Most obviously, the emancipated slave was portrayed as a sexual predator—a "buck"—while the "mammy" or "butler" type was lauded as a more natural black condition.[16] To compound matters, economic interests helped shape the character of the white racist tropes and conventions that came to dominate Hollywood as it consolidated its business infrastructure during the 1920s.

One of Oscar Micheaux's earliest film efforts, *Within Our Gates* (1920), was a direct riposte to *Birth of a Nation*. The film gained notoriety for its direct engagement with the taboos of lynching and white-on-black rape in its closing scenes. The furor over this violent reappraisal of mixed-race relations overrode considerations of how *Within Our Gates* carefully countered the time/space of blackness on the white screen in telling the absent story of African American migration to the northern cities and in its construction of an image of a black community diverse in both regional and class affiliations. As an attempt to redress the obvious racism of Griffith's film, *Within Our Gates* included a controversial lynching scene and inverted *Birth of a Nation*'s sexual encoding of the race threat in a scene where a white overseer, in his attempt to rape the main black female protagonist, discovers her to be his daughter. This open staging of the iniquitous origins of miscegenation was deemed too volatile by the NAACP—who feared the film would fuel race riots.[17]

As Ruth Vasey has pointed out, in an age where the industry had become increasingly dependent on foreign markets for profit, it did not make business sense to indulge in openly defamatory visions of "other" races. And on the domestic front, in the context of anti-miscegenation legislation, censorship laws dictated that filmmakers should avoid depicting the races in conflict (or in sexual liaison) with each other.[18] The film industry's internal monitoring agency, the Production Code Administration (PCA), made miscegenation inadmissible and outlawed interracial affairs for fear of offending the domestic and foreign markets.

Symptomatically, the PCA file on Ralph Cooper's black gangster film *Dark Manhattan* (1937) includes the instruction that there should be no "indication that the gangsters who muscle in on the racket are white gangsters"—and emphasizes that the film's producers should "eliminate any suggestion of conflict between whites and negroes."[19] And in the case of another gangster race film, *Moon over Harlem* (1939), censors objected to the intimation of a sexual relationship between the major black gangster protagonist, Dollar Bill, and a light-skinned African American woman who could be mistaken for being white:

> The scene of Dollar Bill in the café talking to the light colored girl is questionable, and coupled with the accompanying dialogue is objectionable and quite definitely, if not in fact, inference of sex suggestion. In looking at the picture we were of the opinion that this girl was white instead of colored.[20]

Such forces fueled a tendency to keep the races apart not only offscreen (in terms of segregated viewing) but also on-screen and helped consolidate a very particular cinematic understanding of what "all-Negro" or "all-Colored" cast entertainment should provide and connote. White cinema staged blackness predominantly in a subordinate position within its diegesis—black actors assuming servant roles or appearing as song-and-dance entertainers in sideshow scenes that offered temporary "time out" from the center of dramatic attention, which was the white world. Such a tangential relationship to narrative meaning also enabled editors to cut scenes featuring black performers from reels destined for exhibition to white audiences south of the Mason-Dixon Line without damage to continuity. In this way Hollywood guaranteed that its products would not offend Jim Crow sensibilities with southern audiences and thus maximized chances of making a profit.

On the rare occasions that Hollywood did make a commitment to a fuller portrayal of black experience, this, too, was screened to preserve an ontological distinction between white and black. Hollywood's more benign vision of African American experience came in the form of a plantation cycle. Classic examples such as *Hallelujah!* (1929), *Show Boat* (1936), and *Green Pastures* (1936) situated the scene of blackness in a premodern (often Civil War era) Old South, replete with a spiritual-singing, God-fearing, "natural" and innocent cotton-picking country folk. Here blackness signified most powerfully a lost prelapsarian America set to the nostalgic sound of lamentation songs.[21] Thus even where Hollywood put a black world center stage, this was inevitably encoded as something that had passed before the time and space of the modern (of cinema itself). Although such sounds and visions may have serviced white America's negotiation of modernity's costs, they made it all but impossible for blacks to find representation as a modernizing and urbanizing people. And understanding why race-film makers gravitated to the underworld milieu as the preferred setting for their films can only be fully understood in this context. As a contemporaneous reporter for the African American newspaper *New York Age* complains:

> There are twelve million colored Americans who desire to see members of the race depicted in life on screen other than hewers of wood and drawers of water. Negro life has its tragedy, comedy, romance, running the gamut of emotions in moving, ever-changing and diverse settings. But either due to ignorance, prejudice or "cold feet," the big producer so far has failed to recognize these great potentialities of our native every day existence, and has confined himself very largely to primitive scenes on plantation and on the levee. There is more intense, vibrant gripping drama packed in our congested northern cities than in the rural South or on "Ol' Man River."[22]

For those making race films, it made sense to stage black experience in terms of the underworld for a host of mutually reinforcing reasons. Not only did the underworld milieu offer a chance to contest white visions, but, more significantly, it also allowed the sideshow to become the main event.

The early talking pictures of Oscar Micheaux offer a fascinating insight into the development of a talking race-film style that would come to be dominated by underworld-nightclub settings. In the sound era, of the seventeen films we know he made, at least nine were set in the underworld milieu: *The Exile* (1931), *Ten Minutes to Live* (1932),

The Girl from Chicago (1932), *Harlem after Midnight* (1934), *Murder in Harlem* (1935), *Temptation* (1936), *Underworld* (1937), *Swing!* (1938), and *Lying Lips* (1939).[23] Micheaux had always believed that film could be a powerful agent of racial uplift and moral edification. His talking films revealed, however, that a narrative continuity designed to service the delivery of moral lessons was often at odds with other representational opportunities that sound afforded the black community. Micheaux's early sound efforts are marked by a distinct attenuation of their narrative and diegetic logic. This can be partly attributed to the economic problems brought on by sound for African American filmmakers, who operated on extremely small budgets without access to the same resources as their white counterparts.

A prime case in point is *Ten Minutes to Live*. Much of the film was shot silent and included intertitles. According to Thomas Cripps, *Ten Minutes to Live* is an example of how Micheaux failed to overcome the problem of "limited means": "He lectured his audience on soundtracks fat with stilted verbiage that no American, black or white, ever spoke. He spliced three stories into a plot that ran nowhere over a road pot-holed with variety acts."[24] The sound scenes are primarily devoted to revue talent performing at the Lybia Club, a Harlem cabaret. The tortuously convoluted narrative is taken from short stories that purportedly made up a volume titled *Harlem after Midnight*. Of the film's sixty-three minutes, over half are given over to members of the Primetime Revue in scenes filmed from a fixed camera position and that interrupt and further attenuate an already disjointed story line (partly told in flashback) about a philanderer, faked marriage, vengeful ex-lovers, mistaken identity, and attempted and successful murder. Contributing further to the uneven visual quality was the fact that filming of the "red hot stage show scenes" was directed not by Micheaux but by Donald Heywood, the film's musical score arranger, according to the *Kansas City Call*.[25]

The consequently seamed montage undermines narrative continuity and its attendant moral endgame. As if to compound matters, the African American comedy duo "Gallie and George" (Gallie DeGaston and George Williams) perform an extended blackface routine in which they pastiche the very ideals of continuity and moral mission by misremembering key moments and figures in U.S. history, as well as parodying racial uplift and its most revered agents (such as Frederick Douglass, Booker T. Washington, and Marcus Garvey). All of this constitutes an ironic metacommentary on the burden of the race film itself. In the end *Ten Minutes to Live*'s entertainment value comes to rest mainly on the way it showcases black revue talent. The obvious convenience of a nightclub setting for a story of moral lassitude and criminal intrigue afforded the display of urban black America's most creative and conspicuous resource. In the process, dancers, singers, jazz musicians, and stand-up comedians come to assume a status more center stage than background.

What characterized *Ten Minutes to Live* so drastically can still be detected in Micheaux's less "seamed" efforts in the mid- to late 1930s. He was able to construct a more coherent narrative reason to showcase song-and-dance routines in *The Girl from Chicago*. The film weaves a story of adultery focused on a philandering and criminal town boss, Jeff Ballinger (played by John Everett), and his morally loose lover, Liza (Grace Smith), into another story of moral virtue featuring the growing love between a righteous U.S. Secret Service agent, Alonso (Carl Mahon), and a modest schoolteacher, Norma (Starr Calloway). The plot moves its protagonists from Batesburg, in "dear Old Virginia," and Mississippi, to the sin city of Harlem (understood initially as moving home to Harlem)—where Liza has turned herself into an exotic dancer at the Radium Club and married the Cuban gangster and boss of the numbers racket, Gomez (Juano Hernández). Both Liza and Gomez are subjected to the law of moral compensation at the end—Liza shoots Gomez and is then caught by the police. Additionally, Norma's friend Mary (Eunice Brooks) is rescued from her addiction to numbers playing so that she can return to the sanctity of the South. The film ends with Alonso and Norma embarking on a honeymoon in Bermuda, disabused of their naive notions of Harlem as home. To this extent the film typified Micheaux's reforming view of the costs of so-called progress and the role of the city as a breeding ground for vice and moral turpitude.

At the same time, however, the film's engagement with the underworld-nightclub milieu was more than a matter of moral necessity. Incorporation of revue talent was a prime means to sell a race film's entertainment value to investors and audiences alike. The need to keep costs down also increased dependency on more predictable generic frameworks and topical settings. Not accidentally, then, even Micheaux, the most independent of race-film producer-directors found himself adopting the conventions and tropes of the underworld-nightclub milieu as the optimal way to secure a return on his investments. By the mid-1930s Micheaux further sacrificed his autonomy by going into business with a race-film distribution company, Sack Amusement Enterprises, in order to guarantee the economic viability of his films.

A 1936 Micheaux film that is not extant, *Temptation*, seems to have set the pattern that would dominate his late 1930s movies. The *Philadelphia Independent* reported that *Temptation*'s plot turned on how an innocent, beautiful model is framed for murder by "a mob of gangsters and smugglers." Typically, the review spends an equal amount of time highlighting "the musical sequences which take place in the Mad Mullah, a notorious nightclub" in which "will be seen some of your most famous comedy stars."[26] The PCA file on *Temptation* provides further evidence of Micheaux's sense that he was now limited to working within a gangster-dependent world. Ohio censors requested that he eliminate the following dialogue between two "negro girls":

> *First girl:* "Racketeers always believe in having their molls look good; you better keep lookin' good ef you 'spects to hold them. That closet's fulla clothes—all new. I'll show 'em to you befo' yeh leaves."
>
> *Second girl:* "You know you got to have a racketeer to get anything these days. Them's the only Negroes that even have any money. That can do anything."[27]

By 1937, in *Underworld*, we see the consolidation of a talking underworld race-film formula to the cost of Micheaux's morally reforming interests. Although Micheaux continued to envision the underworld-nightclub milieu as the dangerous scene of moral lassitude for the race, his favored South-North/city-country comparative framework had now been reduced to a bookend convention, with the vast majority of the screen action being devoted to dramatizing urban nightlife. *Underworld*'s plot focuses on the fate of Paul Bronson (played by Sol Johnson), a greenhorn graduate from a black college in the South who gets conned and fleeced by an unscrupulous gambler, LeRoy Giles ("Slick" Chester), in Chicago's underworld-nightclub environment. Paul is framed for the murder of the gangster boss of the Red Lily nightclub, Sam Brown (Oscar Polk), by LeRoy and his numbers-running singer-lover, Dinah Jackson (Bee Freeman), the adulterous wife of the deceased. The film concludes with Paul and his loyal lover, Evelyn (Ethel Moses), leaving for Oklahoma.

Underworld's moral frame narrative tried to suggest that the best chance for black advancement lay outside the city limits and under the guidance of an enlightened middle class. Yet a contradictory message is relayed about the excitement and potential of city nightlife and the revue stage as a primary site of black expression and ambition. The Red Lily nightclub features scene-stealing barmen who provide constant comic relief and background singing, an extended tap routine by "Stringbeans," "The Pope Sisters," a protracted blues number, "The Six Sizzlers," "Harlem's Apache Chorus," and "The Bobby Hargreaves Orchestra." Such "distractions" were rationalized by Micheaux as a means to delivering the Harlem urban experience to southern audiences. As Patrick McGilligan notes, Lorenzo Tucker, one of the actors in *Underworld*, recalls challenging Micheaux about his seemingly arbitrary but relentless use of revue acts: "Why are you doing that? It has nothing to do with the story." To which Micheaux responds, "The poor guys down South want to see some pretty legs—dancing and beautiful girls. We've got to satisfy them."[28] McGilligan corroborates such a view in citing Micheaux's own advertisement of his wares to black theater owners in the 1932 *Film Daily Year Book*:

> GET A LOAD OF THIS, MR. EXHIBITOR: Poor attendance is due, in some measure, to the fact that your patrons are "fed up" on the average diet you are feeding them daily and are crying for "something different." Why not give them one of our Negro features for a change? Many theatres are doing so—and with gratifying success. They are especially good for midnight shows. Modern in theme, which pleases your flapper patrons—each picture has a bevy of Creole beauties—with bits of the floor shows from the great nightclubs of New York, with singing and dancing as only Broadway Negro entertainers know how to deliver—try one.[29]

The same strategy can also be said of two subsequent Micheaux efforts, *Swing!* and *Lying Lips*. *Swing!* again features a South-North conceit in which morally loose and righteous southerners venture north to Harlem and its vaudeville world to be embroiled in the criminal deceits perpetuated by nightclub owners. *Lying Lips* abandons the South-North/city-country comparative frame altogether and focuses exclusively on the traumas of a nightclub showgirl caught up in murder and insurance fraud. Both give ample space for staging a diverse range of revue talent.

No matter how much Micheaux may have tried to tailor and control its meaning in the name of his reforming agenda, the nightclub underworld came across as a space of vital black expression and creative energy. His talking race films provided images of a feisty class-divided urban people located not on the periphery of modern America but right at its heart. Black audiences used to watching both Hollywood and race films would have been entertained by this richer vision of themselves. And black actors would have found roles that testified to a reality so systematically excluded by Hollywood. Most conspicuous in this regard was the appearance of Oscar Polk as a gangster, Sam Brown, in *Underworld.* He had just enjoyed Hollywood acclaim playing the Angel Gabriel in MGM's "all-Colored" cast plantation musical, *Green Pastures*, the previous year.

The race film often provided the few African American actors who had found a Hollywood calling a chance to break with mainstream stereotypes. In *Life Goes On* (1938), for example, the urban criminal setting offered Louise Beavers the chance to be something other than a Hollywood southern "mammy" or northern "maid" whose duties are tied to (pre-)serving the white family. Although cast in a motherly role, she is now fighting (in Harlem as a single mother) to save her crime-oriented son and the structure of her own family. *Gang Smashers* (1939) turned Nina Mae McKinney from a plantation temptress (her role in *Hallelujah!*) into a gun-toting detective who assumes the guise of a cabaret star to infiltrate a ruthless Harlem gangster protection racket. Both films were products of Million Dollar Productions—cofounded by Ralph Cooper and one of the few companies in which African Americans had a stake.

If Micheaux struggled to make the talking race film fit his proscriptive "uplift" agenda, Ralph Cooper seemed free of such problems. Born in 1918 (the year before Micheaux released his first film), Cooper emerged as one of the most significant talking race-film talents (as producer, director, star, and screenwriter) in the late 1930s. Billed variously as the "Bronze Bogart" or "Dark Gable," he based all his race films (except for *The Duke Is Tops* [1938]—a musical revue film) on the gangster formula. Collectively, *Dark Manhattan* (1937), *Bargain with Bullets* (1937; re-released as *Gangsters on the Loose* [1945]), *Gang War* (1940), and *Am I Guilty?* (1940; re-released as *Racket Doctor* [1945]) communicated the meaning of the gangster from a distinctively metropolitan and necessarily theatrical black perspective.[30] Cooper's viewpoint would not reinforce binary moral distinctions between city and country. Unlike Micheaux, who was of rural working-class, mid-American stock, Cooper was a proud Harlemite. Moreover, he was a song-and-dance man brought up on the revue stage.

Before embarking on his brief film career, Cooper had already established a reputation as a vocalist and hoofer and also as the emcee of one of Harlem's most famous revue palaces, the Apollo Theater. As a Harlemite showman and talent spotter, Cooper was ideally positioned to use the talking race film as a vehicle to promote black revue talent. Moreover, as someone sensitive to the dominance of white overlords in Harlem's entertainment industry, Cooper would also find a vicarious pleasure in making movies in which black gangsters were the main players. Throughout the period of Prohibition, gangsters financed 125th Street, Harlem's Broadway; black revue theaters were primary outlets for the sale of illegal alcohol as glorified speakeasies.

In his autobiography Cooper details how the Cotton Club, Harlem's most famous revue venue, functioned also as a gangland flagship. Under the proprietorship of Owney Madden ("a former Hell's Kitchen street-gang leader" and bootlegger), the Cotton Club became "the New York underworld's favorite hangout" (most notably for Dutch Schultz, Legs Diamond, and Lucky Luciano). As a result, "hoods were an attraction almost as powerful as the Cotton Club's music."[31] Not only was the Cotton Club operated by white gangsters, but it also had (like many other Harlem revue palaces) a whites-only audience policy. Yet the club also had a 100 percent black employee policy, and its reputation depended on hiring the best African American revue talent, including Duke Ellington as its main act and bandleader. Like all the other major Harlem theaters, the Cotton Club brought wealthy white trade into the black community to spend money on Harlem's primary legal industry: revue entertainment.

Cooper was to fight successfully against Harlem's theatrical apartheid by helping turn the Apollo Theater into 125th Street's first desegregated house of entertainment in January 1934. This success, however, was somewhat pyrrhic and presaged his flight to Hollywood; breaking the color barrier was only made possible by the disintegration of the white gangster interest in Harlem that had come with Prohibition. As Cooper highlights, with the repeal of Prohibition in 1933, "the bottom fell out of the market for illegal booze, and the white warlords who depended on it began to loosen their bloody grip on Harlem. In February 1936, the mob closed its flagship and moved the Cotton Club downtown."[32] Most of the little clubs that Prohibition had spawned in Harlem went to the wall, followed gradually by the failure of larger vaudeville palaces to sustain live black entertainment. The Alhambra, the Lincoln, the Renaissance, and the Lafayette had all become exclusively movie theaters by mid-1934.[33] Furthermore, white finance traditionally directed toward the revue circuit (such as Round the World and TOBA—Theatrical Owners Booking Association—or "Tough On Black Asses" as performers called it) was redirected into making "all-Colored" cast race films.

By 1936, although Cooper had assumed the role of the Apollo's main emcee (introducing the world to figures such as Billie Holiday), he continued to labor for one of the most unscrupulous and powerful of Harlem's white overseers, Frank Schiffman. According to Cooper:

> Schiffman was a smart businessman. But he was also a ruthless competitor who would do anything, including taking advantage of his black employees and exploit the great black artists who worked for him, in order to increase profits and beat down opposition. Schiffman had a list in his office of all the performers who had offended him and who were not allowed to play the Lafayette. My former dance partner, Eddie Rector, signed one of Schiffman's contracts for one price, and when Schiffman paid him a lesser amount, Eddie flew into a rage. Eddie went home and got himself a pistol and told Schiffman he better honor that contract or he was going to ventilate him. . . . I know a lot of performers who wished Eddie had pulled that trigger.
>
> Several knuckleheaded writers of Harlem show business have glorified Schiffman as a great showman. Believe me, this he was not. He was one of the many self-ordained great white fathers of Harlem. Schiffman and other theatrical managers ran their theatres like small plantations where they were masters of all they surveyed.[34]

Under Schiffman the contingencies of black revue employment in the modern metropolis continued to resemble those of the plantation under a regime described by Cooper as "show business sharecropping."[35] Notably, it had been to Schiffman that Oscar Micheaux had turned for financial backing to make a series of sound films, including his first, *The Exile*—a move, according to Cripps, that spelled the end of "the ideal of a black-controlled cinema."[36] Schiffman would eventually accuse Micheaux of a series of larcenies that led to Micheaux's arrest and public humiliation in the press.[37]

By May 1935, following a protracted battle by Schiffman to gain monopoly control of what was left of the revue industry, the Apollo became the only black vaudeville theater in Harlem, with Cooper as its major master of ceremonies under a manager he loathed. On taking control of the Apollo, Schiffman tried to fire Cooper, but the public protested and a détente was reached. Without any competition the Apollo and Cooper secured a powerful reputation as the best showcase for live black entertainment. Cooper was soon noticed by Twentieth Century Fox talent scouts. Tired of fighting Schiffman, Cooper was lured to Hollywood to work with Bill Robinson and Stepin Fetchit, the lot's only other black contract stars.

Cooper's move to Hollywood was to produce a supremely ironic moment in black commercial arts. In 1937 *Dark Manhattan*, his first race film, premiered at the Apollo Theater, the vaudeville space from which he had flown. Shown after a live act and in a community where revue houses now concentrated on exhibition of movies, this black gangster film performed over the palimpsest of Harlem's lost gangster-sponsored vaudeville past. It brought Cooper (playing the main gangster protagonist) back in the image of the white warlords who had once bossed 125th Street—and it constituted a brief avenging moment against the power of the white Harlem overseers. For Cooper, then, the opportunity to make race films constituted a way to sustain revue talent in more ways than one. As entertainment still in need of an exhibition house, the race film helped sustain the viability of the theaters themselves. As he put it: "I got a big kick out of hearing that when the movie was screened at the Apollo, it broke all attendance records at my home theatre."[38]

The release of a Cooper gangster vehicle was to be valued for something more significant, perhaps, than the content of the film. It was grounds for a first-night black urban gala featuring a live revue program in which the screening was the main event. In a climate where, as one reporter put it, "the nightclub field has dwindled to a joke" and the "big chain of moving picture houses equipped with stages have already sounded the death-knell of vaudeville," a premiere screening of a black film was no small thing.[39] *Dark Manhattan*'s world premiere at the Apollo was anticipated effusively in the black press, with a *Philadelphia Tribune* correspondent commenting that "Harlem is expected to turn out in all its gaudy finery for the first grand opening since Nina Mae McKinney made her personal appearance with *Hallelujah* some years ago."[40] The release of *Bargain with Bullets* in Los Angeles later that year became an excuse for a "dazzling first nite session" in which black Hollywood luminaries such as Louise Beavers and Hattie McDaniel turned out: "Living up to the predictions made by daily papers that Central Avenue and the Negro district would stage a stylish formal premiere equal to the regular first nights in Hollywood, the debut of *Bargain with Bullets* at the Lincoln Theatre last Friday was just that." Appropriately, "luxurious limousines and foreign roadsters" delivered stars of the black screen firmament "under blazing lights" in "formal dress" to be greeted by emcee Clarence Muse (broadcasting the event for KMTR radio) and a host of photographers and autograph seekers.[41]

These gala premieres were major social and symbolic spectacles in which the black community stepped out, strolled, and showed off in a manner that defied the rationale that subordinated them in the mainstream industry. Such expressions of community pride brought the rich mix of black urbanites together under a media glare—and around films that placed black folk very much at the heart of modern America and exhibited, in spite of disadvantaged production conditions, an African American ability to master modern representational technology. Furthermore, these gangster vehicles produced an afterlife for a primary form of black expression, revue talent, whose viability had been threatened by the repeal of Prohibition and the onset of the Great Depression in the early 1930s.

In 1936 Cooper was called in by Twentieth Century Fox to replace the incapacitated Bill "Bojangles" Robinson in a Shirley Temple vehicle, *Captain January*. Cooper did not get cast, arguably because of his light complexion.[42] Instead he was redeployed as choreographer to *Poor Little Rich Girl* (1936), arguably Shirley Temple's best dance film. The success of Cooper's choreography led to his being given a five-year contract:

> Later I was nicknamed "Dark Gable," but Hollywood wasn't really interested in a black leading man. When *Poor Little Rich Girl* wrapped, I hoped for acting work, but all they offered me were Uncle Tom parts. "Yassuh" and "nosuh" dummy parts were all that was available for a young black actor in those days, even one with a studio contract. The stereotypes seem so offensive today; but in the 1930s, it was heresy to think that a black actor could do anything but play the devil or the dummy.... If you didn't want to mug wide-eyed and scared and act the fool, there was no room for you in the big studios.[43]

Cooper "decided that instead of appearing in pictures that demeaned blacks," he "would try to *make* pictures that glorified blacks."[44] Ironically, even though the studio had no use for African Americans as filmmakers, Fox trained Cooper (as a contractual obligation) at their studio school in all the skills required to make movies (directing, scriptwriting, lighting, set designing). This provenance might explain why Cooper's race-film efforts exhibit a style that's closer to Hollywood than Micheaux, who was self-trained.

Ever the entrepreneur, Cooper set up an independent production company, Randol-Cooper Productions, with his dance partner, George Randol, in 1937 to make films destined for a segregated black audience. Randol-Cooper Productions' first film was a gangster film, *Dark Manhattan*. Clearly derivative of the formula consolidated in Hollywood films such as *Little Caesar*, *Public Enemy*, and *Scarface*, *Dark Manhattan* starred Cooper in the leading role of Curly Thorpe, a small-time Harlem hoodlum who eventually makes it to the top of the Harlem numbers racket, only to be killed off at the film's conclusion. Although the film's limited budget guaranteed that this would only be of B quality in terms of production values, it was still a very polished product in race-film terms. Uncomplicated by the mission of uplift that so dogged Micheaux's films, *Dark Manhattan* provided an unapologetic and relatively seamless experience that exploited the special meaning the gangster story held for disadvantaged and ethnically marginalized groups as well as capitalizing on the particular significance of the numbers racket to African Americans.

Dark Manhattan's open identification with the Hollywood gangster film (*Little Caesar* and *Scarface* in particular) pointed to a shared interest between lower-class non-WASP urbanites and African Americans in highlighting the contradictions of a culture built on racialized hierarchies. Hollywood's early 1930s gangsters dramatized white ethnic urban lower-class desires for both economic and cultural inclusion in an America ruled by an Anglo-Saxon Protestant hegemony. Little Caesar's desires to "be somebody" are in part driven by his own sense of exclusion from not only the modern urban economy—but also the cultural protocols associated with high society. He journeys from the country and its world of small-time heists to the urban world of big business and gangsters with names like Diamond Pete Montana and Big Boy. While he eventually succeeds in bossing the gang he joined as a foot soldier, Edward G. Robinson's performance accentuates the gangster's sense of remaining a *cultural* outcast condemned only to ever ape the master culture. He does not feel comfortable in a tuxedo (thinking people will mistake him for a waiter), and his gang, in their attempt to hold a banquet in his honor, fall somewhat short of the mark as no one can make a proper speech, the gift turns out to be stolen, and the whole proceeding disintegrates into a food fight. This representation of ethnic striving can be read as a critique of the absurdity of ruling protocols and the attempt of lower-class ethnics to emulate high society.

Desire for cultural as well as economic capital is very much at the center of *Scarface*, too. Tony Camonte (Paul Muni) rises from the gutter to the top and spends much of his time trying to improve his ability to "pass" for a member of the legitimate culture. He tries to train-up one of his main henchmen as a secretary, indulges in elocution lessons, goes to the legitimate theater, and buys top brand clothing. His sense of taste, however, remains gauche and his attempts to free himself from Old

World Italian peasant associations (encoded in a rejecting mother costumed as a gypsy) lead to self-destruction.[45] Given the story of African Americans trying to fight white racist misrepresentation and socioeconomic exclusion in modernizing America, the early 1930s gangster must have had strong appeal as a figure of identification.

As a "numbers racket gangster film," *Dark Manhattan* linked the unique significance of the black underworld economy to the conventions of the Hollywood gangster film. Much like his Hollywood counterpart, *Dark Manhattan*'s gangster, Curly Thorpe, has his journey from ghetto tough to organization boss measured through improvements in sartorial display and the accruing of cultural capital and good taste associated with the higher classes. He starts out as a cloth-capped brawler who, on receiving employment from the numbers banker, is asked to invest in better clothing. He first buys a white suit (which is noted as being too gaudy). He then learns to dress in something more suave and appropriate—a three-piece black suit. His upward mobility also brings with it expensive cigars, a desk job (replete with a name sign, "Mr. James A. Thorpe"), and a beautiful secretary. Thus far, *Dark Manhattan* can be understood as an emulation of a well-established Depression-era gangster film formula that fed desires for class mobility shared by disadvantaged social groups across the race line. Yet *Dark Manhattan*'s meanings are both more local and more extensive than this.

As a *black* gangster, Curly rises to the top, his ascent signified through his journeying from numbers "runner" to "banker/king" via the stages of "collector" and "controller." As detailed in the previous chapter, throughout the 1920s and 1930s playing policy was an integral part of the urban black experience and was understood more as "business" than racket. The numbers or policy kings and queens held special significance for the urban black community. Far from being figures of fear and hatred, they were revered as proficient operators of a black-owned business in which all citizens had a stake. And in their battles to stop the attempts of white gangsters (especially Dutch Schultz) muscling in on the action, numbers operators only enhanced their status as examples of assertive defiance in the face of segregation and subordination. Moreover, playing and operating the numbers game provided metropolitan black folk with a vicarious experience of participating in a modern exchange economy from which they were otherwise excluded. Numbers results were computed from Wall Street Clearing House reports, and the policy organization also emulated the world of corporate banking and its management structure (with runners, collectors, controllers, and bankers).

As such, the policy racket "signified" on the world of corporate capitalist relations to which black folk had limited access. To African American audiences of the 1930s and 1940s, then, a black screen gangster would have brought with him (or her) these particular connotations.

Indeed, as Cedric Robinson emphasizes, *Dark Manhattan* exploited the contemporaneous publicity surrounding the investigation of the Harlem numbers racket, including one of its leading black bankers, Alexander Pompez, by New York's special prosecutor, Thomas E. Dewey: "Cooper and Randol gambled on the gangster genre because of its immediacy to urban Black audiences. . . . [A]s a Harlem nightclub celebrity before coming to Hollywood in 1936, Cooper was acutely aware of the scandal which was rocking the Harlem Black underworld."[46]

Symptomatically, Larry B. Lee (played by Clarence Brooks), the numbers banker whom Curly later usurps in *Dark Manhattan*, asserts that he runs his bank like a legitimate business: "Hard work, underhand methods are never used—it's love not war, it's business." The whole operation is run behind the legitimate front of a real estate company. All the employees are given white-collar roles (secretaries, accountants, telephone operators) and adhere to the prudent protocols associated with white-collar behavior. Numbers per se, is not, therefore, the problem in *Dark Manhattan*. Numbers sustains and nurtures small-scale black entrepreneurship and enables its participants to work within a sanctioned corporate structure. The line between legitimate and illegitimate business practices is violated only when Curly breaks Larry B. Lee's rules and resorts to underhand methods to bully and intimidate the competition in trying to monopolize control of the numbers game. In this sense what turns the numbers business into a racket evolves from the unfettered desire for ever-greater profits—a counterproductive desire that rides roughshod over the more civic-minded interests of the small business community.

In the highly limited context of African American entrepreneurship, numbers constituted a valid business framework. And in many ways this relationship bears some resemblance to the white lower-class urban ethnic relationship to bootlegging in the context of Prohibition. Like Larry B. Lee, Al Capone insisted that he was just a businessman supplying a legitimate public demand in a discriminatory context. Any analysis of the African American gangster film of the 1930s and 1940s must be sensitive to such parallels if it is to understand how and why the talking race-underworld film is more than a simplistic rehashing of tired Hollywood tropes.

The success of *Dark Manhattan* led to Cooper's setting up a joint venture with white investors to found one of the most successful race-film companies, Million Dollar Productions—in which Cooper as the self-styled "Bronze Bogart" or "Dark Gable" became the major saleable commodity and front man. Cooper's next two Million Dollar gangster films, *Bargain with Bullets* (which he also co-wrote) and *Gang War*, capitalized on his gangster image while also refining the underworld race-film formula as a vehicle to showcase revue talent. *Bargain with Bullets* (with Cooper in the lead gangster role as fur thief "Mugsy") contrived that the main female romantic interest was a radio singer, enabling Theresa Harris to demonstrate her vocal powers with the backing of Les Hite and His Cotton Club Orchestra, Eddie Barfield's Trio, and the Covan Studio Dancers. *Gang War* featured, conveniently, a battle between two gangs for the control of Harlem's jukebox trade (with Cooper in the lead as gangster Bob "Killer" Mead). This contrivance highlighted the importance of the roadhouse/juke-joint to black life and business and gave ample time to airing a hit ballad, "Remember the Moon," by Lew Porter and Johnny Lange.

Cooper's film career swan song was *Am I Guilty?* (1940). Having left Million Dollar Productions earlier in the year, his final film was produced by Supreme Pictures, a company in which he had no stake. The question raised by the film's title invited reflection on Cooper's own indulgence in the underworld-film form (indeed the film was re-released as *Racket Doctor*). The main doctor protagonist, James Dunbar (Cooper), is an idealist who runs a clinic in the deprived inner city. He becomes involved, however, with a ruthless gangster, "Trigger" Bennett (Lawrence Criner), who covertly finances the clinic after Dunbar treats him for an injury incurred during a payroll heist. The ambivalent relationship between the underworld economy and basic institutional care needs produces a moral impasse for the good doctor (who ends up with a prison sentence for his association with gangsters). Dunbar's impasse was in many ways Cooper's as he reached a point of exhaustion with the limits of the race film.

In 1941 he took back the job of sustaining the only venue left for live black revue talent in Harlem. As emcee for *Amateur Night at the Apollo* (for almost fifty years), Cooper went on to introduce the world to a massive range of black talent, including Gladys Knight, the Ronettes, the Shirelles, Patti LaBelle, the Isley Brothers, Wilson Pickett, Jackie Wilson, Dionne Warwick, Ben E. King, Luther Vandross, James Brown, the Jackson Five, and Big Daddy Kane. Cooper also persuaded New York radio station WMCA to air *Amateur Night at the Apollo* as a live broadcast—which was subsequently syndicated to over twenty affiliated radio stations nationwide. In the 1950s Cooper promoted the Apollo's variety talent on his own television show, *Harlem Spotlite*, which aired on Saturday nights on New York's Channel 13. In the process Cooper helped nurture the soundtrack that bridged the years between the race film and the early years of hip hop.[47]

The patterning of Micheaux's and Cooper's films around criminal melodrama that could showcase revue talent became increasingly definitive of the talking race film from the late 1930s onward. This formula is typified in race films other than those associated with Micheaux or Cooper. *Mystery in Swing* (1940), *Murder with Music* (1941), *Dirty Gertie from Harlem USA* (1946), and *Tall, Tan, and Terrific* (1946), for example, all have titles advertising the fact that they are as much revue vehicles as crime melodramas. *Murder in Swing* is a whodunit narrative revolving around the murder of an unpopular bandleader. The consequent nightclub mise-en-scène provides a framework for Ceepee Johnson and His Orchestra to show off their accomplished swing talents at regular intervals. The film was directed by Arthur Dreifus, a German exile often employed to make race films, including *Sunday Sinners* (1940) and *Murder on Lenox Avenue* (1941), both of which gave acting-singing roles to the blues singer Mamie Smith. *Murder with Music* runs for barely one hour, yet it manages to fit in nine musical numbers (with the eponymous murder occurring only in the last five minutes of the film). The main attractions are the singer, Nellie Hill (a popular vocalist of the day), and the swing band, Noble Sissle and His Orchestra. One sequence features a foreshadowing of what would replace the race film. A jungle musical number, "I'm a Bangi from Ubangi," plays out on a *television* screen. Both *Dirty Gertie from Harlem USA* and *Tall, Tan, and Terrific* give a starring role to Francine Everett, a renowned singer (and "the most beautiful woman in Harlem," according to the journalist Billy Rowe).[48] In *Dirty Gertie from Harlem USA*, Everett plays a showgirl on the run with her band from her Harlem nightclub manager, whom she has two-timed. In *Tall, Tan, and Terrific*, Everett is again in trouble with her overseers, being at the center of a struggle over the control of a nightclub—a device that again allows most footage to be dedicated to revue acts.[49]

While these films indicated the waning of the race film as a vehicle of uplift or betterment, there was at least one notable exception. *Moon over Harlem* was the product of a liaison between a group of African American stage and race-film actors and musicians and a disenchanted white Hollywood director, Edgar Ulmer. Ulmer was a secularized Austrian Jew who had made his name in high art productions as the artistic and set director for Max Reinhardt and F. W. Murnau—two masters of theater and film expressionism. His close association with Murnau, most notably as production designer and assistant director for *Der Letzte Mann* (1924), led to him traveling with Murnau to the United States to work on the Oscar-winning films *Sunrise* (1927, as assistant art director) and *Tabu* (1931, as production manager). Murnau's death in a car crash in March 1931, however, left Ulmer without a major patron. With the advent of fascist anti-Semitic rule in Germany and Austria, he found himself in a state of exile condemned to making low-budget Hollywood programs. Although he managed to make one noteworthy film, *The Black Cat* (1934), which was the first film to pair Bela Lugosi and Boris Karloff, Ulmer was deeply dissatisfied with what he called the Hollywood "hash machine."[50]

In the mid- to late 1930s Ulmer turned his back on Hollywood to go to New York to work with ethnically marginalized groups (Jewish, Ukrainian, African American) as part of an attempt to give a social and political purpose to his art.[51] Indeed, he was to describe his attraction to low-budget filmmaking outside the Hollywood system as a way to find "absolution for all the things I had to do for money's sake."[52] And one can see in the film an incipient critique of the corrupting force of capitalist greed, which was to inform most of his subsequent Hollywood work after the war, including *Detour* (1945), in which the main protagonist describes a ten-dollar bill as "nothing but a piece of paper with germs crawling all over it."

Moon over Harlem opens with a stylized title sequence that alludes to Harlem Renaissance paintings and a set of stock 125th Street Harlem nighttime establishing shots. The camera then focuses on a tenement apartment and cuts to a wedding scene within. Dollar Bill is marrying Minnie, a rich widow. The ceremony takes place in Minnie's home and is attended by an array of friends and relatives. Once the nuptial vows are over, the camera pans the room to the accompaniment of Sidney Bechet playing his clarinet, capturing the gossip that Minnie has fallen for the wrong man. Behind the mask of being a businessman, Dollar Bill is actually a gangster out to set up his own extortion (and pimping) operation independent of his white boss overseer. Part of this plan involves procuring Minnie's money. From the outset we are provided with the terrible contradiction that a black male's attempt to gain autonomy from a white master must come at the cost of a black woman.

At the wedding Dollar Bill's underlings attempt to chat up female guests while dancing, only to be rejected for being too fresh and lacking in class. These sassy women contrast starkly with the gullible Minnie, who cannot see anything but good in Dollar Bill. Out of sight from Minnie, Dollar Bill seeks out her daughter, Sue, and demands a blessing kiss. She obliges only to find Dollar Bill forcing his sexual intentions on her. Freeing herself from his grasp, she slaps him and storms out of the room. Sue is at the wedding with her boyfriend, Bob, an educated race man, who has taken up the mission of trying to rid Harlem of its extortion racket. The mise-en-scène of the wedding, then, sets up a series of class and gender oppositions that become the focus of the film's thematic interest.

The black gangster's attempt to own and control his own territory independent of the white boss has its attraction. It is clear that Dollar Bill's desires would have resonated well with African Americans—the white boss/black gangster relation serving as a dramatically interesting metaphor for the wider relationship between black and white cultures. The fact that we only ever see the back of the white boss's head only emphasizes the pervasive and faceless character of white power over the black community. Yet it is clear that Dollar Bill's personal desires are ultimately at odds with those of his community. His attempt to "make it" and be free of white bondage is dependent on extorting money from lower-class black pushcart peddlers and shopkeepers. It is also intimated that he is involved in the control of prostitution. Thus while Dollar Bill's personal desires for autonomy are an extension of a collective frustration with the iniquitous racist state of things, the resulting kind of self-assertion is shown to be highly counterproductive and contradictory.

In the end the film reveals how gangster tactics of survival depend on black-on-black crime. Not only this, but they also depend once again on the victimization of women. When Dollar Bill tries to assert his position as boss, he calls in the "boys from Newark" to shake down a pushcart peddler called Jamaica. He resists, so the goons take it out, not on Jamaica but on his wife. As well as bringing to light the antagonisms between New York's West Indians and indigenous African Americans, the film reveals the ultimate site of gangster violence and control to be the body of a black woman. The demise of Minnie illustrates this point most tragically. Hearing that Dollar Bill has been operating outside his permission and purview, the white boss sends some hit men out to kill him. As they are about to shoot Dollar Bill, Minnie charges into frame and takes the bullets instead.

Running parallel to the story of Dollar Bill and Minnie is that of Sue and Bob. Sue has aspirations to go to college, but these are frustrated by her falling-out with her mother over Dollar Bill. Minnie refuses to believe Sue's claims that Dollar Bill is a sexual predator and throws her out of the house. Sue finds employment as a singer at a nightclub—a situation that appalls and shames her mother. The nightclub is called The Plantation, an ironic yet apt name, if we recall Ralph Cooper's description of the exploitative character of such entertainment palaces. In spite of the problem of resorting to becoming a showgirl, Minnie finds friendship and solidarity backstage with other female performers.

This lower-class women's collective is contrasted with the one Bob is assembling from a women's college as part of his crusade to clean up Harlem. Bob states that the college women need to communicate with a world they have only read about. In the process the film suggests that a cross-class collective effort is required for political progress. The worlds of the showgirl and that of the middle-class student need to be brought together. The film's montage achieves this in part by allowing Sue to travel between and work in both spheres. Thematically, Bob's affection for Harlem means that the film embraces rather than rejects the city and the nightclub as sites of communal regeneration. Donald Heywood's music arrangements augmented by Christopher Columbus and His Swing Crew backing chorus-line dancers, provide an effective audiovisual image of collective organization.

The final scene of the film returns us to the scene of the wedding—now one hosting Minnie's wake. Although the guests are once again a mixture of gangsters and ordinary folk, they are portrayed as a unified group on this occasion as they sing in harmony in honor of the departed. Sue and Bob stare out of a window at a neon-lit nighttime Harlem. Bob declares that this is a world "screaming out for leadership," words that underscore the visual idea that he and Sue (unlike the tragic Dollar Bill/Minnie coupling) are the ones who can carry out this mandate.[53]

Like all other talking race films, *Moon over Harlem* was shot on a shoestring. In this case, the film was shot in only four days using short ends (unused scraps of leftover film stock) and was the only time Ulmer ever used 16mm for a feature-length production. Unlike most talking race films, however, *Moon over Harlem* enjoyed exhibition beyond the African American theater chains and segregated market. According to Shirley

Castle Ulmer (Ulmer's wife and the screenwriter for *Moon over Harlem*), the film was also picked up by the Loews Theatre chain and reached audiences across the color line.[54] While it is tempting to think that the grounds for *Moon over Harlem*'s cross-racial appeal might have had to do with its direct political addressing of the adverse effects of white racism, it is more likely that the film's association with Ulmer (as a reliable director of low-budget films) and Heywood (an African American composer, choreographer, and musical director associated with successful Broadway productions) led to Loews' interest.[55] As with most other talking race films, the potential of *Moon over Harlem* to gain a general audience probably relied as much on the appeal of musical revue as anything else.

As a cycle, the underworld talking race movie inverted the way Hollywood diegesis, with its commitment to narrative continuity, subordinated the space, time, and relevance of black expression on-screen. The ease of affiliation and identification across the racial divide with the gangster story and type provided a conventional, yet opportune, framework (with uniquely African American resonance in the case of films featuring the numbers racket) for a montage that could be set to the rhythm of revue performance and programming. And the distillation of the race film into a musical cavalcade is probably best illustrated through the fate of Francine Everett. The filmmaker and producer William Greaves stated that the star of *Dirty Gertie from Harlem USA* and *Tall, Tan, and Terrific* "would have been a superstar in Hollywood, were it not for the apartheid climate in America and the movie industry at the time."[56] Everett would, however, become a regular performer in "soundies" (featuring in over fifty of these musical shorts)—the logical end game of the race film.

In 1940 the Mills Novelty Company started producing a video jukebox, called a Panoram. These machines ran 16mm closed-loop film reels featuring eight three-minute films. This loop was back projected onto a screen contained in a large cabinet and could be played for a dime. The majority of footage featured musical numbers labeled soundies. Of these three-minute shorts, 1,865 were made between 1940 and 1946, before the Panoram business gave in to competition from television.[57] If African American performers found themselves marginalized on the big screen, the Panoram at least offered them a chance to reach audiences in a variety of congregating venues, from the finer dancing and eating establishments to military PX camps, the Staten Island Ferry, soda shops, and train and bus stations. The Panoram gave a chance for up-and-coming talent to be seen and heard for the first time, as well as giving established stars a chance to expand their market. Additionally, the Panoram could achieve a form of integration in an otherwise segregated culture. Alongside Francine Everett, African American musical luminaries such as Duke Ellington, Cab Calloway, Louis Armstrong, Nat King Cole, Dorothy Dandridge and Ceepee Johnson, Fats Waller, Count Basie, and Louis Jordan were all spliced into loops that could include white peers, such as Jimmy Dorsey, Will Bradley, Mel Torme, Les Paul, Lawrence Welk, and Doris Day.[58]

In some senses the Panoram protracted the life of the race film into the wartime and postwar 1940s. As Thomas Cripps outlines, the advent of the USA's commitment to World War II signaled the demise of segregated entertainment (or at least it undermined its legitimacy). The rationale for keeping alive the notion of the race film was out of step with the nation's declared war against fascism. Lack of resources only compounded matters for small-time producers, as the films continued to be marred by very poor production standards. Ironically, the abandonment of the race film was not replaced by a more openly integrated mainstream cinema.[59] In a climate where the big studios were struggling to deal with the consequences of antitrust legislation, an uncertain postwar future beckoned. A couple of "passing" melodramas, *Pinky* and *Lost Boundaries*, were released in 1949, giving false hope to those expecting a change in the order of things. As in other areas of American life, the African American big-screen breakthrough would be attenuated—and this time without an alternative cinema to at least give some visibility to black experience.[60]

It would take the upheavals of the late 1960s to bring back concerted filmmaking dedicated to black audiences. The combined forces of independent production, relaxation in censorship, and success in targeting niche audiences overlapped with a need to address the obvious social and political tumult associated with African American uprising. Significantly, the so-called blaxploitation cinema of the 1970s shared the talking race film's investment in the gangster story as germane to the experiences and desires of African Americans. Furthermore, the next wave of distinctly African American–oriented films, the hood cycle of the early 1990s, with its gangsta stars and inner-city criminal stories of thug life, made an even more conspicuous connection to the gangster. And like the talking underworld race film, both blaxploitation and the hood film operated as venues to showcase black musical talent.

The challenge remains to refine the connections between these different eras and their films, but we can see obvious structures of resemblance that point to the centrality of the gangster to an enduring tactic of counterhegemonic black self-representation. Echoing *Dark Manhattan*'s relationship to Hollywood gangster fare in the 1930s, for example, blaxploitation's *Black Caesar* (1973) invoked associations with the 1930s film *Little Caesar*, on the one hand, while exploiting the contemporaneous success of *The Godfather* (1972), on the other. Tommy Gibbs (Fred Williamson) infiltrates and destroys the Italian American Cardoza family to become Manhattan's first black godfather, all to the rhythm of a James Brown soundtrack. *Superfly*'s (1972) story of a Harlem pusher trying to get out of "the game" through "the game" was sold as much on the basis of Curtis Mayfield's streetwise funk soundtrack as anything else—and indeed this film's montage and meaning is directly dependent on its soundtrack. The hood films of the 1990s took this logic a step further: gangsta rappers becoming stars of vehicles that not only sold their hard-core raps but that also depended on these raps and rappers for their street credibility with audiences.

The gangster/gangsta relationship has brought attention to a black view on American possibility through cross-racial identification with white gangster icons who strove to make it in America. Black male youth have identified with the irony of the gangster's position: as someone seeking legitimacy but who can only do so through illegitimate means. But as gangstas—as black popular culture producers—they have recognized that being a gangster is at once "the American way," albeit from the dark side. As such they have muscled in and appropriated cross-racial signs of subordination that can be used against the grain. Gangsta rap monikers such as "Capone" and "Scarface" underscore a legacy of cinematic crossing-over embodied most notably in Tupac Shakur's obsession with James Cagney (as Cody Jarrett in *White Heat*) in *Juice*. However, we should not let the interrelationship between Hollywood's gangster and African American gangstas blind us to other fields of reference for the black gangster film. *Hoodlum* (1997), directed by Bill Duke, became the first attempt since the late 1930s to dramatize the high point of the Harlem numbers business—an initial step in the quest to connect the era of gangsta to that of the race film. In this spirit I have suggested that we look at the films of Ralph Cooper and Oscar Micheaux as a revised point of origin for any discussion on the meaning of criminal self-representation in African American cinema.

3 Julian Mayfield, Chester Himes, and the Black Literary Ghetto

Hustlers in the House of Literature

When I fought back through writing [America] decided to kill me, whether because I was a degenerate ex-convict who refused to wear sackcloth and ashes, a Negro who refused to accept the Negro problem as my own, a "nigger" who could not conform to the existence prescribed for niggers, a black man who pitied white women, I will never know. I do know that when America kills a nigger it expects him to remain dead. But I didn't know I was supposed to die. I still had hope. I still believed in the devil. CHESTER HIMES[1]

With the passing of the race film in the late 1940s, African American popular cultural production lost a dimension that it would not regain until the late 1960s with the advent of blaxploitation cinema. This did not mean that representations of the race problem disappeared from the big screen in the 1950s and 1960s. Hollywood co-opted the issue of race representation in a series of "passing" melodramas, such as *Pinky* (1949), *Lost Boundaries* (1949), *Band of Angels* (1957), *Imitation of Life* (1959), and *Black Like Me* (1964). It also made the first black movie superstar out of Sidney Poitier, who enjoyed unprecedented and sustained box-office popularity for an African American screen actor throughout the 1950s and 1960s, including the garnering of a best actor Oscar in 1964. Poitier's success, however, was not greeted with enthusiasm by all sections of the black community. By the late 1960s, in a more militant climate of black self-assertion in the context of civil rights activism and assassinations, Poitier's continued acceptance of ascetic, assimilationist, and saintly sacrificial roles that seemed to pander to white liberal and black bourgeois ideals about integration was deemed to be atavistic at best or a form of "Uncle Tomism" at worst. Although Poitier had become one of Hollywood's highest-earning actors by 1968, earning $9 million in that year, he was accused by those associated with the growth of a more militant black arts movement as being "a million-dollar shoe shine boy."[2] To these critics, at least, Hollywood's "cinema of integration" remained a compromised form of black attainment—one that continued to reveal limits to the terms of an acceptable black image and purveyed, arguably, a more sinister form of white racism under the guise of white liberal guilt.[3]

Stagolee, however, did not go into cultural hibernation. The criminal aesthetic was kept alive by black writing (especially from the expatriate perspective). In the late 1930s Richard Wright's "Blueprint for Negro Writing" declared a need for black writers to break with bourgeois prerogatives—especially those that led to pandering to white readership and the avoidance of the grittier urban truths confronting African Americans.[4] The publication of *Native Son* in 1940 consolidated Wright's reputation as the vanguard black protest writer. A best seller and critical success, *Native Son* attended to the way the ghetto was a defining aspect of black physical and psychological life. It exhibited Marxist, Freudian, and naturalist-determinist understandings of the black inner city and shared much with the kind of urban sociology that broke new ground in the 1940s—most notably that exemplified in St. Clair Drake and Horace R. Cayton's *Black Metropolis: A Study of Negro Life in a Northern City*—for which Wright wrote the original introduction.[5]

Wright assumed a presence of behemoth proportions in the postwar 1940s and the 1950s. Literary debates about the future of black writing were conducted primarily in relation to his proscriptions. It is not my intention to regurgitate the problematic history of Wright's legacy. Rather it is to highlight the degree to which other writers in the "Wrighteous" mold may have been overlooked as lesser overly derivative figures—or aspects of his influence may have been underexamined because critical attention has been primarily devoted to the high "literary" altercations that developed between Wright, Ralph Ellison, and James Baldwin. The work and careers of Chester Himes and Julian Mayfield, both of whom acknowledged their indebtedness to Wright, suggest other ways in which the development of a militant urban realist aesthetic mobilized African Americans.

Neither Himes nor Mayfield is well represented in anthologies of African American literature. Indeed, Mayfield, until recently, has been almost entirely neglected, while it is only Himes's early protest work that has been given any space. A case in point is the *Norton Anthology of African American Literature*, which includes a short story by Himes and nothing on Mayfield. The fact that Himes published more stories in major black and white commercial magazines (such as *Opportunity* and *Esquire*) than any other African American writer in the 1930s counts for nothing.[6] And his Harlem detective fiction of the 1950s and 1960s is discounted because it was written in exile, a condition that made him "among the least read of the postwar writers," it is claimed.[7] This seems a somewhat specious argument given Himes's own claim that he was effectively blacklisted by American publishers over this period, and it does not take into account the fact that his detective fiction *did* eventually prove highly successful with American readers once Random House picked up the imprints in the late 1980s.

If Himes's underrepresentation can be explained (albeit contentiously) as a result of exile and belated publication of his popular fiction, it is perhaps more perplexing that Mayfield has been overlooked given that he wrote two Harlem ghetto novels in the late 1950s, a political thriller in 1961, and established a contemporaneous reputation as a leading advocate of a militant black aesthetic in a series of scholarly essays. Recently, Kevin K. Gaines has drawn attention to Mayfield's political significance as an exile internationalizing the cause of civil rights as an aide to the Kwame Nkrumah regime in Ghana—but Mayfield's earlier domestic work and history remains underresearched.[8] Marginal as both Himes and Mayfield appear to have been to the major currents of black literary aesthetic experiment in the 1950s and 1960s, it is my contention that they represent a significant and overlooked link between the world and era of Wright's call for urban realism and that of blaxploitation.

Although they appear to have never met, both Himes and Mayfield shared in a struggle for domestic acceptance, membership, and disenchantment with the Communist Party USA (CPUSA), allegiance with Malcolm X and his ambivalent attitude to the nonviolent discourse of civil rights, an experience of exile, and a signal interest in the ludic features of Harlem street culture (numbers and voodoo).[9] They extended part of the Harlem Renaissance's sociological poetics (embodied in Rudolph Fisher and Claude McKay) into a more active era of black assertion against white racism at home and abroad. And they provided a critical vision of the limits of black political struggle that would prove unpalatable to the NAACP while remaining germane to those disillusioned with the way apparent gains at the legislative level failed to transform ghetto realities.

Himes started out with protest writing in a Wright-like vein but found his métier in the writing of absurdist detective fiction, a kind of writing that found its eventual audience through director and black activist Ossie Davis's highly successful 1970 transcription of *Cotton Comes to Harlem* into one of the earliest examples of blaxploitation cinema. Mayfield's Harlem ghetto novels presaged a controversial political career as champion of armed militant action during the civil rights era and as exiled writer in residence and aide to sub-Sahara Africa's first independent government, that of Nkrumah in Ghana. He took his Black Power advocacy into the realm of commercial cinema in 1968, having been asked by socialist and once-blacklisted Hollywood director Jules Dassin to co-write the screenplay and star in *Up Tight!* (1968), a film, alongside *Cotton Comes to Harlem* (but without the same box-office success), that is cited as a progenitor for blaxploitation cinema.

African American literature in the period between the end of the Harlem Renaissance and the Second Black Arts movement is defined by the rapidity and the character of African American urbanization. The period from 1940 to 1960 is one in which African American movement to the central city from rural America intensified alongside white flight from the inner city to the suburbs. White departure from urban centers also meant that employment opportunities sought by migrating black folk disappeared with them. Residential segregation on the basis of race ensured that the character of the black urban experience would be one of sequestration from the life chances proffered to white Americans. The word *ghetto* became synonymous with the black metropolis.[10]

African American writers responded to the transformation of black life by devoting themselves to the development of an urban realist aesthetic. The primary advocate of this mode of representation was Richard Wright, whose best-selling seminal novel, *Native Son* (1940), accounted for the urban alienation of its main protagonist, Bigger Thomas, as the product of vicious environmental determinism. Tenement Chicago incarcerates Bigger's mind—as internal ghetto, breeder of violent reaction, and a consciousness alien to itself. Bigger, the proletarian street-savvy lover, exists in tension with his status as rapist-murderer.[11] Wright professed that he wanted to turn away from the aesthetic indulgences of the Harlem Renaissance in the name of a more gritty depiction of the abject character of black urban existence.[12] For Wright it was a matter of urgency that the black aesthetic be harnessed primarily to social(ist) protest that serviced working-class rather than middle-class ideals. Sharing in this turn toward an uncompromising social realism was a generation of black writers that included Chester Himes and Julian Mayfield.

One of the ironies, perhaps, of having been overly under Wright's influence is that this may have led to both Himes and Mayfield being overlooked as significant contributors to the development of a black aesthetic over the period in question. Arguably, Mayfield's novels could be interpreted as following Wright's proscriptions too closely for him to have gained a distinctive-enough voice. This alone, however, is not a reason to perpetuate the critical neglect of a multifaceted and controversial black political artist. Less obviously than *The Grand Parade* (1961) (an exposé of the political chicanery involved in the attempted racial integration of a southern town), Mayfield's earlier Harlem novels, *The Hit* (1957) and *The Long Night* (1958), are precursors to his agitated militancy. These street novels provide an index to a peripatetic future that would condemn Mayfield to being peripheral in terms of the critical memory of the period, when he was actually quite central to the times as an outspoken theorist of the black aesthetic and as a political militant/miscreant invoking both the ire and affection of prominent black cultural and political commentators.

Alongside Lorraine Hansberry and Harold Cruse, Mayfield edited Paul Robeson's *Freedom* newspaper in the early 1950s.[13] In the early 1960s he took issue with the NAACP's nonviolent strategy in a article for *Commentary* (at the time a prime venue for left-wing opinion) titled "Challenge to Negro Leadership: The Case of Robert Williams."[14] And the militancy that informed Mayfield's advocacy of armed self-reliance influenced his reflections on the revolutionary future of black arts. That his essays "Into the Mainstream and Oblivion" and "You Touch My Black Aesthetic and I'll Touch Yours" were included in two seminal collections of African American cultural criticism, *Black Expression* (1969) and *The Black Aesthetic* (1971) (both edited by Addison Gayle Jr.), highlights Mayfield's contemporaneous significance.[15] Even in exile, as a founder of the first overseas branch of Malcolm X's Organization of Afro-American Unity (OAAU) in Ghana, Mayfield continued to enjoy a reputation as an important facilitator of African American political development.[16]

Mayfield's multifaceted career trajectory—from schooling at the Harlem Writer's Guild, to militant activism, to exile, to screenwriting and starring in a proto-blaxploitation film—has parallels with that of Himes. Having started out by writing social protest novels, Himes went into exile and took to writing in a popular form, leading to his appropriation by 1970s filmmakers as a basis for blaxploitation cinema. Himes's journey from socialist protest writing in the vein of his literary mentor, Wright, in the 1940s to more absurdist representation in the form of his popular detective fiction represents a turn that led to his critical disappearance during the 1950s and 1960s—and revitalization in the 1970s. Himes's inability to reach an American audience in the 1960s might be construed as a deficit—as the product of a lack of sensitivity to the civil rights discourse of the era compounded by the distance between Europe and the United States as a writer in exile. Yet Himes's choices were precisely informed by an early disillusion with the terms of black American political assertion. His ironic and violent visions were corroborated by the descent of the civil rights crusade into a period of riot, assassination, and debilitating schismatic in-fighting. In not too dissimilar ways to the story of Malcolm X's reception, what made Himes unpalatable in one period made him entirely and urgently germane to what was to come.

If Richard Wright bookends the beginning of the period in question, Malcolm X stands at the other end. As hustlers in the house of literature, Malcolm X, Mayfield, and Himes dramatized the way ethical ambiguity and ambivalence continued to haunt and define what made black literature and the black predicament "black." The metaphor of the ghettoized hoodlum world serviced a need to represent the real lived conditions of black folk in the period and to critique the way aesthetic categories continued to buttress racial ontology.

Malcolm X's self-staging as an "ex-"hoodlum-thief-pimp in *The Autobiography of Malcolm X* is of seminal importance in black writing—most specifically in our rethinking of the value of criminal aesthetics and its "ill-logic." As Black Panther leader, Bobby Seale, once expressed it, "Staggerlee is Malcolm X before he became politically conscious. *Livin' in the hoodlum world.*"[17] *The Autobiography of Malcolm X* was published in 1964, and its prescience and popularity was amplified by the assassination of Malcolm in 1965. This work is normally located canonically and generically as part of a political tradition, traceable from Douglass and Du Bois as an example of autobiography as self-actualization—or as a militant frame story to the Second Black Arts movement. Here I wish to situate *The Autobiography of Malcolm X* differently, as a work that links and lends sanction to a range of contemporaneous popular black writing experimenting with street aesthetics. For as much as Malcolm's story attests to political awakening, it also draws its plausibility and credibility from a specific lived ghetto experience. Although Malcolm's story is meant to be understood as one of deliverance, this does not mean that we should attribute strictly negative value to his supposedly fallen state.

As Kenneth Mostern so eloquently argues, *The Autobiography of Malcolm X* enacts a conflagration of hoodlum and activist identity—where the former legitimates the latter: "The identitarian rhetoric of the book, inasmuch as it is addressed to an audience of potential political allies, comes to this: trust me because I represent your (actual or potential) untrustworthiness."[18] In other words, the tropes of criminal self-representation are not enlisted to service an epiphany that is cleansed of ambivalence and paradox. *The Autobiography of Malcolm X* established against the grain and logic of race advancement rhetoric that living in the hoodlum world and owning the status of hoodlum could be prerequisites to being "trusted" with the interests of black folk as an activist representative.

Indeed, as Nikhil Pal Singh elaborates in the case of the Black Panthers, the black radical imagination drew quite explicitly on the criminal badman tradition as a means to engage and recruit the otherwise alienated urban poor to a political cause—channeling proclivities to hustling and violence toward a disciplined and organized struggle. Symptomatic of their quest to "capture the imagination of their primary audience: black youth in the ghettos of Oakland and Richmond,"[19] for example, is the story Bobby Seale told about his son's naming: " 'The Nigger's name is Malik Nkruhmah Stagolee Seale.' Malik for Malcolm X, Nkruhmah to commemorate the first successful African revolutionary, and Stagolee for the hustler, bad man, and outsider of black folklore."[20] The Panthers understood that the mobilization of their community and critique of the state depended on the cultivation of a provocative self-image—one that constituted "an insurgent form of visibility, literal-minded and deadly serious kind of guerrilla theater, in which militant sloganeering, bodily display, and spectacular actions simultaneously signified their possession and yet real lack of power."[21] The Panther strategy of developing a language that could bridge the gap between the inchoate disorder of the street and militant political organization openly drew on the success of Malcolm X's self-staging as someone with a criminal provenance.

The Autobiography of Malcolm X was a best seller and, as such, did much work to increase the cultural capital of black underworld writing that had borne a liminal (or ludic) relationship to the overworld of prevailing literary standards. Malcolm's story, then, is an ironic bildungsroman—one that would help sanction the production of an unapologetic hard-core urban black experience faction that viewed the street and prison as an organic form of schooling, embodied most graphically in the work of Robert Beck and Donald Goines.[22]

Both Mayfield and Himes respected Malcolm, and the respect was mutual. Mayfield shared in Malcolm's advocacy of armed self-reliance and an internationalist perspective on civil rights. He is remembered fondly by Malcolm for his initiative as an organizer of the first overseas branch of the OAAU:

> The author Julian Mayfield seemed to be the leader of Ghana's little colony of Afro-American expatriates. When I telephoned Mayfield, in what seemed no time at all, I was sitting in his home surrounded by about forty black American expatriates; they had been waiting for my arrival. . . .
>
> I simply couldn't believe this kind of reception five thousand miles from America![23]

Mayfield would later accompany Malcolm on a consequent journey to Egypt.

According to Himes, Malcolm had been influenced by Himes's earlier social protest fiction, especially *If He Hollers Let Him Go*.[24] For his part, Himes stated that alongside Richard Wright's *Black Boy*, *The Autobiography of Malcolm X* was the black autobiography that most moved him.[25] Indeed, Himes would compare his Harlem ghetto fiction with Malcolm's autobiography: "My books are set in the Negro ghetto. . . . They are as authentic as the *Autobiography of Malcolm X*. But I don't strain after authenticity when I write them. I tell it like it is, and the truth comes out as a matter of course."[26] And the truth was as uncomfortable for black readers as it was for anyone else. Himes felt that Martin Luther King and his nonviolent stance was a "godsend to white people."[27] Like Mayfield, Himes had far more affiliation with Malcolm's militancy and way of interlinking the quest for black American rights to an international postcolonial agenda. Such a position necessarily placed both authors at odds with the "mainstream" of civil rights integrationist action. And the occasion of Malcolm's assassination clearly had an impact on Himes's understanding of the futility of adopting a nonviolent platform in the United States:

> There is no way you can evaluate the American scene and avoid violence, because any country that was born in violence and has lived in violence always knows about violence. Anything can be initiated, en-

> forced, contained or destroyed on the American scene through violence.... The only people that the white community in America has tried to teach that it is Christian to turn the other cheek and to live peacefully are the black people.[28]

Malcolm's death seemed to corroborate his previous ideas on the psychopathology resulting from white racism that infects both white and black. One of Himes's most significant enthusiasts was Frantz Fanon, one of the most significant thinkers of colonial trauma and postcolonial possibility. In *Black Skin, White Masks*, Fanon cites Himes's *If He Hollers Let Him Go* as one of the best treatments of how white fantasies of the black male as rapist leads to perverse forms of wish fulfillment. He poses the awkward question: "Does this *fear* of rape not itself cry out for rape?" And he recommends Himes as an author prepared to be most candid about the pathological terms of miscegenation: "In *If He Hollers Let Him Go* ... the big blonde trembles whenever the Negro goes near her. Yet she has nothing to fear, since the factory is full of white men. In the end, she and the Negro go to bed together."[29] By 1959 Fanon, at the forefront in the struggle to bring independence to Algeria as part of the Front de Liberation Nationale, was working at the University of Tunis and was giving lectures based on Himes's work.[30] In the United States, however, Himes remained an unknown entity.

Mayfield shared Himes's skepticism, advancing an anti-integrationist (anti-commonsense) theory of black literature and politics in a number of articles, including "Into the Mainstream and Oblivion," in which he warns:

> The Negro writer is being gently nudged toward a rather vague thing called "the mainstream of American literature." This trend also would seem to be based on common sense. But before plunging into it he owes it to the future of his art to analyze the contents of the American mainstream to determine the full significance of his commitment to it. He may decide that, though the music is sweet, he would rather play in another orchestra. Or, to place himself in the position of the black convict in *The Defiant Ones*, he may decide that he need not necessarily share the fate of his white companion who, after all, proffers the hand of friendship a little late.[31]

Mayfield's reference to the 1958 film *The Defiant Ones* was designed to illuminate how literary assimilation and integration into the American mainstream constituted a self-defeating sacrifice. In the film Sidney

Poitier, a black prisoner on the lam, is chained to another convict who is a white racist bigot (played by Tony Curtis). As Mayfield puts it:

> Each hates the other intensely, but soon both realize that if they are to find freedom they must cooperate for their mutual good. By the time their actual chains are removed, they have come to believe that they are bound in a larger way—that their fates, their destinies, are intertwined—so much so that in the end, most remarkably (and, one hopes, not prophetically), the Negro forgoes his chance for freedom because his white comrade is too weak to escape.[32]

Finding the symbolism dubious, Mayfield took sides with those African Americans who were outraged by the film's conclusion, which literally seemed to undermine the promotion of a liberated sense of a black self. As Donald Bogle recounts: "Poitier alienated a certain segment of the audience. When he saved his honky brother, he was jeered at in ghetto theaters. Black audiences were consciously aware for the first time of the great tomism inherent in the Poitier character."[33]

As we shall see, beyond placing his fictional characters in a no-win situation vis-à-vis hegemonic notions of black uplift, Mayfield's literary choices rendered him an "outsider." His first two novels, set as they are in the Harlem ghetto, exemplified his commitment to a social realist treatment of black impossibility in white America. While integration into the mainstream meant oblivion to Mayfield, adopting this stance also seemed to put an end to his career as a fiction writer; *The Grand Parade*, Mayfield's third and last novel, was published in 1961. Significantly, this novel was precisely about the odds stacked against meaningful civil rights political organization. Turning away from fiction to commit himself instead to political activism at home and overseas, Mayfield was to declare: "Let another generation deal with the niceties of beauty and art. This generation of black men and women has its work cut out for it."[34]

Like Mayfield, Himes was wary about any ambition to be included in the mainstream. Rather than abandon a writing career, however, Himes actually rediscovered one. As a jaded and embittered *ex*-activist, Himes's understanding of exile and outsider status was different from Mayfield's. Having served a prison sentence in the late 1920s and early 1930s for armed robbery, during which he discovered his talent for writing, Himes had initially achieved some success as a protest writer. His first two novels, however, underscored the problems of African American left-wing political affiliation. Written in 1945 and 1947 respectively, *If He Hollers Let Him Go* and *Lonely Crusade* detail how the cause of racial equality was suppressed in the name of a supposedly greater cause. Both novels' major protagonists (Bob Jones and Lee Gordon) are black male college graduates employed in wartime defense plants whose leadership talents are constantly thwarted or overlooked because of their race. The psychological damage of white racism is pervasive, infecting political and sexual relationships in equal measure. Emotional attachments to white women are the source of constant danger and compromise. Bob Jones becomes the victim of false rape accusations by a white female co-worker. Gordon Lee's marriage to a black woman is poisoned by an internalized sense of emasculation and inferiority; a problem he attempts to remedy through an ultimately counterproductive affair with a white member of the Communist Party. For Himes, then, the personal is political; traumas and betrayals associated with miscegenation are inseparable from those that trouble political programs that engage the struggle for racial equality.

Himes himself had very mixed experiences with white women. His cross-racial romantic liaisons counted against him in his younger years when he was convicted of armed robbery and sent to jail. He could not sustain a marriage with his first wife, Jean Johnson,[35] who was black, or a long-term relationship with Alva Trent Van Olden Barneveldt—a white ivy-league American heiress who had left the comfort of her white world, Dutch husband, and children for a far more precarious relationship with Himes. As he put it: "The greatest failure for any man is to fail with a woman.... I had failed with my black wife in my native country and now I was failing with a white woman whom I loved in a foreign land."[36] Toward the end of his life Himes found a degree of happiness with Lesley Packard, a white Englishwoman and longtime companion in exile.

In *If He Hollers*, Bob remains wary of the party—at odds with one of its representative's statements that "the problem of the Negro industrial worker... is not so much racial as it is the problem of the masses. As soon as the masses, including all of our minority groups, have achieved economic security, racial problems will reach a solution of their own accord."[37] Asked if he agrees with this idealist proscription, Bob's riposte, built as it is on his firsthand experience of the stigma attached to intimate cross-racial association, is telling:

> No ... It's a state of mind. As long as the white folks hate me and I hate them we can earn the same amount of money, live side by side in the same kind of house and fight every day ... the only solution to the

> Negro problem is a revolution. We've got to make white people respect us and the only thing white people have ever respected is force.[38]

The awkward relationship between socialist ideals and overcoming Jim Crow is developed even further in *Lonely Crusade*. Lee Gordon becomes a CPUSA activist but finds himself the victim of dissimulation. His white lover, Jackie, has only feigned affection for him in order to seduce him into the party ranks. In an act that is tantamount to prostitution, Jackie uses sex to exploit the asymmetry of white/black relations in order to curry favor with the party leaders. Lee's conflicted experience of socialism is reflected in Himes's own withering critique of the CPUSA:

> I don't believe that Communists have ever really worked toward any solution to the Negro problem in the United States. I think the whole strategy of the Communist Party has been to use the civil rights struggle to help the cause of Communism.... All of the important black writers who belonged to the Communist Party in the early 1940s left it long ago.[39]

Himes left the United States in 1953. From an embittered position of self-imposed exile in Europe he chose to deliver a literary critique of black possibility in white America through a series of Harlem detective novels written from the late 1950s to the late 1960s. Much like Rudolph Fisher, both Himes's and Mayfield's work is deeply informed by the problem of finding an adequate literary form that could resist the pitfalls of adherence to dominant aesthetic categories. And again, like Fisher, these writers, as a consequence of their aesthetic choices, ran the risk of being forgotten or undervalued.

MAYFIELD'S HARLEM: THE ESTRANGING VIEW FROM WITHIN

A stage and screen actor, director, playwright, screenwriter, novelist, academic, militant political activist, and aide to the heads of the first postcolonial regimes in Ghana and Guyana, Julian Mayfield was in many ways a remarkable self-styled Renaissance man. He was born in 1928, in Greer, South Carolina, and raised in Washington, DC, where he attended Dunbar High School. After a year at Lincoln University, Pennsylvania, Mayfield moved on to New York to study at the Jefferson School of Social Science and to pursue his passion for acting and drama.[40] He got his break when he took over the major role of Absalom from his friend Sidney Poitier (for whom Mayfield was the understudy) in Kurt Weill and Maxwell Anderson's 1949 production, *Lost in the Stars*—a musical-cum-operatic version of Alan Paton's anti-apartheid novel, *Cry the Beloved Country*, directed by Rouben Mamoulian.[41]

This chance provided a platform for other mainly off-Broadway and Harlem theater acting roles as well as giving him the opportunity in 1952 to codirect and produce Ossie Davis's first play, *Alice in Wonder*—for which he also wrote two one-act prelude plays, *A World Full of Men* and *The Other Foot*. As part of this intense creative arts apprenticeship, Mayfield joined the Harlem Writer's Guild in the 1950s, honing his craft to produce three novels, *The Hit*, *The Long Night*, and *The Grand Parade*. In the process he became part of a vanguard group of guild writers at the time, all of whom produced their first major works through a system of daunting peer-group criticism, including John O. Killens, *Youngblood* (1954); Paule Marshall, *Brown Girl, Brownstones* (1959); and Ossie Davis, *Purlie Victorious* (1961).[42] Given the quality of this group's oeuvre and the subsequently successful literary careers of his colleagues, it is surprising that Mayfield's work disappeared into relative obscurity until very recently.

Perhaps under the influence of Killens (who led the guild at the time), a devotee of Richard Wright, Mayfield developed a pronounced social realist view of Harlem-as-ghetto, examining the mutual relation between inner and outer worlds. Central to Mayfield's work is the need to combat recourse to self-delusion and illusion as a means of surviving the social and material immiseration of living in a racially segregated inner city. Playing the numbers is a critical element to both novels—the numbers, as we have seen, being a quotidian feature of Harlem life. Numbers is itself an expression of a superstitious inclination—one encouraged in a world where the only certainty is that the real world is not one of opportunity for a black person. For Mayfield playing numbers constitutes a black way of investing in the American Dream.

The Hit's major protagonist, Hubert Cooley, lives in perpetual hope, convinced that his "luck" must change, that he will be able to leave Harlem for San Francisco, leave his wife for Sister Clarisse, leave his son and his paternal burden—when his number finally hits. Hubert lives for an irresponsible future, one kept alive through his dreams. In such a state he is constantly condescending about the present social reality; indeed, he doesn't seem to live in it at all. He has a disparaging view of almost all other black folk, a projection of a sense of self-loathing rooted in his wish that he had not been born black.

As he wanders the Harlem streets, he remains unaware of how far he cuts a strange and estranging figure to others, many of whom think he is "peculiar in the head."[43] Yet Mayfield connects Hubert's withdrawal from external realities with a more general black condition where, ultimately, everyone is peculiar in the head. Hubert's desires for freedom from the ghetto, freedom from the family, and freedom from the color of his skin provide an ironic vision of the American dream, of what *freedom* connotes.

Hubert is disgusted by the inability of black folk to adopt behaviors that ensure white success: "All these years of freedom had not taught them the most important thing about being free: to hold on to your money and make it work for you. Wasn't that the way the big white man stayed on top?" (6). Through Hubert's eyes we see a Harlem composed of scenes of indolence, profligacy, and irrational superstition, which he views with disdain. Such are the conditions, however, that fuel the black inner city's version of the dream—one in which even Hubert must participate. As he acknowledges, albeit repressing the contradiction: "If the good Lord would let Hubert catch one of those lucky numbers he would show everybody that there was one Negro who knew how to put his money to work" (6). He, too, trusts to the policy wheel. He, too, believes in dreams. Indeed, he draws his winning number, 417, from a particularly vivid one (16–17).[44]

Mayfield's authorial interjections provide a context that explains Hubert's contradictory complicity in the system he despises:

> The most popular game in New York City, and especially in Harlem, is the numbers. The poorest, most miserable creature can play. To try his luck, all he needs is a penny, and if his guess is right the numbers bank will pay him six dollars in return. . . . Its volume of business is steady, and it is seldom in crisis, for it is based on that most solid and persistent of all American phenomena—the dream.[45]

The irrationality of racism guarantees, ironically, that in Harlem the tenets of the American Dream are very much alive. The nightmare of the present only intensifies investment in and exploitation of dreams. And Hubert is not alone in this regard. As he wanders down 125th Street at noon, Mayfield reflects on how the dream is constantly renewed, black style:

> Preachers napped and dreamed of churches larger than the Abyssinian. Lawyers and petty real-estate brokers planned and schemed and gamblers figured. A con man dropped a wallet with a hundred-dollar bill in

> it to the sidewalk in front of the Corn Exchange Bank and waited for the age-old game. A hustler sat in her apartment on Sugar Hill sipping cocktails with a white merchant from downtown who was taking a long week end, sized him up, estimated his worth. Madam Lawson shuffled her cards, Madam Fatima stared into her silver ball, and turbaned Abdul Ben Said of the ebony skin mumbled an incantation to the black gods of old, and lo! all of them saw glory in the morning if not sooner. There near the top of Manhattan Island, Harlem sizzled and baked and groaned and rekindled its dream under the midday sun. (77–78)

The metonymic link between superstition and money articulates Harlem as an endless con game.

Hubert's bet on 417 is collected by an ambitious numbers writer trying to establish himself as a banker, John Lewis. Lewis's dream is to become something more than a middleman between player and those who made the real profits. When 417 comes in as the winning number, Lewis does not have the funds to pay out and takes flight to Grand Central Station and a destination beyond to start again. Just as Harlem constantly rekindles dreams, it necessarily defers them. As James Lee, Hubert's son, says to his waiting father, "He never comes, Pop. Don't you see that? John Lewis never really comes" (153). Hubert, however, remains in his own catatonic state, still believing that he has finally made it.

By contrast, James Lee, bearer of the reality check, has traveled his own journey out of self-deception. Driven by a desire *not* to become like his father, James Lee is committed to a life without commitment. Unable to see behind his father's dispassionate face, without access to Hubert's remarkably similar desire for a life free of responsibility, he lives the life projected by his father. James Lee sees the loveless relationship between his mother, Gertrude, and his father as a sign of how commitment is a sign of death. His restless desire to remain independent is reinforced through his job as a cabdriver—a mobile nomad within urban limits. His infidelity to his girlfriend, Essie, is sanctioned as a positive attribute, the sign of freedom in contradistinction to the trap of matrimony embodied in his parents. The relationship is haunted, however, by an abortion—something James Lee insisted on to preserve his independence and which figures metaphorically as a way to characterize the flawed basis for a future together. Epiphany comes too late to save his relationship with Essie, for her self-realization is dependent precisely on leaving James Lee. He at least frees himself from the delusion that his behavior is in any way productive. In the process the simple opposition of values coded by the antagonism between generations is subject to a degree of deconstruction. James Lee learns to see that in resisting his father he reproduces the very thing he detests.

The quandary that we are left with at the end of *The Hit* is taken up and reshaped in *The Long Night*. Once again a father/son relationship is central to the narrative. This time we are provided with a perspective on ghetto life through a ten-year-old, Frederick "Steely" Brown. Although named after the great black abolitionist leader, Frederick Douglass, the boy prefers to use his gang moniker, Steely, as a junior member of the Comanche Raiders. Steely's imagination is fired by his father Paul's stories of Toussaint Louverture, the leader of the slave revolt that freed Haiti from Napoleon. Such black pride figures, however, take second place to Davy Crockett and Superman in Steely's order of heroes, because they were more famous. In this sense Steely represents a drift away from the nationalist desires of his father.

Yet *The Long Night* features an epiphany that is more optimistic than *The Hit*. The action is motivated by Steely's assignment to collect on a winning bet placed by his mother and the consequent trouble in trying to recover the $27 winnings when it is stolen. The young son is serendipitously reunited with his estranged father when he mistakes him for a drunk he can roll for the lost money. Paul pawns his suit and watch to help Steely get his $27. Steely persuades Paul to come home; in the process a different kind of paternal reconciliation is achieved compared to *The Hit*. Where Hubert remains trapped in a dreamworld, Paul is able to come to a form of self-knowledge, a way to recover his dignity by being honest with himself and his son (rather than remain in a drunken stupor). The returning father is an optimistic motif here—compared to his continued self-deception in the earlier novel. Paul owns up to his condition as a man who failed to pass the exams that would have allowed him to progress to his dream job beyond the ghetto as a lawyer, and who subsequently took to the bottle in shame and out of a desire to hide away. Coming home in *The Long Night* constitutes an awakening to responsibility—and literally a new dawn.

Initially, Steely, as a member of the new generation, is seen to be distanced from the dreams of his father. Moreover, as a victim of the more powerful white heroic myths that substitute Davy Crockett for Toussaint Louverture, he is distanced from the memory of slave rebellion. Only strange and faint echoes of this lost agency survive. Mayfield chose to introduce *The Long Night* with an epigraph drawn from a Haitian voodoo incantation: "Agwé Arroyo, protect your children, Sea-shell in hand, care for your little ones." This quote is taken from Maya Deren's *Divine Horsemen: The Living Gods of Haiti*, a classic work on voodoo, which was published in 1953. Agwé is the "loa"/"lwa," or god of water, the "sovereign of the seas," protector of sailors, ships, and the waterborne diaspora.[46] Using lines from the prayer to Agwé as a preface to a story about a long night in Harlem is consistent with Mayfield's complex understanding of the African American predicament.

He gives the Arawak and Creole words of this prayer to a zombielike figure, Black Papa, a lost Haitian sailor condemned to navigate the streets of Harlem as a junk-cart-pushing tramp. Black Papa missed his boat home and now haunts the streets droning: "Cina, Cina, Cina, Dogwe sang, cina lo-ge."[47] These words are sadly unintelligible to the spooked Steely, who struggles to imagine him as one of Toussaint's people. On one of the three occasions that Steely encounters Black Papa during the long night, he describes him as a "shriveled old man" whose visage under the streetlamp "glowed luminously white. His black skin showed ashen, and his eyes seemed darker and deeper than they ever had by daytime... they seemed not to be eyes at all but empty sockets like the two top holes in a grotesque Halloween mask."[48] That Black Papa is so clearly depicted as a member of the living dead constitutes an obvious but significant way of representing the despondent state of black America. Yet he also embodies the dormant possibility of reconnecting to a lost tradition—back to Africa by way of Haiti, the land of the great liberator, Toussaint Louverture.[49] More intimately, Black Papa is a double for Steely's lost father. Black Papa's imploring that Agwé protect his children is answered in the end through Steely's discovery of his father in an alleyway and the reuniting of the family.[50]

The incorporation of paranormal tricksterlike characters into narratives that seem otherwise committed to gritty social realism is entirely consistent with the "reality" Mayfield's protagonists inhabit. This is a world in which the folkloric, superstition, and dissembling constitute means to survival and possible transcendence. To this extent Mayfield underscores the understanding of Harlem's fortune economy dramatized in work by McKay, Fisher, and Fauset in the 1930s and 1940s into 1950s Harlem. And in *The Hit* he updates black trickster badman behavior in the context of African American integration into the wider postwar national engagement in the cold war.

Caught up in a traffic jam, James Lee's mind wanders back in time to his Korean War experience. He bears the mark of war in the form of irremovable shrapnel lodged in his right buttock. A constant source of irritation, this wound reminds him of his encounter with the most savvy and tricksterlike figure in the book, McGowan, a fellow black invalid in the hospital ward. Like Black Papa, McGowan knows his badman folkloric history. He attempts to enlighten James Lee as to the absurdity of literally putting your ass on the line as a black man for your country for reasons never made clear to you. Seeing the war as just another con, McGowan outwits the system first by feigning a stomach ailment that keeps him bedridden instead of at the front, and then through faking madness once this ruse is found out. Significantly, he takes to chanting the popular Tin Pan Alley coon song "Shine" (first featured in blackface routines and, at the time of *The Hit*'s publication, most associated with Louis Armstrong) as part of this new dissembling exercise. As hospital orderlies struggle to put him into a straitjacket, McGowan starts to dance and sings the refrain: "'Cause my hair is curly, 'Cause my teeth are pearly … That's why they call me Shine."[51] As he is dragged from the ward, McGowan winks at James Lee, mischievously highlighting the irony of having to fake madness to escape the absurdity of the war.

That McGowan's ruse is also predicated on the incantation of a song not only associated with blackface routines but also with a folkloric black badman only intensifies the game that this trickster plays with white fantasy. Shine was also enshrined as part of a famous toast, "Shine and the *Titanic*." The rhyme narrates the story of a black stoker who, having warned of the impending disaster to the ocean liner, decides to save his own soul ahead of the passengers. The less bowdlerized versions of the toast include Shine's rejection of sexual favors being offered by white women on the upper decks in exchange for him carrying them to safety. Far from being understood as a negative behavior model, Shine highlighted a certain kind of ironic heroism in the context of a time (1912) when Jim Crow laws dictated that no black folk could travel as passengers on the *Titanic*.

For Mayfield, then, "idiots" such as McGowan and Black Papa complement children in being able to speak truth to a deluded adult world. Harlem itself is constructed as trapped in a permanently infantile state. This is a dependent economy where the conjoining of the words *black* and *work* adds up to subservience and exploitation:

> Here on One Hundred and Sixteenth Street factory girls and shopgirls and office girls hurried homeward in wedged heels and bargain basement

> dresses; here hurried also the factory boys, the stock boys, the shopboys, the garage boys, the kitchen boys, and the messenger boys; the handlers, the day laborers, the unskilled helpers; rushing toward pocket-sized apartments with their mustard-colored pay envelopes containing their rewards for services rendered to downtown commerce. It was still early for the petty pimps and the two-fifty whores, but a few of these already loitered on the corners near the saloons like hungry, impatient birds of prey. For all these people—the producers and the parasites, the black, brown, yellow, and white, and all the shades thereof—Saturday night exploded with unrepressed fury, releasing stocked-up passions and recharging dwindling hope and wavering confidence.[52]

The "employed" share a similarly servile class of job. These producers turn out to be saps, exploited by downtown commerce away at work, becoming prey for a parasite class on returning home. This is a world where work never equals the chance to rise above a certain rank or station. And the consequent feelings of victimization, repression, and frustration fuel desires that can only be met through an explosion of sensual indulgence, intoxication, and sex, the domain of a different form of exploitation.

Mayfield's no exit rendition of black possibility marginalizes political discourse; a situation compounded by the way we see most things from the naive perspective of Steely. The child can only hear through a keyhole the heated arguments over "the big question" between Lester and his father in the back room (74). He only half-hears and comprehends a dispute over black nationalism between the pharmacist Mr. Litchtstein and a black customer (57). And he can only overhear his mother's complaint to his father about "filling his [son's] head . . . over color and race" while on a subway ride to watch Jackie Robinson take on the white world at Ebbets Field. "I been hearing that nonsense all my life and it ain't never did anybody any good as far as I can see," she opines (63).

Yet even as they only have indirect access to the contradictions of the adult world, it is the children who harbor any hope in Mayfield's writing. In different ways both James Lee and Steely provide the possibility of something other than a defeatist outcome in inverting the paternal relationship by the end of each novel. Where this might lead, however, is left suspended. And given that Mayfield provides such a compelling vision of the way the ghetto feeds self-delusion and fatalism, the forms of self-awakening that are achieved remain pyrrhic in the case of James Lee and quite embryonic in the case of Steely.

HIMES'S HARLEM: STRANGER THAN FICTION—THE VIEW FROM EXILE

Like Mayfield, Himes provides a cynical view of the ghetto's ability to profit from its own immiseration. As he puts it so graphically in a passage from his first Harlem Domestic Series novel, *A Rage in Harlem*:

> Looking eastward from the towers of Riverside Church, perched among the university buildings on the high banks of the Harlem River, in a valley far below, waves of gray rooftops distort the perspective like the surface of a sea. Below the surface, in the murky waters of fetid tenements, a city of black people who are convulsed in desperate living, like the voracious churning of millions of hungry cannibal fish. Blind mouths eating their own guts. Put in a hand and draw back a nub.
>
> That is Harlem.[53]

What is latent in Mayfield is taken to extreme in Himes. Self-awakening has no progressive force in his novels. In Himes's Harlem, the only truth that emerges is that behind every mask lies another, ad infinitum, because, ultimately, "Black people are so gullible ... somebody's always out to cheat them."[54]

Spanning a period from 1957 to 1969, Himes's Harlem Domestic Series—crime stories featuring two tough black detectives, Grave Digger Jones and Coffin Ed Johnson—provide a sustained critique of black aesthetic and political possibility during the period of civil rights struggle. They reflect a point of view probably enhanced by the experience of writing in exile—a situation that fed an angry disposition toward the United States and enabled a caustic distance from the contradictions that defined the black experience. As part explication for why he chose to use Harlem almost exclusively as the locale for his writing once in exile (and indirectly account for why he used the nomenclature *domestic* to describe his detective fiction), Himes was to adumbrate: "I guess the only place I am at home, really at home, is in Harlem, but I could never possibly live there. My mind is shattered by the injustice of it."[55] He preferred to use the term *domestic* when describing his Harlem novels to counter any criticism of his portrayals of the black inner city as exaggerated and fantastic. The violent absurdity of Harlem was not a fiction designed for sleuth resolution; it was simply and terrifyingly quotidian, part of the "daily routine" in Harlem, where "reality was stranger than fiction."[56]

Of interest here is both the political and aesthetic distance between the Himes who wrote these formula crime fiction novels in the 1950s and 1960s and the Himes who wrote social(ist) realist protest novels in the

1940s. While there are similarities between the Harlem detective fiction and the uncompromising toughness of perspective of *If He Hollers Let Him Go* and *Lonely Crusade*, the differences are critical. Behind the putative disintegration of his original politically motivated writing into the surreal absurdist ambivalence of his detective fiction lies a path toward a far more complex understanding of the terms of struggle than overtly programmatic ideological agendas allow:

> I am not protesting against anything in my [Harlem detective] novels. I just write stories about crime in the ghetto, and those kinds of stories need a definite solution, just like an arithmetic problem. But more and more readers have realized that the essence of these stories lies in the fact that there really are people who live like this, and because they do, this is the way they will act when living under racist oppression. Recently people have begun to think that these stories represent a bolder kind of racial protest than the explicit protest novels I wrote years ago.[57]

Addison Gayle also noted that Himes belonged to a generation of novelists who tried to view the "black problem in Marxist terminology," but who "despite the insistence upon a naturalistic literature, infused with Marxist denouement, found it difficult to adhere to literary rules based upon superficial realities, which said little about the reality of black life in America."[58] Himes fit the description of "ambivalent Marxist" in his early writing, and his increased skepticism about political proscription made him one of those "unable to accept the image of the black man as Christ figure or eternal victim." Rather, the commitment was to giving "conscious motivation" to characters who were "outsiders." And in adhering to the idea that "Blacks must save themselves," Himes "created images which angered and shocked ... liberal and Communist critics and advisers."[59]

In this regard, Himes makes interesting distinctions between activism and rebellion. He sees the first as severely proscriptive and the second, although inclined to disorganization, ultimately, the more effective and organic form of revolt against white racism:

> I don't consider myself an activist.... I believe it was Flaubert who said that rebellion was the most effective tool in politics. I share his opinion. I believe in rebellion although up to now it has really been disorganized and ridiculous. Yet Negro activism in the 1960s had more success than anything since the Civil War. Since that period of activism, though, no more progress has been made.[60]

The Harlem Domestic Series, then, runs as a qualifying parallel discourse to the integrationist and nonviolence language and action of civil rights—a commentary from abroad, as it were, one that reserves judgment on the kind of organization that might best serve black interests in white America. As an introspective world of black-on-black crime, these novels systematically interrogate the distance between activism and rebellion, between the world of the political and the ordinary.

Himes had been in exile in France since 1953. Desperately short of income, he had taken up a challenge issued by the translator of his first novel (*If He Hollers Let Him Go*), Marcel Duhamel, founder of the Serie Noire imprint for the publishing house, Gallimard, that he write a detective novel. Serie Noire was dedicated to publishing hard-boiled paperback thrillers, especially translations of major American crime writers such as Dashiell Hammett, Raymond Chandler, Horace McCoy, and Jim Thompson. Duhamel thought Himes's writing already demonstrated a hard-boiled disposition that would transpose well into crime fiction. Himes's first Harlem detective novel appeared as *For Love of Imabelle* in the United States in 1957 and was reissued as *A Rage in Harlem* in 1965. While the novel gained little attention in the United States, its translation into French as *La reine des pommes* earned Himes the prestigious Grand Prix du Roman Policier for 1957.

The first French edition included promotional dust jacket blurbs by literary and artistic luminaries Jean Cau, Jean Cocteau, and Jean Giono. Giono's went: "I give you all of Hemingway, Dos Passos and Fitzgerald for this Chester Himes."[61] High praise that Himes saw as laying down a transatlantic gauntlet that would further isolate him: "I knew Americans couldn't take it. I knew Americans couldn't accept a black writer being so highly praised unless he's writing protest novels. They would take it as a personal affront."[62] Equally, Himes acknowledged that he would only have qualified acceptance among the French literati as the African American who broke the color line in Serie Noire detective writing: "I became a person ... not to be thrown away ... comparable to Richard Wright, and the French didn't know what to do with me because I wasn't attacking America but looking at blacks with their extreme absurdity."[63]

The novelty of providing readers with crime fiction written by an African American was amplified by Himes's decision to feature not one but two detectives as central to his stories. The doubling of perspective—a black view split, as it were—allowed Himes to innovate within the familiar structure of the detective novel in ways that amplified rather than suffocated what made black inner-city experience distinctive. As buddies these detectives highlight how being on the outside is not simply a property of individual alienation exemplified by "classical" white sleuths, such as Philip Marlowe and Nick Charles. Rather, such problems are shared, collective by default. Significantly, the double act also allows for wry and witty interchange that is often obscure and unintelligible to white line-managers.

In many ways Himes takes the inversions of Rudolph Fisher's *Conjure Man Dies* to a more nihilistic extreme.[64] As I have argued, Fisher's writing pitted the "logic" of (white) deductive reasoning against the putative irrationality of African witchcraft to deconstruct the dyadic/oppositional framework—one that informed a racial differentiation between science and superstition. To Himes, logic only ever appears as the reasoning supporting exploitation, both in terms of white exploitation of black social impoverishment and black-on-black crime. Thus Himes extends Fisher's questioning of the detective form in terms of its adequacy to black experience, especially with regard to the use of analytical reasoning. In such a context, reason is itself absurd(ist).

A Rage in Harlem focuses on the trouble that ensues when its central protagonist, Jackson, an undertaker's assistant, falls for a confidence trick called "The Blow." A gang of scam artists blow into town looking for a sucker. Jackson is the "square" who is duped into believing they can turn $10 bills into $100 denominations through a chemical treatment and use of an oven. Jackson invests his entire savings in the enterprise, only for the oven to blow up and with it the cash, seemingly. In the pandemonium that ensues, the con artists escape just as another gang member impersonating a cop bursts in. Jackson is the only one left in the room. The fake cop tells Jackson that he can escape arrest for a bribe. To this end Jackson steals a further $5,000 from his employer's safe and gives it to the con man.[65]

A man of faith, Jackson goes to the Reverend Gaines to confess his sins and ask for help, which he receives in the form of some pat appeals for God's intervention and ironic proverbs (such as "The Lord helps those who help themselves, Brother Jackson"). Jackson takes this as an excuse to recover the lost money (especially that which he stole from his employer) through gambling. In true Harlem tradition he resorts to the fortune economy and places bets on every numbers gig imaginable—including those that connoted bad luck ("to be on the safe side," a black inversion of fate):

> He played the *money row*, *lucky lady*, *happy days*, *true love*, *sun gonna shine*, *gold*, *silver*, *diamonds*, *dollars*, and *whiskey*. Then to be on the safe side he also played *jail house*, *death row*, *lady come back*, *two-timing woman*, *pile of rocks*, *dark days* and *trouble*. He wasn't taking any chances.[66]

He then joins an all-night crap game that only worsens his financial predicament.

In this opening chapter Himes takes up core themes definitive of the black urban environment. Harlem is the ultimate clip joint, where its celebrities were crap shooters and pimps with monikers such as Red Horse and Four-Four, where you were either a member of the patsy congregation or a charlatan-trickster con man. Himes gives his gullible protagonist the name of Jackson—without ever clarifying if this is either his first name or surname. Jackson stands in for a type: a greenhorn square who is easily taken in by every ruse and masquerade. His belligerent innocence extends to his blind love of Imabelle, who is clearly in on the scam that has landed Jackson in trouble.

All appearances are deceptive in Himes's Harlem. Eager to track down the con men, Jackson seeks the aid of his twin brother, Goldy, who earns his living posing as a Sister of Mercy (Sister Gabrielle) collecting charity money from customers outside Blumsteins, Harlem's most upmarket department store with its shop windows teasing passersby with promises of bourgeois comfort. Goldy is a street-savvy junkie and part of a group of female impersonators whose transvestism enables them to be involved in various forms of vice, including Lady Gypsy, a fortuneteller/numbers prognosticator, and Big Kathy, who is a prominent brothel madam.

The twin brothers, one who is innocent and the other who feigns innocence, allow Himes to play further with how appearance operates at all levels in Harlem. Goldy knows that his brother's transparent innocence (or squareness) will only ever make him a victim and will hinder his pursuit of the con men. By contrast Goldy uses his innocent facade or masquerade to help in the search for the con men—but this can only be done after he has drugged Jackson to keep him off the street.

Himes takes up issues we have seen raised by Fisher and McKay about Harlem as a series of "fronts." Most specifically Himes revisits Fisher's use of doubling (two detectives, two jesters/twins, and the play between scientific rationalism and superstition) to emphasize that in Harlem deception is the norm and is misunderstood by outsiders. Moreover, it is this inside knowledge that enables Harlemites to outfox a white surveillance culture. Goldy, for example, states that "the best way to fool a white cop in Harlem was to quote foolishly from the Bible."[67] He is able to hide behind the projected stereotypical image of black folk as superstitious. Yet among Harlemites themselves, such a ruse is less likely to fool anyone, precisely because it is understood to be a front. Grave Digger, for example, tells Goldy to "can that Bible-quoting crap."[68] Fronts are so much taken for granted within the community that the sight of a Sister of Mercy trawling bars, leafing through police files, asking questions about the whereabouts of dangerous con men is never remarked on as strange by Harlemites.[69] As Himes put it: "My domestic novels rarely deal with racism explicitly, except *Blind Man with a Pistol*. These books are really about ghetto hustlers getting around the law to make a living. They show you how you can beat the law in ghetto situations and the solutions are pretty simple, even mathematical."[70]

Consistent with this understanding of how the black world remained hidden from the law and white comprehension through such dissembling practices, Himes suspected his French readers constantly misconstrued what was at stake in his work:

> They thought I was depicting black Americans as buffoons like in the time of the slavery. I got news for them. I had taken much of my writing from slavery: the poem in *La Reine des Pommes* "*Run nigger de paterroller catch you*" is a slave chantey which reads in straight English "Run nigger run, the patroller will catch you." I wasn't showing the Negro as an oppressed, downtrodden people, as the French have been taught to believe, but simply as an absurdity. I must again quote the present-day Negro dialogue that makes the joke: "You ain't cut me, nigger, you done clean missed me." "Missed you? Shake your head, nigger, it gonna fall off."[71]

The chantey is what runs through Jackson's head as he flees from the botched attempt to trap the gang over another con they are running. Jackson is too square to figure out why this folk rhyme haunts him.

It had been rumored that the gang members were about to try another standard con ("the old lost-gold-mine pitch"), this time using a trunk full of fool's gold to encourage investment in a mining enterprise.[72] Playing on black desires for autonomy from white financiers, they make themselves even more attractive to investors through selling their scheme as a strictly blacks-only venture. Grave Digger and Coffin Ed set up a trap that can con the cons. They send out Jackson as the sucker-bait to track down the scam artists. And the plan is successful because the confidence tricksters and detectives alike have no doubt about Jackson's "squareness."

What results from this dissembling game is a dizzying violent showdown in pitch-darkness between the gang and the detectives in a disused warehouse that was once a Father Divine temple or "Peace Heaven." Behind this legacy of fronts, Coffin Ed has acid thrown in his face and in the confusion knocks out his own partner. From now on in the Domestic Series, Coffin Ed will bear this new scarified mask as testament to the grotesque and disfiguring character of Harlem's masquerade. And as he stumbles around in agony, we get a strange premonition of Himes's last novel in the series, *Blind Man with a Pistol*: "He was going crazy with pain, in there blind, with a loaded pistol, ready to shoot anything that moved."[73]

One blind and the other unconscious, the detectives are rendered helpless to arrest a deadly chain of events. Goldy has his throat cut, "from ear to ear, straight down to the bone," and is left to die on the street "jerking and twisting ... in death convulsions as though having a frantic sex culmination with an unseen mate."[74] Dispassionately dispatched, Goldy's corpse is subject to further abuse. His brother Jackson races through Harlem in a stolen Cadillac hearse carrying what he believes to be a trunk full of gold, unaware that the "gold" is actually Goldy. The morbid humor of the situation is heightened when the corpse eventually falls through the doors of the hearse onto the street as Jackson rushes to try and pay off the debt he owes his employer, the appropriately named undertaker, Exodus Clay. Jackson arrives only to find out that Clay has benefited from the deaths of the con men. He intends to claim burial costs of $8,000, the sum that was found on the deceased. Jackson's unwitting involvement in these events means that he is relieved of any debt and is retained in Clay's employment. Himes's mordant view of serendipity is compounded when Imabelle returns to Jackson, who remains blind to her deceptive behavior. Gullible to the end, Jackson learns absolutely nothing from what has unfolded, completing what we might call an "anti-bildungsroman."

These arbitrarily violent and darkly ironic episodes emphasize the displacement of the detectives' capacities to resolve anything, and become a blueprint for the whole series in terms of the sense of impotency accorded these law enforcers. Jerry H. Bryant argues that the detectives have a superegoic relation to the chaos of Harlem, as agents who can dispense justice in a world where both underworld and the law interfere or hinder righteous prosecution. Yet Bryant's own description of the terms of the detectives' authority suggests that they will never be able to bring order and resolution to the domain they patrol:

> Their effectiveness as cops in black Harlem depends upon their keeping the respect of the community they protect, and keeping that respect requires the violence for which they are renowned. . . .
>
> The letter of the law is perhaps not safe in the hands of two such cops, but justice is. Knowing they are on the "right side," Ed and Digger can sidestep the law in order to make justice prevail."[75]

Such a formulation resembles that of the Western outlaw-cum-sheriff who famously can save the community from evil but sacrifices his right to live in it because of the means used to this end. The problem with Himes's Harlem is that this logic no longer obtains. Using violence against the violent, while it indeed links the detectives to both the Western outlaw and the black badman tradition, is not restorative of the social order (and perhaps reflects ironically on the death of the outlaw as a regenerative figure in American culture).

The two black detectives do not have as central a role in *A Rage in Harlem* as they do in subsequent novels. But their marginal relationship to the dramatic action—and their liminal place between black and white worlds—is something that defines their frustrated status. Indeed, by the time of the last novel, Himes makes every effort to highlight the absurdity of being both black and detective.

In *Blind Man with a Pistol*, Himes's absurdist view reaches its apotheosis. And given his maxim that in Harlem reality is always stranger than fiction, Himes could also claim that *Blind Man with a Pistol* is "a sociological story about race relations."[76] The novel consists of several parallel narratives that at times intersect and at other times break up any sense of a coherent time-space continuum. One story is that of the two detectives trying to solve the murder of a white man who had been cruising for gay sex with black men in Harlem. Another concerns those involved in a sperm elixir scam (an echo of Fisher's *Conjure Man Dies*). The other stories involve attempts to organize different political rallies, all of which converge violently in the center of Harlem. And the narrative concludes with the arbitrary tale of a blind man on the subway who takes to randomly shooting people.

Himes stated that "*Blind Man with a Pistol* was meant to be the end of the series. Everything I'd tried to do in my previous stories came together in that one. . . . But I didn't offer any solutions to the race problem."[77] To this end the very logic of the "whodunit" structure is made the subject of the novel. "Who started the riot?" "Who murdered the white sex tourist?" None of these mobilizing questions are answered—or indeed are answerable. The detectives are constantly pressed by their white line managers, Lieutenant Anderson and the Captain, to come up with solutions. They can only ever answer cryptically. To the question "Who started the riot?," for example, they give this signifying response, one that Anderson describes as "an act":

> "Some folks call him by one name, some another," Coffin Ed said.
>
> "Some call him lack of respect for law and order, some lack of opportunity, some the teachings of the Bible, some the sins of their fathers," Grave Digger expounded. "Some call him ignorance, some poverty, some rebellion. Me and Ed look at him with compassion. We're victims."
>
> "Victims of what?" Anderson asked foolishly.
>
> "Victims of your skin," Coffin Ed shouted brutally.[78]

Coffin Ed and Grave Digger do get a lead about who may be behind much of the pandemonium in Harlem. But the figure concerned, an infamous black numbers racketeer who has masked his homosexuality behind a fake marriage to a lesbian partner, is too important to bring down. The black detectives find themselves blocked by a police-endorsed cover-up. The absurdity of their mission is thereby compounded. Despite their seeming normalcy in comparison to the Harlem of freaks that they patrol, they end up looking like the ghetto's most absurd and redundant creatures. Deprived of a raison d'être, the end scene features them reduced to practice shooting at rats escaping tenements that are being demolished. Amid the detritus of collapsing buildings, the madness of their situation is exacerbated by the sight of a blind man emerging from the 125th Street subway station arbitrarily shooting at people.

On the way to this inconclusive outcome, Grave Digger and Coffin Ed become embroiled in a series of unmasking activities. They embark on a hunt to find a mysterious Jesus Baby, a gay "steerer" who masquerades as a militant activist sporting a red fez with "Black Power" emblazoned on it. He had taken the white john to the Hotel Theresa and was later seen running away with his client's trousers. The bare-from-the-waist-down white man appears shortly afterward with his throat slit and dies in Grave Digger's arms.

In the very next scene another scam-associated murder takes place—this time involving the ill-fated attempt of one Reverend Sam (who is really a numbers banker and pimp running a feral brothel full of whores masquerading as nuns) to purchase a tonic to extend his life expectancy. The purveyor of the "sperm elixir," Dr. Mubuta, subscribes to a particular "solution to the Negro problem": "We're gonna outlive the white folks. While they has been concentrating on ways of death, I has been concentrating on ways to extend life. While they'll be dying, we'll be living forever"(39). Although Sam's chauffeur, Johnson X, interjects with a rational voice, "Does anyone in their right state of mind ... believe that shit?," this moment of reason coheres with the fear expressed by other members of Sam's coterie of son, daughter-in-law, lawyer, wife, and mistress, that he is going to fall for the scam and give away his entire fortune to Dr. Mubuta. Violent chaos breaks out when Sam's wife, Viola, tries to kill Mubuta, who in spite of overcoming this attempt on his life by killing both Viola and the lawyer, is knifed to death as he tries to escape through the kitchen by the fez-wearing steerer who just happens to be entering the room. Himes's sole concern is with characterizing black fate as something violent and random. We are deprived of a sense of where and when this incident takes place or of why it is of any significance in terms of plot. Instead we are subjected to a moment of arbitrary narrative collision in dislocated space.

Thematically, Himes constantly suggests that politics is only a front for something more fecund. A gay prostitute wears a Black Power fez. Sperm elixir is the "solution to the Negro problem." While "Black Power" is given overtly homoerotic connotations, Himes's also provides a witheringly ironic vision of interracial brotherhood as an extension of the vice business—another confidence trick run by people who are "extraordinarily stupid" and completely unaware of the ridiculous image they strike to others (25). As a novel written in the immediate aftermath of Martin Luther King's assassination, *Blind Man with a Pistol* sees the old gospel of integrationist, nonviolent, direct action reduced to the status of an advertising slogan that works on the principle of deferred gratification. Symptomatically, the rally leader, Marcus Mackenzie, sells his political vision with these words: "*Brotherhood! It can be more nutritious than bread. More warming than wine. More soothing than song. More satisfying than sex*" (22).

Marcus has a rich Swedish girlfriend, Birgit, whose fascination with "brotherhood" is intertwined with "brothers as lovers."[79] She takes him to France, where they concoct the idea of themselves symbolizing the possibility of interracial brotherhood. Birgit and Marcus ride in a command car at the front of the March for Brotherhood, followed by forty-eight integrated black and white marchers. For Himes, Birgit, Marcus, and the marchers sum up the self-delusional character of liberalism. The leaders see themselves as serious politicians guiding a procession for black rights. Yet the march itself gave the "illusion of an orgy" to all "amazed" onlookers. A motley crowd of black and white folk disgorge from bars, brothels, poolrooms, alleyways, and seedy hotels to join "the carnival group thinking they were maybe headed for a revival meeting, a sex orgy, a pansy ball, a beer festival, a baseball game. The white people attracted by the black. The black people attracted by the white."[80]

The integrationists are revealed to be victims of their own "squareness"—the leaders are self-deluded about their followers' sincerity. By contrast, the other two protest organizations that feature in the novel are run by charismatic figures capable of galvanizing (and exploiting) real commitment from their followers. Capitalizing on the psychopathology of the miscegenation/misogyny overlap in interracial relations, the Black Power leader, Dr. Moore, is a supreme gangster-pimp-manipulator whose organization is financed by the use of black whores to con rich white johns and the use of protest and pride rhetoric to fleece black folk. He cuts the image of a Mafia Don surrounded by muscle-bound bodyguards. This kind of charlatanry is pitted against the more ambiguous force of the Black Jesus Baby movement. Led by Ham, a character whom we have been duped into thinking is an imbecile from the beginning of the novel, this organization is located in a disused movie theater. The idea of the front is doubled here most obviously by the fact that the "Temple of Black Jesus" was once a place that sold celluloid dreams. Ham argues, precisely, that the way forward for the race is through an attack on dissembling itself. He starts out with the demand:

> Don't call me a prophet. . . . A prophet is a misfit that has visions. All the prophets in history were either epileptics, syphilitics, schizophrenics, sadists, or just plain monsters. I just got this hairlip. That doesn't make me eligible. . . . Neither am I a latter-day Moses. . . . Moses was a square. Instead of leading his people out of Egypt he should have taken over Egypt, then their problems would have been solved. (75–76)

Through the logic of negative definition, Ham turns out to be the most honest figure in the city of dissemblers. He rejects the status of race leader or prophet and assumes that of soldier-general. He rejects the white Jesus, because "believing in the philosophy of forgiveness and love . . . [is] whitey's con. . . . We're gonna drop the praying altogether" (77).

Instead, Ham proposes a surreal agenda, to feed whitey on the flesh of the Black Jesus "until he perish of constipation if he don't choke to death first"—an idea based on his observation that if the white Jesus sacrament has been so enduring, imagine how much more powerful and infinite that of the Black Jesus will be given that black flesh is so much tougher (77). He announces that he intends to purchase loyalty to the cause brazenly through use of bribes and dancing girls marching under a banner reading "Jesus Baby" and behind a lavender Cadillac convertible with an effigy of the Black Jesus strapped to its hood. Absurd as this plan appears, it remains compelling because of the honest logic that informs it. The Black Jesus Baby movement is not out to con anyone.

The three marches converge on Nat Turner day. What enfolds repeats the confusions surrounding the memory of Turner as a leader of a bloody slave revolt in 1831—a short-lived outburst rather than a sustained rebellion. Believing he was divinely ordained to lead slaves against their masters, Turner's brief uprising involved killing his master's family and over fifty whites before he was captured and subsequently executed. The terrorizing nature of this extremely violent murder spree (and the horrifying character of white retaliation against slaves) made Turner an ambivalent culture hero. Himes's attraction to Turner—his choice to locate the political marching on a day celebrating Nat Turner—however, has everything to do with Himes's elaboration on violence and the black experience.

The day of protest disintegrates into violence and looting. The leather-clad Black Power marchers ("like Nazi SS Troopers in blackface" [100]) beat up the integrationists and then move on to punching prostitutes, while the Black Jesus Baby members play out a miscreant role in hindering the police from being able to stop things. The onlooking crowds experience all this as the "best show they'd had in a month of Sundays" and as an excuse to loot (101).

This sense of decadent degeneration is captured in Himes's nostalgic lament for the heyday of the Harlem Renaissance where the Hotel Theresa was not a knocking shop, but a place where the great and the good gathered—including Rudolph Fisher. This signifies self-consciously on the distance between the time of Fisher and that of Himes, and invokes comparison between *Conjure Man Dies* and *Blind Man with a Pistol* (Himes reinvigorates the sperm elixir scam, for example).

Himes summarized what he intended in the writing of *Blind Man with a Pistol* in this way:

> You know what I see out there in the real world? Instead of organizing a well-structured political movement capable of efficient action, the

> Black Panthers waste their time playing "cops and robbers." And the American press, which likes nothing more than to titillate its readers with stories about crime, has undercut the Panthers' revolutionary potential. If the black masses ever thought that the Panthers might improve their lives, they know better now. The opportunists of both races are manipulating the Panthers for their own purposes.[81]

To Himes, the logic of the ghetto means that organization or collective or group action constitutes the chance for the big con, especially when co-opted by publicity. Himes believed strongly in organized violence[82]—but with a particular caveat:

> All the so-called leaders of the black people in the United States are effectively neutralized by publicity. I have never fully endorsed the black movements, although I have supported both the Black Muslims—I was a friend of Malcolm X—and the Panthers. I don't think they will succeed because they are too used to publicity, and a successful revolution must be planned with secrecy, security.[83]

This is a world where revolution is constantly reduced to empty publicity slogans, such as "BROTHERHOOD! Brotherly Love Is The Greatest!" and "BLACK THUNDER! BLACK POWER!"[84] Once again the conditions of white racism become the basis for exploitation of its victims. Politics is just another scam, no different from religious cult organizations or the numbers racket. And the only view on political formation in such a context that "makes sense" is necessarily absurd. As Grave Digger sums it up in *Blind Man with a Pistol*, responding to black youths who accuse him as a cop of being on "whitey's side": "Go home and grow up. You'll find there ain't any other side."[85]

CONCLUSION

Understanding both why Himes and Mayfield have been forgotten and in turn need remembering has everything to do with how their work bore an uneasy relationship to the heroic action and rhetoric of the civil rights struggle. Yet the unfinished (anti-institutional) character of their ghetto-centric writing keeps readers alive to the contradiction of integration. Taking Mayfield and Himes seriously necessarily involves sidelining the grand narrative of the period's civil rights struggle in order to make available those unresolved and apparently more ephemeral street stories that refuse the politics/ideology of closure. That Mayfield and Himes dissented from supporting what Victor Anderson calls the "cult of black heroic genius"[86] should not be construed as a political failure or race betrayal:

> For African Americans, cultural fulfillment has all too often been tied to the ways that African American cultural activities represent the genius of the people. But this aesthetic consciousness is also a mirroring of the neoclassicist moral consciousness that was teleologically developed in the European Enlightenment and Romantic heroic self-understanding.[87]

The skeptical and often absurdist view of agency advanced by both Mayfield and Himes can be seen as an extension of concerns at the heart of the writer who most influenced them, Richard Wright. As Abdul Jan-Mohamed elaborates, Wright's work explores the problem of the African American's aporetic relationship to choice and freedom. Building on Orlando Patterson's description of the slave as a "socially dead being," Jan-Mohamed highlights the nihilistic terms of "life" that confronted the slave and that continued to inform the black predicament as a death contract during Wright's lifetime. While it is clear that no human enters voluntarily into a contract as a slave, the "relationship between master and slave remains a 'contract' to the extent that the slave can always 'choose' to die instead of remaining a slave." Choosing to die (or to kill) via suicide or rebellion becomes the ground for refusing and negating the death contract and remaining a slave, "but, because we 'normally' see this as an insanely 'drastic' and 'irrational' choice, we in effect refuse to recognize it as a viable choice."[88] Yet under such circumstances, the "choice" of actual-death becomes the only way to free oneself from absolute or perfect subjugation as a socially dead subject. And it is only when we approach criminal self-representation as a means to renegotiating the death contract that we can see the "reason" and political potential underlying the badman's aporetic maxim, "I'll die before they kill me."[89]

This chapter has extended insights made about the crises confronting the more canonized members of the black literati of the 1940s and 1950s (especially Wright and Ellison) into the work and world of black writers committed to more popular forms. At stake are bourgeois aesthetics, or rather the relationship between social and aesthetic legitimacy. And I have argued that what makes the criminal aesthetic "criminal" in the writing under review is that it disorganizes the high/low distinction on which not only cultural taste but also racial hierarchy is built under the regime of bourgeois aesthetics. Much has been written about the problematic reception of and status accorded to Richard Wright's work in this regard as "artist manqué."[90] This understanding probably applies even more to writers such as Himes and Mayfield, both of whom made a self-conscious effort to produce what might be classified as an "*écriture* manqué" (or bLack literature). That their literary journeys prefaced the emergence of (or provided blueprint screenplays for) blaxploitation cinema should not be taken as a forlorn conclusion to failed writing careers. Rather, this connection invites us to reconsider the value of blaxploitation as a signal form of black popular, or grotesque, cultural production.

4 The Changing Politics of Baadasssss Cinema

From *Up Tight!* to *Dolemite*

In the April 1961 edition of *Commentary*, Julian Mayfield declared that "in what is essentially an attempt to overthrow an entrenched political and economic power, the Negro leadership class will be faced with a crisis, for its purely legalistic (or passive resistance) approach will clearly not be able to control the dynamics of the Negro struggle."[1] Mayfield's militant position came on the back of his meeting and befriending Robert F. Williams, whose advocacy of armed self-reliance in confronting white racism in Monroe, North Carolina, had led to his suspension as head of this chapter of the NAACP in 1959 by the organization's executive leader, Roy Wilkins. Mayfield's drift toward Williams's way of thinking can be detected in his third novel, *The Grand Parade*, also published in 1961, which dramatized the traumas of attempted desegregation of a North/South borderline city called Gainsboro.

In a story full of graft, kickbacks, and fixed electioneering, various protagonists' political ambitions are subject to ethical and moral corruption. Black political progress is seen to be dependent on forging counterproductive alliances with white racists and black gangsters, all compounded by a heady dose of adultery. Randolph Banks, the aspiring black politician at the heart of the work, negotiates the problems of McCarthyite/FBI threats to his career because of his brother Lonnie's membership in the CPUSA. Although sympathetic to Lonnie's political commitment, he does not understand Lonnie's inability to make compromises in order to avoid being expelled by the party in the first instance, or to testify to the state to avoid blacklisting. And he tries to persuade Lonnie to name names before a senate loyalty committee to save both their careers. Indeed, Randolph betrays at several levels. His political conscience is constantly compromised by a willingness to strike deals with corrupt authorities whom he subsequently outs as criminals in order to progress further up the greasy pole. At a more intimate level he also engages in systematic infidelity with Patty Speed, a numbers racket queen with major politicians in her debt. Randolph tries to get her to use her influence to stop the attempted integration of Lee Junior High because he fears a race riot that would blight his image. In her response, Patty, the gangster, is revealed to be one of the only figures with a moral compass:

> Oh, Randy, don't you see we aren't getting anywhere your way? There must be another way to fight. I don't want violence, but why turn our backs on it if it's necessary? Don't you see, we can't afford to be the best Christians in the country. We're too poor, too far behind. We've got to fight any way we can.[2]

The novel's denouement duly features a race riot consequent on the forced integration of Lee Junior High. In the process Mayfield revisits the scene played out most infamously at Little Rock Central High in 1957 but with a sense of bitter irony. For Mayfield this moment in the civil rights struggle is one that represents the dead end of passive resistance.

Mayfield's embarkation on a militant activist career was inspired by his relationship with Robert F. Williams. Mayfield had first encountered Williams in Cuba as part of a group of African Americans (a delegation that included LeRoi Jones, John Henrik Clarke, and Harold Cruse) invited by the Fair Play for Cuba Committee to witness the progress of the embryonic communist regime on the occasion of its first anniversary in 1960.[3] Williams invited Mayfield to come to Monroe and view firsthand the kind of political organization it took to combat the Ku Klux Klan (KKK). Impressed by Williams's tenacity and courage, Mayfield took to defending the notion of armed self-reliance against the grain of NAACP beliefs in nonviolent civil disobedience. Most significantly, he admired Williams's ability to mobilize and organize lower-class African Americans. In the process he identified a problem in the way the NAACP's strategy disenfranchised a major section of the black constituency:

> The most decisive factor in the conflict will probably be the Negro laboring class, heretofore unheard from. These are the great masses of the unskilled, who belong to no labor unions or civic organizations.... A casual walk through any colored section of a Southern town or city will reveal him, standing on the corner, lounging near the bar, slouched on

> the doorstep, staring into the uncertainty that is his future. The "they" in his life, those who make decisions that vitally affect him, are not only the governments, federal, state, and local . . . but even the Negro middle class and the striking students, all of whom seem to be going some place without him. It is not *his* children that all of the school desegregation furor is about; he is lucky if he can keep them in the colored school. No one can currently claim to speak for this man, not church, union, nor NAACP.[4]

In the late 1950s, given Governor Luther Hodges's lack of action against the Ku Klux Klan's night-ride terrorizing of Monroe's black neighborhood, Newtown, Williams made his NAACP chapter a National Rifle Association (NRA) chapter. This proved to be an effective policy against KKK aggression. Williams gained national attention when his armed defense group successfully reversed a KKK motorcade following an attack on the home of NAACP member Dr. Albert E. Perry. While KKK night riding halted, state authorities and the NAACP executive became increasingly concerned about Williams's armed power.[5] In an increasingly hostile climate in 1961, Mayfield helped run guns "obtained from New Jersey gangsters with the assistance of writer LeRoi Jones" from Harlem to Monroe to aid Williams.[6] In August 1961, under the pretext of reporting for the York, Pennsylvania, *Call and Daily*, Mayfield made his last trip

The incendiary situation that emerged was, in part, the ironic consequence of internecine differences over protest and resistance among civil rights advocates. The Student Nonviolent Coordinating Committee (SNCC) and other supporters of nonviolent civil disobedience had mounted an interracial demonstration in Monroe, in front of the town hall, in an attempt to show how this strategy of passive resistance was preferable to Williams's one of armed self-defense. For their efforts the members of the nonviolent group were attacked and beaten up by a white mob. Mayfield and Williams decided to rescue the beleaguered demonstrators and escort them to Newtown under armed guard—exchanging fire with the white mob.

In the midst of this violent altercation, a white couple had mistakenly ventured into Newtown and found themselves at the mercy of angry black denizens. Again Williams provided protection to the unprotected, providing sanctuary in his own home for the errant white couple. White onlookers (including law enforcement officials) interpreted this as a brazen act of kidnapping designed to fuel violent confrontation.

Williams decided to run. In the first instance, Mayfield drove him and his family away from the scene, negotiating military roadblocks. Once placed on the FBI's most wanted list (for kidnapping), Williams needed Mayfield's further help in getting out of the country into Canada (from where he was to find exile in Cuba). For his part, Mayfield was to take flight first to London and then on to Ghana with his wife and child in December 1961. In many ways the experience of political entropy that characterized the Monroe incident would inform Mayfield's screenplay for *Up Tight!* (1968).

Mayfield admired Williams's constant bypassing of the domestic media, whom he felt were complicit with white racism. While in Monroe, Williams had fed the Cuban News Service with news of the USA's racial strife. Cuban radio proved to be a conduit through which protests could be organized all over the world to expose what mainstream American media suppressed. Once in exile in Cuba, Williams would continue to circulate embarrassing truths about the USA's domestic problems to international and home audiences through Radio Free Dixie, broadcast from Havana. Mayfield would also adopt an internationalist perspective on the cause of racial equality while in exile in Ghana.

Mayfield's exile was marked by the distinction of becoming writer in residence to the first postcolonial sub-Saharan independent African nation, Ghana. Alongside other distinguished African American expatriates, Mayfield was keen to be part of a new world of international black self-determination. The newly independent African states set the precedent for possibilities yet to be realized in the United States and offered encouragement and sanctuary to a host of embattled African American activists and intellectuals. The pan-African, transatlantic movement was certainly a source of inspiration, even as it became increasingly fraught with problems. Mayfield was founder-editor of the *African Review*, official chronicler of the 1962 international peace conference at the Accra Assembly, hosted Malcolm X's visit in 1964 as one of the organizers of the first international branch of Malcolm's Organization of Afro-American Unity (OAAU), and was a leading critic of U.S. foreign policy with regard to Africa. Whatever Mayfield's achievements, however, his associations and frustrations with a growingly discredited Nkrumah, an estranged relationship with his wife, Puerto Rican activist Ana Livia Cordero, led to him leaving for Spain in February 1966, just three weeks before the military coup overthrew the government.[7]

In Spain, Mayfield wrote a reflection on the Nkrumah regime's significance, "Lonely Warrior." While he believed this was necessary as a corrective to what he saw as more prejudicial and politically expedient accounts of the failure of African independence, the manuscript was not taken up by publishers, partly because they felt Mayfield's insider and putatively "balanced" perspective lacked sufficient grounding (his papers having been confiscated by the junta). The Spanish sojourn came to an end with his successful application for a postdoctoral fellowship (with a waiver of the PhD requirement) to Cornell, for the 1967–68 academic year. A return to the United States had been driven by his disappointment with the neocolonialism of the new African regimes and his desire to be part of a new black revolutionary movement at home. His friend Conor Cruise O'Brien (who had served as chancellor to the University of Ghana while Mayfield was in exile there) earmarked Mayfield as someone to lead in teaching the relationship of black American to African literature in liberation struggles across two continents. On finishing his postdoctoral appointment at Cornell, Mayfield accepted O'Brien's invitation to take up a post in the Albert Schweitzer Program in the Humanities at New York University. And it was exactly at this moment that Mayfield received an invitation to work on a Hollywood film, *Up Tight!*, with another returnee from exile, director Jules Dassin.[8]

UP TIGHT!: MAKING WAY FOR BLAXPLOITATION

Perhaps it is coincidence that a long-standing relationship with Conor Cruise O'Brien, a leading Irish republican, would culminate in Mayfield's decision to work on a film based on Liam O'Flaherty's *The Informer* (1925), a novel about betrayal within the ranks of Irish revolutionaries fighting for independence. O'Flaherty's American cousin, the director John Ford, had turned the novel into an Oscar-winning film in 1935. In 1968 Jules Dassin, himself a Hollywood dissident famous for his uncompromising films noir and victim of the anticommunist blacklist, chose to make a return to America after twenty-five years abroad, by using *The Informer* as a basis for a film about the contradictory state of the Black Power movement (and, perhaps, as an ironic reflection on the culture of naming names that had led to Dassin's own banishment by red scare–mongers). To this end he recruited Mayfield not only to co-write the screenplay (with himself and the black actress Ruby Dee) but also to take on the informer role itself. With the additional talents of Booker T. Jones and his racially integrated Memphis soul band, Booker T. and the MGs, providing the movie's soundtrack, *Up Tight!* ought to have realized the potential of internationalist solidarity in popular cultural form. It was, however, too candid about the obstacles to such collective action.

In many ways the experience of political entropy that characterized the Monroe incident would inform Mayfield's contributions to *Up Tight!*

Up Tight! was released at the very end of 1968 (December 28). Its action was set four days after the assassination of Martin Luther King on April 4, 1968. The title sequence gives way to archive footage of the funeral cortege outside the Ebenezer Baptist Church in Atlanta with Judy Clay singing a gospel song, "Children, Don't Get Weary" (a form of homage to Mahalia Jackson, who sang "Precious Lord," King's favorite hymn, at the funeral).[9] The setting shifts to Cleveland, where King's funeral is relayed on television accompanied by a recording of his "I Have a Dream" speech. Julian Mayfield, as Tank, is watching, having drowned his depression in a bottle of hard liquor. A car approaches his apartment. Tank's best friend, Johnny Wells (Max Julien), and other members of the "Movement Committee" are on their way to rob an arms warehouse. "Wrong night, guys!" shrieks Tank, rejecting the revolutionary brothers' pleas that he fulfill his duty as part of the heist. Tank cannot match this call to action with his need to mourn the passing of Martin Luther King. The discourse on armed militancy and nonviolent civil disobedience flows from this point; King's death signals the demise of the nonviolent program. As Johnny explains to Tank about King, "Listen to me. He was a big man ... but he was holding us back. And Memphis proves the answer is guns, more guns."

The heist goes ahead without Tank, whose absence slows the operation down. Johnny removes his shirt, hot from lifting crates of guns into the van. The delay means that the gang falls foul of a white guard doing the rounds. The van takes off leaving Johnny, who knocks out the guard and takes flight and leaves his labeled shirt ("J. Wells") behind. The guard dies in the hospital; a warrant is put out for Johnny as wanted for murder. The Movement Committee expels Tank from their ranks, placing the blame for Johnny's plight on Tank's drunken indolence. Tank is left to wander Cleveland's streets at night contemplating his desperate situation. Alone and feeling guilty, he has a series of encounters with different figures that only compound his situation.

While observing a street corner speech by a Black Power advocate, he encounters Clarence/"Daisy Girl" (Roscoe Lee Browne), a gay black police informer. Clarence tempts Tank to inform on Johnny as there is a $1,000 reward to be won. Tank outwardly rejects such a suggestion, reminding Daisy that he had a reputation as a union member in the steel mills for beating up informers and scabs. He questions Daisy's conscience: "How much do you get for the head of a brother? What's the going rate? ... How do you feel when you sell a man?"[10] Tank moves on, seeking sanctuary with his girlfriend, Laurie (Ruby Dee), only to disturb her attempts to placate a welfare agent keen to remove her benefits. Tank hates the idea of welfare, yet he himself is unemployed and unable to support Laurie and her kids. Laurie intimates that she has taken to selling herself to make ends meet, suggesting that life would be better if Tank disappeared from her life and leave her free to find a sugar daddy.

Feelings of rejection exacerbated, Tank stumbles down the street only to encounter the fugitive Johnny, who is trying to see his mother before he takes exile after having procured a passport. Johnny asks Tank to tell the head of the committee, B.G. (Raymond St. Jacques), that he needs some of the brothers to watch the apartment in case the police are around. Eager to please (and to seek a way back into the ranks of the movement), Tank accepts the task and asks Johnny's forgiveness for abandoning the heist. Johnny divulges that he could never blame Tank, because he is a romantic atavism: "You're from another time. You were great in the mills. The steel, fire, the old union bit. And when you came on strong, all of us kids knew it. But revolution is not your stick. The disciplines are too tough for you."

This sense of redundancy and obsolescence is elaborated further when the narrative cuts to a meeting in a bowling alley between the Black Power separatist movement and representatives of old school integrationist beliefs. Prominent black integrationist Kyle (Frank Silvera) seeks an audience with the separatists to highlight the error of their violent armed agenda. To the consternation of the revolutionary brothers, he brings with him a white activist, Ted (Michael Baseleon). On being asked to leave, Ted reminds one of the separatist leaders, Corbin (Dick Anthony Williams—dressed in dashiki and sporting an Afro), that "we were together in Selma ... they threw us in the same jail." Corbin responds, "Other times ... things have changed." And B.G. adds with measured finality: "We're wasting time. Selma, lunch-counters, Birmingham. Yesterday. A phase we went through together. Now we don't walk together anymore. It's policy now. No whites." In a similar tone he dispatches Kyle: "[The nonviolent program] is dead. Killed by white violence, April 4, 1968, in Memphis."

Tank arrives and tells everyone that Johnny needs help in seeing his mother. B.G. honors the request but rejects Tank's plea that he be accepted back into the movement, stating that Johnny had sought Tank's expulsion. In a state of total disillusionment, Tank finds himself wandering the streets. Subjective camera work provides a stumbling point of view as Tank walks into the precinct police station where he informs on Johnny's whereabouts. Residents of the tenement complex where Johnny's mother lives show solidarity in trying to protect the fugitive from the police. Projectiles are hurled from crowded balconies and staircases. This resistance dissipates, however, once the police start firing bullets into the air and tear gas into the crowd. Johnny is killed in a shoot-out.

The scene changes to Tank spending conspicuously at a bar. His joviality is broken by a sense of conscience about Johnny. He makes his way to the steel mills, where he remonstrates with the chimney stacks about twenty years of labor forgotten, finding solace, however, in the industrial noise. The discourse about Tank's primitive attraction to steel—and his embodiment of obsolescent labor—is highly redolent of Eugene O'Neill's *Hairy Ape* and its main protagonist, Yank. The Yank/Tank relation is one that adds a layer of meaning to how Dassin and Mayfield may have thought about the political choices of 1968 in quite modernist terms. We shift from Tank's confrontation with the steel mill to a surreal scene in an amusement arcade. Here he repeatedly outdraws a robotic cowboy much to the amusement of a group of white folk disgorged from a Rolls Royce. Tank's shooting is accompanied by Booker T. and the MGs' instrumental track "Deadwood Dick," a musical allusion to the most famous black Western outlaw. The onlooking Caucasians are "slumming it," excited visitors to the black neighborhood staged as arcade-cum-jungle. Tank plays with their stereotypical assumptions. They ask: "Is all this target practice part of 'The Plan'?"; and "Sir, are you one of those militants? Would you really like to kill all of us?" Tank feeds their appetite for the apocalyptic in a room of distorted mirrors, telling them that the plan will take force "next Thursday" when white folk will wake up to a world in which there is no water and telephones will be "out of order due to black folks" and when "you turn on TV and all you see is a big black face like mine saying 'we done took over.'" The banks will be black, and white folk seeking to escape from Cape Canaveral will find that the plug has been pulled on all space rockets.

The film returns to a more realist vein when Tank realizes he should attend Johnny's wake. There he mistakenly thinks everyone suspects him of having informed. Paranoid, he tries to leave, depositing a conspicuously generous $20 in the wake collection plate. His behavior arouses B.G.'s suspicion. Two committee members are sent out to retrace Tank's steps. They discover that he had come into a lot of money but had no real explication for this save an ill-thought idea that he had hit big on the numbers. B.G. subjects Tank to a kangaroo court interrogation. Tank cannot name the winning number and resorts to saying that he gleaned his money from selling blood. This alibi fails when he gets the price of blood wrong. The metaphor of selling blood condemns Tank. Against the protestations of Kyle, who has gate-crashed the proceedings, B.G. instructs two of his lieutenants to take care of Tank.

Although Tank escapes this situation, his freedom is only temporary. He has time to confess his sins to Laurie before deliberately leading his executioners to his chosen place of death. Back at the steel mills, Tank clambers over slag heaps and scales waste disposal conveyors. Waving to his pursuers from a steel tower he is shot and falls to his death on the slag below.

Vincent Canby of the *New York Times* and Roger Ebert of the *Chicago Sun-Times* both saw *Up Tight!* as a groundbreaking effort, potentially the first of a Hollywood cycle that would finally broach the problems of race and racism in the United States more candidly.[11] And as Paula Massood notes all too briefly, *Up Tight!* was significant because it was one of the first Hollywood race-focused productions that was set in an urban context.[12] That the film failed (in box-office terms) to live up to the potential identified by major mainstream film critics probably has to do with the undecided character of the story and the eagerness of the critics to overlook the film's flaws as a vehicle of entertainment because of the urgent quality of the film's topic. Although promoted as a film made by the director of *Rififi* (1955), *Topkapi* (1964), and *Never on Sunday* (1960), the hallmarks of a "Dassin" feature were overburdened and suffocated by the polarizing rhetoric and blunt staging of the militant-nationalist/nonviolent-integrationist conflict. The mise-en-scène is redolent of Dassin's style: the heist has echoes of *Rififi* and the caper in *Topkapi*; his predilection for on-location shooting in films noir such as *Naked City* (1948) and *Night and the City* (1950) is reiterated. Thematically, *Up Tight!* resembles *Brute Force* (1947), *Thieves Highway* (1949), *Night and the City*, *Rififi*, and *Never on Sunday* in the way it replays Dassin's long-standing concern for social justice and the dignity of the hapless outsider and social rejects (whose victories are only ever pyrrhic).

Dassin had employed the Oscar-winning cinematographer Boris Kaufman (Academy Award for *On the Waterfront* [1954]) for *Up Tight!* Kaufman, a Russian émigré at the forefront in bringing a neorealist style to Hollywood, had most recently been associated with director Sidney Lumet as cinematographer on *12 Angry Men* (1957), *Long Day's Journey into Night* (1962), and *The Pawnbroker* (1965). As the brother of Soviet filmmaker Dziga Vertov and cinematographer for the anti-authoritarian/

anarchist French filmmaker Jean Vigo, it is surprising that Kaufman had not teamed up with Dassin earlier, given similar political leanings and a shared commitment to a rebellious neorealist aesthetic.

Kaufman had remained conspicuously underemployed during the postwar 1940s and early 1950s. This can be explained in part by the fact that his late arrival in Hollywood (in 1942) meant he was excluded from feature-length film work by guild regulations. His associations with Soviet filmmakers and Vigo, however, meant that he was also under surveillance at the height of the Red Scare. Kaufman's "break" in being offered the chance to be the cinematographer for *On the Waterfront* was somewhat ironic. He overcame the threat of blacklisting partly because of this association with the director, Elia Kazan, who had turned into a friendly witness before the House Committee on Un-American Activities.[13] The fact that Kaufman had been involved in *On the Waterfront*, itself a film about the ethics and morality of informing, invites interesting comparisons with *Up Tight!* Questions of collaboration and betrayal resurface as thematic material. A self-conscious reflection on how Hollywood should intervene and mediate moments of major political crisis is engaged at the level of visual style. Arguably, however, the subtleties of neorealist mise-en-scène and the complex characterization of Tank's quandaries are compromised by the more overbearing and somewhat simplistic treatment of the political impasse confronting African Americans in the immediate aftermath of King's assassination.

While *Up Tight!* was brave enough to seize the moment, it inevitably reduced the complexity of that moment in trying to dramatize the choices confronting those wishing to resolve the problems of racial inequality. The film acknowledges from the start that questions of representation are very much in the hands of mass media. King's funeral is presented as a television event (a form of docudrama). The mawkish potential of this media attention to underscore a black and white liberal integrationist message is vociferously rejected by Cleveland's revolutionary brothers and sisters. Such moments so early in the movie are a clear and shocking deviation from the Hollywood line, encapsulated in Poitier's successful integrationist message vehicles from 1967, *In the Heat of the Night* and *Guess Who's Coming to Dinner*. To this extent *Up Tight!* is a very self-conscious political departure from the big-screen rules on representation of racial discord. Yet the proximity of the film to the event of King's assassination means that its terms of reflection are too immediate and rushed. Much like the problem confronting Tank (who remains perplexed by his choice to inform on Johnny to the end, and who finds himself considered a political dinosaur), the film doesn't have the luxury of time or distance in contemplating the crisis. Indeed, as the main musical hit from the film proclaims, "Time Is Tight" in 1968.[14]

The movie's best gesture is in giving militant separatist voices equal airing and moving the terrain of the race-focused Hollywood film to the black inner city—even if this is done within an overly simplifying dualistic storytelling structure. Some critics attribute this flaw to making the issues confronting African American political choices map over *The Informer*, a story about a different revolutionary moment involving a different nation. While this may be a fault, it does not ultimately mean that Dassin and Mayfield had to construct the dichotomy of political progression in polarizing terms. The film's suggestion is that these are endemic to the internecine infighting within the post-King movement. It is the either/or rhetoric of Black Power and the program of Black Nationalism that is debilitating. The film's simplistic oppositional framework can be read, then, as a deliberate product of Mayfield's frustrations with the terms of African American political development, informed by his experience of other black liberation struggles in Africa. The film cultivates sympathy for a man who no longer belongs in this new world. Tank is understood as a sentimental relic of a former time of socialist agitation at the steel mills—when there were unions. As such, Tank could be regarded as a figure of nostalgic identification for not only Mayfield but also Dassin, who was an old-time leftist, victim of the anticommunist witch hunt, attempting to return to a changed America. The film's pathos is derived from the way it shows that the time of *Up Tight!* is beyond such traditional understandings of organization and filial loyalty.

Up Tight! is both too late and too early. While the film "failed" as a project for avowedly political (and thus perhaps atavistic) commentators such as Dassin and Mayfield, it gave starring screen time to two actors who would help shape blaxploitation cinema in the 1970s. Raymond St. Jacques (B.G.) would find popularity as Coffin Ed Jones, one of the Harlem detectives in the screen version of Chester Himes's *Cotton Comes to Harlem* (1970). He had previously starred in *Change of Mind* (1969) as a black man with a white brain transplant. He would go on to play Imir in *The Final Comedown* (1972), a film about a black militant betrayed by hypocritical white radicals, renew his Coffin Ed Johnson role in *Come Back Charleston Blue* (1972), direct and star in *The Book of Numbers* (1973), before settling on an acting career primarily in television.

Max Julien (Johnny Wells) would not only star in one of blaxploitation's most famous films, *The Mack* (1973), but would also produce and star in *Thomasine and Bushrod* (1974) (a black take on *Bonnie and Clyde* in which the vigilante protagonists steal from rich white folk and redistribute the wealth to poor blacks and Mexicans), and coproduce and write the story and screenplay for *Cleopatra Jones* (1973).

In spite of *Up Tight!*'s box-office failure, Mayfield continued to try his hand at filmmaking. A screen version of *The Long Night* was made in 1976, directed by black theater producer Woodie King Jr. and redeployed the acting talents of Dick Anthony Williams, who played Corbin in *Up Tight!* The film, however, had extremely limited release and circulation as the only American entry to the New York New Directors and New Films Festival at the Museum of Modern Art in April.[15] The film was commercially released in June by Howard Mahler Films (a small-time distribution company for mainly exploitation material, such as soft-core erotica, gore, and X-rated Hong Kong horror and martial arts films). There is evidence that the movie was retitled as *Steely Brown* (posters for the film under this title exist), but there is no record of a release under this name.

In addition to the screen adaptation of one his novels, Mayfield's memoirs reveal that he wanted to make a film about the Haitian leader Henri Christophe and the slave revolutionary Toussaint Louverture with his friend William Marshall.[16] Marshall was one of America's finest black stage actors but also made a name as the eponymous star of the blaxploitation horror film *Blacula* (1972). This project extended Mayfield's fascination with Haiti first articulated in his novel *The Long Night* (with its references to Toussaint as a role model for Steely and the haunting figure of the lost Haitian sailor Black Papa, who chants incantations to the voodoo gods). Moreover, the idea for the film appears to have been fueled by his further ventures in exile, this time in the Caribbean, working for the Forbes Burnham regime in postcolonial Guyana. Henri Christophe was a legendary independence fighter who had honed his skills under Toussaint Louverture and went on to be Haiti's first black leader. His appetite for power, however, would ultimately corrupt him and turn him into a tyrant. The parallels with problems Mayfield himself had experienced with the first generation of postcolonial leaders such as Nkrumah in Ghana and Forbes in Guyana are intriguing. Sadly, entreaties to Marshall to help produce and star in the proposed film never came to fruition.

MUSICAL INTERLUDE: THE FUNK AND POST–CIVIL RIGHTS DISILLUSION

On June 17, 1966, during a civil rights march to Jackson, Mississippi, two SNCC activists, Willie Ricks and the organization's leader, Stokely Carmichael, introduced the chant of "Black Power." Born in part out of frustration with the character of nonviolent protest and the slow pace of change associated with integrationist protest strategies, this militant call signaled a deep rift in the civil rights movement.[17] While *Up Tight!* represents one understanding of how the old refrain of "We Shall Overcome" would be drowned out by nationalist rhetoric, there were parallel shifts going on across African American popular culture, especially in music.

Up Tight!'s soundtrack had been composed by Booker T. Jones, who led up an integrated band, Booker T. and the MGs. That the band stemmed from Memphis, the very site of Martin Luther King's assassination, lends additional pathos to the difficulty confronting those who still believed in an integrated movement. One could argue that the turn represented in *Up Tight!* was carried through in funk. The changing attitudes of two of funk's most important representatives, James Brown and Sly Stone, embody how a split with integration ideology would run a troubled course.

Brown is credited with pioneering the move from soul to the "on the one!" principles of funk with the song "Cold Sweat" in 1967. The subordination of melody, harmony, and chord progression to often single-chord-based rhythms and grooves brought the rhythm section to the fore. The shift in priorities celebrated arguably Afrocentric elements, with the drum and bass becoming the focal point. While funk's dance appeal and uninhibitedly visceral attitude to sex was vital to its success, the way it tapped into changes in the political environment also made it timely. There was a short distance between Brown's demand in "Cold Sweat" that he "satisfy your pulse" and his cry that black folk "Say it loud: I'm black and I'm proud" in 1968. Yet there was also only a short distance to retreat back to a more hedonistic and narcissistic use of the groove. "Say It Loud" gave way to "Get Up (I Feel Like Being) a Sex Machine" in 1970, as the energy of militant protest dissipated through a mix of internal division and external repression.

For Sly Stone, funk's optimism gave way to a profoundly nihilistic view on the possibilities of a harmonious society. As the leader of an integrated band, Sly and the Family Stone, he championed songs that advocated peace and love in the psychedelic spirit of 1960s San Francisco. The very sight of a mixed-race band was novel for the day, made all the more extreme through their wild fashion choices and sporting of Afros and blond wigs. The 1969 album *Stand!* epitomized what the group stood for at its most optimistic. Featuring songs such as "Everyday People" (their first number-one single) and "Don't Call Me Nigger, Whitey," the album attacked group hatred and provided a soundtrack to unify everyone and take them to something higher. The defiant but loving spirit of *Stand!* led to the band being featured at Woodstock later in the year. The seeds of dissipation and disillusion, however, were endemic to the very same grooves that seemed so affirmative.

In 1971 Sly released *There's a Riot Going On*. The album's bleak themes were underscored by an overdubbed recording sound. The final track on the album, "Thank You Africa for Talkin' to Me," constituted a grim reflection on the redundancy many of his songs to date mixed in with a notion that he had encountered the devil:

Lookin' at the devil
Grinnin' at his gun
Fingers start shakin'
I begin to run

Caustic memories of older songs surface through an overdubbed aural haze: "I wanna thank you falettinme be mice elf agin," "dance to the music," "everyday, everyday, everyday people," all allusions to previous optimistic hits, all qualified as part of a former life by the stanza:

I wanna thank you for the party
But I could never stay
Many things on my mind
Words in the way

As Greil Marcus highlighted:

> The record was no fun. It was slow, hard to hear, and it didn't celebrate anything. It was not groovy....
>
> *There's a riot going on* was an exploration of and a pronouncement on the state of the nation, Sly's career, his audience, black music, black politics, and a white world. Emerging out of a pervasive sense ... that the good ideas of the sixties had gone to their limits, turned back upon themselves, and produced evil where only good was expected.[18]

Negation supplanted affirmation as Sly sought solace by increasing his self-destructive drug consumption while providing bitter reflection on how the old music was now only "a soundtrack for a world that didn't exist."[19]

If Sly's trajectory into a PCP-fueled depression signaled a loss of hope, George Clinton's acid-based P-Funk represented an almost religious alternative. The funk as it was developed by Parliament and Funkadelic in the 1970s became an end in itself. "Funk is its own reward," professed Clinton, who had taken to developing elaborately staged concerts in which his alter ego, Dr. Funkenstein, would descend from space in the Mothership Connection to fight Sir Nose D'Voidoffunk.[20] If funk's hellion possibilities could no longer tap into the reality of post–civil rights disillusion, it could sustain a fantasy ideal. Clinton as a black star-child could head up a new church of ecstatic worshipper-participants, "one nation under a groove," all "up for the down stroke," if only for the duration of a P-Funk event.

The solipsism, hedonism, and excess reflected in the gravitation of funk away from political militancy had parallels with the cinema they accompanied, blaxploitation. If *Up Tight!* represented a dysfunctional moment in the struggle against discrimination, at least in terms of a more traditional notion of political agitation, this did not herald the termination of troublesome African American popular cultural production. Sly's nihilistic turn and P-Funk's surreal excess were consonant with the absurdist outlook of Chester Himes.

TIME FOR HIMES: *COTTON COMES TO HARLEM*

If Mayfield's return to the United States via film was an aborted effort, the same could not be said for Chester Himes. Significantly, a major militant activist (and friend of Mayfield) would turn to Himes for his first filmmaking endeavor. Rather than engaging the political problems of the time, Ossie Davis opted to transcribe Himes's absurdist view to the big screen. And this proved successful. The terms of success suggest how a cinema that engaged and exploited the black predicament in white America by 1970 necessarily had to adopt a different politics. *Up Tight!* had in many ways dramatized the impossibilities of working with older paradigms (both those associated with Poitier's message movies, on the one hand, and those associated with a pure separatist mandate, on the other).[21] The idea of either integration or a collectivist sense of Black Power had been undermined. The black niche audience was jaded on such diatribe. The way had been paved for the arrival of blaxploitation's politically ambivalent and irreverent vigilantes, such as Sweetback, John Shaft, and Youngblood Priest (main protagonists in

Sweet Sweetback's Baadasssss Song [1971], *Shaft* [1971], and *Super Fly* [1972], respectively).

While the screen adaptation of *Cotton Comes to Harlem* is less acerbic than the novel, it retains Himes's satirical view of black folks' gullibility and black leadership's unconscionable exploitation of the community's enduring and belligerent faith in a better day coming. The storyline is faithful to the novel, centering on a crime caper in which $87,000 is stolen from the Back-to-Africa movement. Himes's detective duo, Gravedigger Jones (Godfrey Cambridge) and Coffin Ed Johnson (Raymond St. Jacques), are charged with finding the money as well as trying to solve the mystery of a cotton bale that has appeared in the heart of Harlem. The leader of the Back-to-Africa movement, the Reverend Deke O'Malley, is a confidence trickster who mixes old time appeals to Christian charity with a nod to black pride and Afrocentricism (he dons a dashiki) in order to fleece the community at his rallies. The stolen money is hidden in the cotton bale that falls from the getaway vehicle. A relic from the rural South, Uncle Bud (Redd Foxx) recognizes the bale as high-class Mississippi cotton and appropriates it. The serendipity of his knowing the value of cotton as a displaced southerner with memories of the plantation leads him literally to a fortune. All this happens unbeknownst to everyone else. In the end the bale is recovered, but the money has disappeared. Uncle Bud solves the crime by sending a card from his new home, having used the money to buy a plantation in Africa. As Massood highlights, "Uncle Bud's return is twofold: a return to his rural roots *and* a return to his African roots."[22]

Himes's irreverence to authority—especially to religious and political power—finally found its audience in the post-1968 environment. The uneven register of the film, its mix of tragedy and comedy, violence and laughter, was redolent of Himes's discordant style. It also made the film difficult to evaluate and categorize. Clearly critical of message rhetoric, yet neither recognizably crime or comedy generically speaking, *Cotton Comes to Harlem* signaled the arrival of blaxploitation cinema, even as it puzzled critics. Vincent Canby, for example, while praising the film for its "honest black idioms and actors," chastised the film for "employing terrible white stereotypes of black life."[23] The desire for a film treatment of black experience free of stereotype (especially from the viewpoint of a major white film critic) might seem praiseworthy. Yet it is also indicative of a pervasive and particular awkwardness of the white onlooker to putatively counterproductive self-representations by African

American popular culture producers. As Himes constantly highlights, sincerity is all too often the mask of the charlatan. In a world of dissembling, playing with stereotype is a mode of survival. And forging unholy alliances is no less grotesque than being fooled by the dishonest preacher. Mayfield's and Himes's disconsolate perspective on collective political action tapped into a post-King sense of disillusionment and prepared the ground for the arrival of outsider individualist antiheroes such as Sweetback, Youngblood Priest, and John Shaft on the black screen.

Cotton Comes to Harlem was successful enough to encourage producer Sam Goldwyn Jr. and distributors United Artists to invest in a second Harlem film based on a Himes novel. *Come Back Charleston Blue* (1972) was based on *The Heat's On*. Again the film was to be directed by an African American. This time the job was given to Mark Warren, an Emmy Award–winning director with a background in directing the comedy television series *Rowan and Martin's Laugh-In* and *Sanford and Son* (the black American version of British *Steptoe and Son*, starring Redd Foxx and Demond Wilson). Following *Come Back Charleston Blue*, Warren went on to be part of the directorial team responsible for the most successful transposition of blaxploitation cinema onto the small screen with *Get Christie Love!* (1974), which ran for one season (twenty-two episodes) featuring a sexy, smart, black undercover LAPD agent, played by Teresa Graves, who, like Warren, was a veteran of *Laugh-In*.

Although these new visions of black experience were proving popular, the terms of their success proved highly controversial. The denigrating epithet of "blaxploitation" was leveled at this series of films in 1972 by Junius Griffin, president of the Beverley Hills–Hollywood branch of the NAACP. The African American magazine *Jet*, in a column titled "Civil Rights Groups Attack Black Films," described Griffin as leading "a resistance movement against the motion picture to fight 'Black exploitation' films."[24] Griffin headed up the formation of the Coalition Against Blaxploitation (CAB), whose members were drawn primarily from the NAACP and the Congress of Racial Equality (CORE) and whose ideas were supported by Jesse Jackson's People United to Save Humanity (PUSH). *Ebony* highlighted how PUSH shared in Griffin's contention that a film such as *Super Fly* was retrogressive, for "the switch from the Stepin Fetchit stereotype to the Super Nigger is proof that black film portraits have come full circle." According to Griffin, *Super Fly* was "an insidious film which portrays the black community at its worst. It glorifies the use of cocaine and casts blacks in roles which glorify dope-pushers, pimps and grand theft."[25] Alongside *Super Fly*, *Shaft*, *Blacula*, *Sweetback*, *Cotton Comes to Harlem*, and *Come Back Charleston Blue* were targeted as "offending movies."[26]

Amplifying the problem was the increased dependency of such filmmaking on white financing and control—all of which would lead to an even more deleterious situation in which African Americans would contribute to their own degradation. One of the few redeeming features of *Super Fly* had been the fact that it had been backed by black financiers and directed by an African American. B. J. Mason voiced fears that the sequel, *Super Fly TNT* (1973), was "being readied—*minus* the talents of Phillip Fenty, the black writer, Gordon Parks Jr., the black director, and the original black financiers."[27] In the case of *Super Fly TNT*, Mason's fears were only partially realized. Not only was Fenty retained as original writer but also the more famous African American author Alex Haley wrote the screenplay. Although Gordon Parks Jr. did not direct, he was replaced by the film's African American star, Ron O'Neal. Yet the very success of these films still depended ultimately on black moviegoing support. Moreover, the fact that African Americans went in disproportionate numbers to the movies only made the problem of blaxploitation doubly exploitative. As Conrad Smith, western regional director of CORE, emphasized: "The intolerable conditions of Blacks being systematically exploited by an industry which was failing miserably during a recession three years ago, but is now being saved by a 40 percent Black box-office, can no longer be ignored by any *Black* individual or organization."[28]

While reporting such campaigns against the "Super Nigger Trend," both *Jet* and *Ebony* reserved judgment. The same edition of *Jet* that covered Griffin's attack on the perpetrators of blaxploitation also included a major feature, "How Watts Festival Renews Black Unity." This report on the Wattstax 1972 benefit concert followed on immediately from the column devoted to Griffin and featured a lead picture of Jesse Jackson. Yet the bulk of its content and subsequent photographs paid homage to a host of African American celebrities associated with "offending movies." Primary among these were "Richard (*Shaft*) Roundtree," "Melvin (*Sweetback*) Van Peebles," "Fred Williamson," and "Isaac Hayes ... who also served as grand marshal of the Watts Festival [and] led the audience through his theme from *Shaft*, which garnered him an Oscar, a Grammy and other awards."[29] The key figures supporting the Watts Festival, an event designed to restore dignity and hope to this inner-city Los Angeles community since the rebellion of 1965 (an event Darius James described as "Woodstock goes to the ghetto"),[30] turned out to be an admixture of civil rights crusaders *and* blaxploitation stars—including musicians such as Hayes, who featured on Stax records soundtracks to blaxploitation cinema. *Ebony* also couched its understanding of the blaxploitation phenomenon in undecided terms. B. J. Mason's feature piece was titled "The New Films: Culture or Con Game?" (subtitled "Rash of 'black' movies draws both condemnation and praise").[31]

A study of the trajectories of Mayfield's and Himes's work hopefully prefaces a need *not* to be complicit with those who summarily dismiss blaxploitation as bad art and counterproductive to black needs. There is a forgotten history to the evolution of this kind of ambivalent and devilish cultural production that should help in qualifying the argument that blaxploitation was the worst form of black complicity with white racism. While blaxploitation could be open to accusations of complicity because of its reliance on white mainstream resources—especially in terms of white direction and distribution—it also opened up other possibilities. The remainder of this chapter attends to an example of criminal blaxploitation filmmaking that is far less easy to chastise because of its guerrilla-like independent production qualities, even as it is perhaps all the more offensive for continuing to indulge putatively counterproductive representations of the black experience.

SIGNIFYIN' CINEMA: RUDY RAY MOORE AND THE QUALITY OF BADNESS

In spite of being acknowledged by major rap artists as a signal influence on the hip hop generation, Rudy Ray Moore remains an overlooked figure in the study of black popular culture. In straddling the worlds of rap and film, Moore has suffered, perhaps, from being awkward to categorize. The fact that his popularity with two generations of black youth has been derived from the under-the-counter character of his X-rated comedy records and the ultra-low budget and handmade quality of his film productions have contributed further to his critical neglect. Moore's movies, however, are "bad" in ways that should invite rather than dissuade scholarly attention.

In looking at Moore's films, we encounter a set of limits about our expectations of something called black cinema. The kinds of judgments that are brought to bear when looking at *Dolemite* (1975), *The Human Tornado* (1976), *Petey Wheatstraw: The Devil's Son-in-Law* (1979), and *Disco Godfather* (1980) raise questions not so much about the status of the films themselves (as "films," per se) than about the inadequacies of the paradigms we use when approaching this kind of cultural production.

Given the way Moore's films uniformly display signs of flawed filmmaking (such as boom microphones creeping into shot, discontinuous editing, badly choreographed martial arts fights), it is tempting to attribute the source of their enjoyment solely to their extreme low-budget camp characteristics. This, however, would be to overlook critical ways in which the pleasure that contemporaneous black audiences and the hip hop generation derive from Moore's films is generated from something other than how they fail to meet hegemonic understandings of good filmmaking. I shall argue that understanding Moore's popularity with black youth of different generations has everything to do with his necessarily irreverent attitude to the laws that govern mainstream moviemaking.

In the context of a long history of white racism on- and off-screen, African American filmmaking has had to work under an interrelated burden of improving representations of the race in a manner that might separate itself from dominant cinematic modes of production. Black filmmaking autonomy, however, has come at a cost. Attempts to break with hegemonic rules have necessarily meant operating with very limited budgets and without the benefit of extensive distribution and releasing arrangements. In spite of such restrictions, the critical-scholarly community has worked from the axiom that the good black film is one that can still demonstrate high-quality filmmaking acumen while at the same time addressing issues germane to the fate of African Americans.

If one uses such a paradigm, Rudy Ray Moore's films might appear to be abject failures and examples of counterproductive self-representation. They are manifestly low-budget handmade fare but without evidence of cinematic artisanship. They are concerned with black experience but do not adhere to a politically progressive or uplifting mandate. To this extent Moore's film output could be construed as embodying the very worst features of the cinema to which he contributed, namely, blaxploitation.

As we have chronicled, blaxploitation is a contentious nomenclature. It openly acknowledges the way a cycle of films in the 1970s took advantage of an African American audience and its desire to see black heroes involved in black exploits on the big screen. Made with limited funds and distributed and released to niche ghettoized urban markets, the first major examples, *Shaft* and *Super Fly*, set up a contradictory model for emulation. Investors (mainly white) were attracted to a formula that ensured low-budget films could gross disproportionately well at the box office, especially in an era of financial crisis for the film industry.[32] Initially, this formula depended on stories that addressed black urban or ghetto realities in putatively realist ways. Innovations on this theme led to increasingly sensationalist and outrageous treatments of black experience but without the benefit of increased budgets, which would have countermanded the appeal of this kind of cinema to potential investors. The cycle's popularity was linked, then, to venal attributes (such as exploiting desires for sex and violence) that seemed to compromise other ways in which such filmmaking could have been seen as advancing the interests of the race. To cultural and political guardians, the blaxploitation film was to be shunned, its double crime being that it fed the wrong impression of the race and further ghettoized the economic conditions for the production of black film.

To Donald Bogle, for example, black-oriented commercial cinema of the 1970s was inevitably a complicit vehicle of white racism at worst or a lost opportunity at best:

> For the most part, the films were heady male action fantasies with tenacious buck protagonists performing deeds of derring-do, while self-righteously paying lip-service to the idea of political commitment. The films would have us believe the heroes were out to clean up the ghetto of its ills. Actually, the best way to have cleaned up the ghetto might have been to have first rounded up the producers of some of these vehicles.[33]

Moreover, as Ed Guerrero highlights in a paraphrase of a hostile contemporaneous *New York Times* article by Clayton Riley, there was nothing new about blaxploitation films. They were "no more than thematic templates reworked with black casts," using "updated stereotypes that reconfirm white expectations of blacks and serve to repress and delay the awakening of any real political consciousness."[34]

The expectation that a true black-oriented cinema be aligned with a progressive mandate is driven, accordingly, by the search for pure forms, which is itself highly problematic. As Peter Stanfield argues:

> It may be precipitous to dismiss blaxploitation films as "degraded" because of their failure to meet a responsibility for articulating explicit political platforms. . . .
>
> The question of how the social experience of the audience is addressed is a properly political one, even though the nature of blaxploitation films makes appeal to direct political intervention ultimately unproductive.[35]

Blaxploitation evinces a growing sense of political enervation and determinism in which black agency had become strictly "limited only to the streets."[36] As Massood adumbrates, such representation emerged out of a wider field of sociological, political, and television news representation in which "black" had become synonymous with "ghetto" destitution and violent inner-city uprising.[37] In this sense, even as blaxploitation was indirectly indicative of energies released by the climate of protest in the late 1960s and early 1970s, it was also expressive of growing disillusionment with the way political action had failed to deliver substantial change on the ground.

Furthermore, blaxploitation's skepticism toward political authority becomes a formal property. As George Lipsitz suggests, although the cycle's films do indeed deal in stereotype and rework familiar templates, generically speaking they might be better described as "uneasy hybrid[s]" reflective of the way prevailing genres were inadequate to black experience.[38] Such recombinant impurity (mixing of action, gangster, martial arts, horror) certainly characterizes Moore's films, whose disorienting effects are exacerbated by their ultra-low production values. And explaining how this might be a source of pleasure to black audiences has involved confronting the racially proscribed limits of the aesthetic values critics employ in judging such "bad" popular film production.

Mikel Koven, for example, states that *Dolemite* "is perhaps one of the worst films I have ever seen. . . . Watching *Dolemite* was the only time during the preparation of this book [*Blaxploitation Films*] that I actually felt white."[39] That *Dolemite* is not accessible in normative terms, as reproducing the pleasure of coherent narrative cinema, estranges the (white) film critic. Alienating as this experience may be, Koven also recognizes that the film's "[unrivaled] success with contemporary black audiences" had everything to do with "forms of speech" and "modes of presentation" associated with Moore's established reputation in reciting folkloric tales of black badmen known as "toasts."[40] Darius James, in an irreverent investigation of his experience of the 1970s as a black adolescent, makes this the essential characteristic of Moore's films: "Unlike most of the commercial cinema's Black-market movies, which rely on the story formulas of their honkoid counterparts, the movies of Rudy Ray Moore are rooted in the structure, imagery and motifs of Black oral narrative known as 'The Toast.'"[41] While James, Koven, and Eithne Quinn[42] note but do not elaborate on this point, it is an invaluable place to start when trying to (re)evaluate the ambivalence of not only Moore's heroic creation but also blaxploitation more generally.

Dolemite's story features Moore in the main role as a nightclub owner-entertainer and pimp serving time in prison, having been framed by a rival for drug dealing and a fur robbery. Queen Bee, Dolemite's brothel madam and business partner, secures his release, which resulted from a confidential agreement with the warden and the FBI that he help uncover the real bosses of the narcotic and gun racket in Los Angeles. Out of prison, Dolemite finds out that he has lost his nightclub to bad Willy Green (whom he also knows is the man who framed him in conjunction with corrupt cops and racketeer Mr. Big) and that Queen Bee has been retraining his stable of hookers as an all-girl army of kung fu killers. He buys back the club, much to the consternation of Willy Green and Mr. Big's mobsters. The film concludes with an extended martial arts battle in which Dolemite and his street-savvy female hustlers kick out the mob.

Such a simple revenge narrative is a skeleton that supports Moore's real priorities. In the first instance, Dolemite's profession and moniker is vital. As a nightclub entertainer who goes by the name of a folkloric badman, Dolemite is Moore's double. Moore entered the business of making movies on the back of a reputation gained as a stand-up comedian who specialized in explicit renditions of a badman folk poetry repertoire, which he committed to vinyl in a series of popular party records. His signature toast was "Dolemite," which was the opening track on his first and most famous party record, *Eat Out More Often* (1970). Moore's oral rendition tells us about a badman protagonist who immediately upon birth in San Antonio usurps his father's authority. He learns to drink whiskey and gin from the age of one. His uncle, Sudden Death, is called in to sort him out, but Dolemite tears his leg off. One hundred of the "baddest" men in town eventually bring him down and get him jailed. Having served his time, Dolemite is released at the age of thirteen and embarks on a terrorizing world tour (which features him kicking lions in Africa and copulating with steers in South America). He returns to the United States to see a heavyweight boxing match and then travels from Kansas City to Chicago. Here he engages in a sexual gauntlet with the madam of all brothel madams, Chi Mabel. Dolemite emerges victorious after having conquered her venereal powers and leaving her dead from sexual exhaustion. Dolemite eventually dies, but at his funeral "his dick was still hard."

The toast is an expressive form where the emphasis falls on the individuality of the delivery and performing of otherwise well-known and oft-repeated tales of mythical hellion figures such as the mischievous Signifying Monkey and the murderous Stagger Lee. Parallel to the moment of blaxploitation cinema in the 1970s, there also arose an anthropological fascination with the invigoration of oral wit in urban black communities, especially with African American street and prison poetry that celebrated the badman as culture hero.[43] Folklorists, however, have struggled to make sense of how the destructive badman figure—who seems so indiscriminate and asocial in his violent acts and who appears to be as much a peril to black community as white—can hold such strong appeal to black folk. John W. Roberts argues that the use of Anglo-American norms in evaluating heroic creation has led to a misunderstanding of the black badman:

> While white Americans have had every reason to view the law as supportive of their interests and rights, and to conceptualize outlaws as heroic only under extraordinary conditions and within well-defined situations, African Americans have had few reasons to view the law as anything other than antagonistic to their interests.... [T]he folklore of the black badman did not develop within a tradition of folk heroic creation in which retaliatory actions against the established power structure required expressive justification.[44]

In correcting predominant understandings of the folkloric black badman, Roberts situates the appeal of the badman myth in the specific context of changes in black culture consequent on manumission—and understands the badman as a figure of special appeal to those African Americans participating in the new secular lifestyle in which the law was both absent and your foe. Freedom had a contradictory connotation of being free of the law. And the sites of freedom were always potential sites of lawlessness. Jooks, saloons, and nightclubs proffered opportunities for intoxication, gambling, entertainment, and violence. In such a context, black activity was often demarcated as illegal by default, and "the black characterization of badmen as 'bad' derived from their association with a kind of secular anarchy peculiar to the experience of free black people."[45]

If Roberts outlines how freedom was ironically configured in the late nineteenth century following emancipation, Moore's reinvigoration of the badman toast in the 1970s is similarly engaged with disappointments consequent on another failed promise—this time that of civil rights legislation. Moore himself notes how much the kind of cultural production he was involved with was frowned upon by the National Association for the Advancement of Colored People (NAACP):

> The NAACP and the big black groups did complain about the movies we made in that period. Not mine, per se, but a lot of them. They were talk-

> ing about the image, but I've got to say this. None of these groups did not finance no movies of a different status for anyone. So I say today that should we have tried to make a movie like the so-called groups would have liked us to, it would have died at the box office the first day.[46]

Clearly, Moore's badman tales, first on record and then on film, spoke to a particular part of the black community at odds with the moral and political vanguard and whose needs were better met by the contradictory image of black empowerment that Moore articulated. His badman toasts were sold under the counter (because of their risqué content and covers)—symbolic of the awkward status of this kind of heroic configuration. The kind of blue humor that went with this territory was the first on record and paved the way for Redd Foxx and Richard Pryor, more well-known black exponents of the X-rated stand-up act. Moore financed *Dolemite*, his first film, with money earned from the sale of his party records (around $100,000), which featured explicit renditions of the exploits of "Petey Wheatstraw," "Shine," "Pimping Sam," "The Signifying Monkey," and "Dolemite."[47] These recorded versions of essential parts of his blue stand-up comedy routine had given him an underground following as a latter-day griot. Replete with covers of himself and go-go dancers in a state of undress, his first two party records, *Eat Out More Often* and *This Pussy Belongs to Me*, made Billboard's soul chart top 50 in 1970.[48]

At one level, then, on film Moore further conflates his own persona with the badman characters he impersonates on record. His films could be said to take on the quality of the toast, where, in comparison to prose, pleasures are derived primarily from performance and rhetorical style rather than "reading for the plot." At the same time, Moore's discontinuous montage or pat attention to plot is motivated by his background as a variety show entertainer who had first worked as a song-and-dance man performing under the moniker of "Prince DuMarr" for a traveling revue company in the 1950s before trying his luck as a soul singer in the 1960s.[49] Such experience, in conjunction with his eventual success as a stand-up comedian, clearly influenced his understanding of what would make for good cinematic entertainment.

Not surprisingly, perhaps, not only does *Dolemite*'s story have a nightclub at its dramatic center, but so too do all his other films. Such mise-en-scène allowed Moore to indulge his own stand-up talents in delivering toasts such as "Shine and the Titanic" and "The Signifying Monkey" as well as enabling him to edit according to the loop-logic of a variety show. That is, the plot is reduced to being a means to rationalize the stringing together of otherwise arbitrary acts of showmanship. Significantly, the musical genre notwithstanding, this kind of montage inverts the mainstream cinema's understanding of the time and space conventionally given over to black talent on white screens.

In Moore's films the entertainer is not treated as minor or "time out." The conceit of making the predominant theme the struggle for control of entertainment venues and the main protagonist a stand-up comedian certainly helps to lessen the sense that the time and space of entertainer performance is diversion from more serious narrative pleasures. In making a stand-up comedian an action hero, however, it is clear that Moore is not interested in substituting black for white actors in stories that resemble or emulate established Hollywood formulas. Dispensing with generic guidelines, Moore compounds the prioritization of performance and spectacle over narrative and character development and coherent diegesis by making expertise in martial arts a critical part of the stand-up comedian's repertoire.

The integration of martial arts into blaxploitation had been precipitated by the success of *Enter the Dragon* (1973) with black audiences. *Enter the Dragon*'s main star, Bruce Lee, embodied a nonwhite form of self-defense that turned violence into a performance art. The film also exhibited the talents of the black karate champion Jim Kelly, who went on to star in *Black Belt Jones* (1974), the first movie that successfully blended the twin fascination for martial arts and black action among black audiences. Moore's *Dolemite* continued the trend (albeit in a more maverick fashion) that made kung fu a vital part of the revue world.

While Moore's irreverence for diegesis and generic stability is particularly pronounced, the strategy of making the nightclub the primary mise-en-scène for black-oriented commercial cinema is nothing new. Moore continues a tradition established by the talking race films of the 1930s and 1940s, which, as I have argued extensively in a previous chapter, were also conveniently focused on nightlife and the revue stage. Such films paid only lip service to narrative, which was often reduced to being merely a device to rationalize the splicing together of "soundie"-like footage featuring discrete stage acts. As one-reel mini-films, soundies featured popular entertainers doing musical, comedy, and burlesque revue routines. These reels were looped together for use on specialized jukeboxes known as Panorams in the early to mid-1940s and functioned as publicity for groups trying to sell records. As I have argued, we can see the soundie not only as a structuring force in talking race films but also as a significant precursor to the music video. Moore's films constitute an inventive continuation of this black cinematic revue aesthetic and its way of inverting patterns of screen subordination and racial etiquette. And in their content and style they prefigure the raunchier features of hip hop music video.

Moore's second film, *The Human Tornado*, for example, demonstrates these stylistic priorities from the outset. The opening credits start with a fade-in to a close-up shot of Rudy Ray Moore's face, sporting an Afro. To the tempo of a funk soundtrack, he turns and disappears into a roadside ditch with a tarpaulin sheet draped around his back that tells us "Rudy Ray Moore is Dolemite." Beneath a series of superimposed hand-painted titles and credits, Moore reappears in different guises through a sequence of abrupt cuts. First he pops up on the roadside edge with cap, striped pants, and a red shirt that he proceeds to take off strip-show style to the rhythm of the ongoing funk music. Following a series of idiosyncratic martial arts moves and poses, a cut brings about his transmogrification into a fakir character, replete with African robe and conjurer's turban, who acts out a range of hammy prayerlike gestures. To the audio cue of the first lyrics ("He's a human tornado"), another cut reveals our protagonist briefly in "pimp" style, wearing a baby blue, 1970s flared suit with platform shoes, before a further cut brings him back as the dashiki-clad Afro-conjurer executing some magical kung fu against foes reflected in two mirrors. We then experience a jump cut to a Stutz Blackhawk (the ultimate 1970s celebrity automobile) pulling up outside a house. Moore is revealed to be the driver, who gets out wearing a dapper pinstripe suit and two-tone shoes, to be greeted by a joyful woman (presumably delighted at the sight of the new "fly" car). We then jump-cut again to a new scene, with Moore dressed in a white tuxedo posing in front of a wall decorated with his party album covers. The final director credit is a cue for Moore to exit frame right. The subsequent cut takes us to a mirror ball and the interior of a nightclub where Moore, now in a black tuxedo with one of his party records under his arm, is introduced to an audience as "Mr. Dolemite." He proceeds to deliver a stand-up routine consisting mainly of jokes about sex and sexual endowment at the expense of overweight members of the audience, each joke in a different tuxedo, all to the beat of a funk band rhythm section and the gyrations of a female burlesque dancer dressed in a jungle-patterned g-string bikini.

Very little of this opening seven minutes helps locate the audience in a stable relationship to the time and space of the narrative or within a consistent generic world. We are provided instead with a self-promoting impressionistic collage that conflates Moore with Dolemite as a trickster-like, identity-shifting figure. Effectively, the story only begins with the next abrupt cut. Dolemite arrives at his palatial home in a white luxury sedan. He announces to a gathering of various black religious and civic interest groups that he is donating his house to help fund the building of a boys' home.

The strange juxtaposition of explicit, politically incorrect comedy and a philanthropic act of civic virtue is indicative of the way Moore's films swing radically between different registers. The apparent "crudity" of montage (foreshadowed by the credits) pays little respect to maintaining temporal or spatial coherence. Thematically, however, such shifts are interesting precisely for the way they position the different value we accord narrative and performance. The fact that immediately following his moral pronouncement to support a worthy cause, Dolemite disappears into his back bedroom to service sexually a paying white female customer—who also turns out to be the sheriff's wife—only compounds matters. Servicing the good cause of racial advancement is pitted against bad behavior, first as a blue comedian and second as someone conforming to the image of the black stud of the white imagination.

Inverting priorities, Moore displaces any investment in the teleology of the progressive uplift narrative. The local redneck Abelmonte police force, eager to stop the integration of the neighborhood, raids Dolemite's house. The sheriff discovers his wife in bed with Dolemite, at which point she screams rape (comically revisiting an all-too-familiar white racist trope). Dolemite flees the scene, naked, abandoning his house and all his possessions, only this time for reasons of self-preservation rather than moral sacrifice. He embarks on a journey from this southern space of "nigger-haters" to Los Angeles and his old partner and confidante, Queen Bee. There will be no progression as such, only a set of repetitions, as Dolemite finds himself once again embroiled in a feud over nightclub ownership. Indeed, following on from *Dolemite*, *The Human Tornado* is more repeat than sequel. As James points out, it "is the same story except more so," as our protagonist helps Queen Bee regain her nightclub from the white mob who have kidnapped two members of her kung fu working-girl army.[50]

Not being fettered to a political mandate gives Moore a certain degree of freedom—freedom to play with the possibilities of montage once released from any obligation to continuity or generic consistency. The naked Dolemite jumps down the hillside from his house, headfirst. Halfway down, the action is frozen. Over the freeze-frame, Moore interjects with a voice-over directed at the audience: "So y'all don't believe I jumped, huh? So watch this good shit." We are then subjected to a reverse motion shot of Dolemite flying back up the hill, followed by a replay with the title "instant replay" printed across the screen.

With the caricatures of redneck white folk and the tongue-in-cheek self-presentation as a naked overweight action hero, this play with the elasticity of the medium contributes a cartoon character to the movie. Mixed generic register (action, gangster, gore, slapstick, martial arts) and abrupt shifts in mood disturb any stable orientation to character, story, and plot. Dolemite's sexual liaisons, for example, swing from comic fantasy to something resembling romance. He has a genuine courting African American partner in Hurricane Annie (also drawn from one of his toasts). The possibility of consummating their love is constantly thwarted by phone calls and unwanted intruders (a motif repeated in Moore's next film, *Petey Wheatstraw*, with love interest Nell). Yet even when the opportunity arrives, the otherwise tenderly rendered lovemaking is intercut at a delicate moment (of off-screen cunnilingus) with a brief scene of both Annie and Dolemite in a diner feasting on pork ribs.

His encounter with the wife of the mob boss, Cavaletti, provides for the film's most indulgent fantasy sequence. Posing as a door-to-door salesman of artwork featuring interracial bodily entanglement, Dolemite seduces Mrs. Cavaletti in an attempt to secure information about where the kidnapped women are being held. We enter Mrs. Cavaletti's fantasy world, one in which she reclines in a negligee on alphabet bricks spelling BED, while various black bodybuilding suitors emerge from a toy box to entertain her. This subjective shot and scene gives way to a more objective but no less slapstick one in which we see a bed bouncing, walls shuddering, pictures falling, and a ceiling collapse.

Dolemite, the sexual tornado, is reliant on stereotypical visions of miscegenation. Knowledge of the clichéd way in which others perceive you is vital to Dolemite's trickster behavior. Consistent with this visual play on the surface of things as the site/sight that matters is Moore's recourse to highly stylized oral rhetoric that intrudes on other more "natural" speech forms and performance styles. *The Human Tornado* contrives a set of situations where Dolemite can arrest the real-time flow of the narrative to deliver braggadocio rhymes. At the beginning, having escaped from his house, he sets up a roadside trap for the pursuing sheriff and his goons. With his shotgun pointed at the police car, Dolemite delivers the following rap to a funky backing track:

I'll stop this longhaired dilapidated sheriff now,
'Cos he just wanna follow me anyhow
He thinks he's bad. Ain't got no class,
I'm gonna . . . this shotgun up his muthafuckin' ass.

In a move that anticipates the development of the Dolemite idea in directions even more clearly related to the toast, we see our hero fake his own death in order to live on. Having rescued the kidnapped women from a torture chamber, Dolemite recites:

Mules kicked me and didn't even bruise my hide,
Rattlesnakes that bit me have crawled off and died.
Yes, I fought my way in here 'cos I'm rough and ready,
So girls, let's go and get that muthafucka, Cavaletti.

Having defeated the mob, however, he is hunted down and shot by the cuckolded sheriff. Left for dead, it turns out Dolemite has been wearing a bulletproof vest. The film closes with Dolemite laughing at the camera. He may have outwitted "the Man" by appearing to be dead, but his terms of survival necessitate a change in identity. The more prosaic features of the first two screen versions of the badman will give way to a more supernatural take in his third film, *Petey Wheatstraw: The Devil's Son-in-Law*.

While the first two films certainly demand suspension of disbelief even as they are set in realist time and space, *Petey Wheatstraw* makes such suspension more "logical" if only because it is concerned more directly with the badman's contract with Satan. In doing so Moore connects his own art and act to a legacy we can trace back to the eponymous bluesman of the 1930s (subject of chapter 1) and the trickster figures who haunt Mayfield's and Himes's work. Dolemite's rap to Cavaletti toward the end of *The Human Tornado* includes the line "you got a one-way ticket straight to hell." *Petey Wheatstraw* opens with Moore lit up in red in front of flames delivering a toast:

Yes, I'm Petey Wheatstraw, the devil's son-in-law,
The high sheriff of hell.
I went with notorious Fannie,
Even made love to Lula Bell.
I took back today and brought back yesterday,
Took the 4th of July and put it in June,
And made leap year jump over the moon.
I'm not here to brag, nor here to boast,
I can sit on a tombstone and produce baby ghosts.

Although this is a tempered version of the far more explicit "Petey Wheatstraw" narrative that Moore delivers on his party records, the mise-en-scène effects a cinematic transition into the world of the toast. The flame-lit Petey reflects on his birth in the midst of the great Miami storm, which cues a flashback to his mother in labor. A white doctor helps deliver first a watermelon, followed by a full-grown youth who proceeds to beat up the medic and insult his own father. This scene reworks not so much one from the "Petey Wheatstraw" oral story (whose birth is not recounted) as the opening of Moore's "Dolemite" toast, in which:

> the day he was dropped from his mammy's ass,
> he slapped his pappy's face
> and said "From now on cocksucker, I'm running this place."

The young Petey finds wisdom through an aged martial arts guru, Bantu, who teaches him the ancient oriental ways. In spite of this training and background, Petey insists that his real ambition has always been to be a comedian! With this image of a kung fu fighting stand-up comic in mind, we cut to an older Petey (now played by Moore) onstage doing his usual "dissing the audience" routine prior to taking his show on the road. Moore has once again contrived to conflate the image of the folkloric badman with that of the peripatetic entertainer in fashioning a distinctively black culture hero.

What unfolds is once again a story about nightclub feuding. This time Petey finds himself in competition with the comedy duo Leroy and Skillet who have secured a $100,000 loan from mobster "Mr. White" to open a new club, The Twenty Grand. They have promised the gangster an immediate return on his loan on the basis of being the only act in town at a time when most revue entertainers are on tour. Petey's arrival in Los Angeles to perform at another venue, Steve's Den, at the same time as Leroy and Skillet's opening night threatens to ruin things. The duo hires thugs to try and resolve matters. They end up killing the young brother of Petey's loyal friend, Ted. Following a serious and quite moving death scene, a funeral takes place at a Baptist church. As the pallbearers take the coffin down the church steps, the entire cortege, including Petey, the lead gospel singer, and the preacher, is mowed down by two hit men with machine guns. *Petey Wheatstraw* is the most generically recombinant of Moore's films. Like previous screen efforts, it pays homage to cheaper forms such as Bruce Lee martial arts and schlock supernatural horror. It combines this with loftier Faustian themes and more firmly anchors its representational mayhem and irreverence in the hyperbole of badman folklore. The somber image of body-strewn church steps is relieved through the arrival of a bearded man sporting a wide-brimmed hat who seeks out the dead Petey, giving him his visiting card, "Lou Cipher." Lucifer makes Petey a proposition. He can return Petey to the living world and let him take revenge on the scheming assassins on condition that on completion of this mission Petey marry his daughter and sire a son. Although Petey has his fears about the ugliness of Satan's daughter confirmed on seeing her photograph, he agrees to the arrangement. With reverse motion, the dead funeral cortege is returned to life, and Petey sets out not only to bring down Leroy and Skillet and Mr. White but also to destroy the devil himself.

Armed with Lucifer's magic cane, Petey is able to ruin Leroy and Skillet's opening night by casting a spell that forces the duo to disrespect the wife of their mobster sponsor seated in the front row and to admit that they dilute the club drinks. Having destroyed the building, however, Petey continues to stall his return to hell, using the cane as an instrument of "uplift" and goodwill mission with ghetto-style irony. Backed by an upbeat funk soundtrack, we see him saving a kid from being hit by a car while chasing a ball across the street, making an obese woman thin, transforming a malfunctioning rusty automobile into a brand-new one, and turning a cheating husband into a small dog at the request of the jilted wife.

Petey's mischievous plans to renege on his promises to Lucifer culminate in confrontation. Lucifer sends in his shock brigade of red-horned karate disciples sporting capes and orange and purple leotards. The devil himself finally appears in "real" form, in a red, flared jumpsuit replete with glitter belt, Dracula cape, and werewolf hair. Despite the camp costumes and poorly choreographed martial arts fighting, Petey maintains his dignity, emerging the victor after having hurled Lucifer in a ball of flame to his apparent death from the top of a building.

A joyful Petey gets into what he thinks is his accomplice's car, only to discover that he is sharing the backseat with an all-too-alive Lucifer and his daughter, with new recruits to the world of the undead, Leroy and Skillet, in the front. The film ends with the words, "Now you may kiss the bride," the lifting of the daughter's veil, and a freeze-frame of Petey's screaming face. Outsmarted by the devil (the ultimate trickster), the badman has found his match.

Notably, Moore's next film, *Disco Godfather*, brought his filmmaking to an end. Having self-financed all his productions, he was vulnerable to box-office failure. *Disco Godfather* bombed, bankrupting him. There are various reasons for this change in fortune. At one level Moore knew that he had exhausted the *Dolemite* formula; *The Human Tornado* was an improved version of *Dolemite*, while *Petey Wheatstraw*, which constituted a yet more imaginative way to keep the badman toast structure going, essentially played out similar ideas and tropes. *Disco Godfather* may have been one film too many, but it was also the product of miscalculation on Moore's part, as it departed from the elements that had made his work popular with audiences.

Outwardly, *Disco Godfather*'s concatenation of generic expectancies associated with *Saturday Night Fever* and *The Godfather* promises a "typical" Moore experience. The abuse of the Bee Gees soundtrack album for *Saturday Night Fever* as a surface from which to snort coke alongside the roller-skating disco dance act and the drug trip sequences (in which the Disco Godfather is transmogrified into a machete-wielding voodoo "angel of death" confronting the zombie victims of PCP/angel dust addiction) evokes the previous films' humorous excesses. And the suspended ending, in which we are left unsure about whether the Disco Godfather will recover from having been subjected to angel dust by his gangster nemesis, is consistent with the tenor of both *The Human Tornado* and *Petey Wheatstraw*.

Yet while *Disco Godfather* does have Moore hallmarks, too much time is spent on a forced antidrug diatribe. The Disco Godfather himself is an ex-cop turned deejay, providing a background that realigns and delimits the protagonist's motivations and rhyming within a moral and diegetically coherent world. His behavior is motivated by an unambiguous civically virtuous message, and his rhymes are stripped of profanity and rationalized as strictly part of the disc jockey's art in managing the dance floor (limited to a range of one-liners, such as "Put your weight on it," "Put some zip in your hips," and "Put some slide in your glide"). In many ways the film fails because Moore tried to make a film that organizations such as the NAACP would have liked: "*Disco Godfather* was a film I should never have done. It's because I was trying to change my structure and do things that would be a little more positive."[51]

CONCLUSION: SIGNIFYIN' ON HOLLYWOOD

In a footnote to his observations on *The Human Tornado*, Darius James provides a suggestive aside, recommending that Moore link up with black literary theorist Henry Louis Gates Jr. to write a book-length study of his films in terms of the toast tradition.[52] Gates's theorization of the black cultural practice of signifying highlights how the relationship between vernacular tradition and literary artistry is definitive of a black difference (what is "black" about African American literature). He attends to black American literature's "double formal antecedents" (vernacular and Western) as a way to think about blackness as something beyond categorical or ontological essence.[53] Likewise, cultural theorist Stuart Hall stresses that

> in black popular culture there are no pure forms at all. Always these forms are the product of partial synchronization, of engagement across cultural boundaries, of the confluence of more than one cultural tradition, of the negotiations of dominant and subordinate positions, of the subterranean strategies of recoding and transcoding, of critical signification, of signifying.[54]

Moore's films play out a confluence or double formal indebtedness, and in the process they signify on mainstream film and the expectations that come with it. His films subordinate narrative pleasures to ones associated with the performance and spectacle of the black revue stage act, on the one hand, and music video, on the other.

Accounting for the appeal of Moore to the hip hop generation, however, involves analysis not only of his filmmaking aesthetics but also of the guerrilla nature of his production financing. Moore's relative autonomy from strictures governing black-oriented filmmaking was derived from the way he could self-finance. He had honed marketing skills first in figuring out how to merchandise the toast on vinyl. This extended to the exploitation of desires for explicit rap humor on the records themselves and also to the packaging of his material with controversial "adults only" album covers:

> That's where my head was at; to get business and a piece of the rock... by the covers being so daring it helped them to sell.... The record stores just put them under the counter and when somebody came in and asked for it, they put it in a brown paper bag and the customer went on home with it.[55]

He put out his first party album, *Eat Out More Often*, on his own record label, Comedy International Enterprises, which allowed him to steer clear of meeting fees and percentages demanded by larger companies and retain the profits for himself. Using the money gained from his records, he was able to do something similarly entrepreneurial with his movies. Although reliant on a small niche-market distributor (Dimension Pictures), he was able to produce his movies under his own company, Comedian International Pictures. Thus the on-screen battle to wrest control of entertainment venues from the likes of Mr. Big and Mr. White is doubled by Moore's off-screen ability to make films independent of larger syndicates. As he says:

> I'm self-made. I've had no training, no studying, or nothing. I just have the will power and the mother wit and the gift to structure things and work on them to make them better. Throughout the years, I've become a genius in what I'm doing. . . . I'm probably the greatest X-rated comedian in the world today.[56]

Hubris comes with the territory when one is a toastmaster, but there is a larger significance to proclaiming oneself as "self-made" through badman merchandising that extends beyond the seemingly parochial world of Moore's films. Moore holds an appeal with today's hard-core rappers because he set out a blueprint for their entrepreneurial hustle in supposedly counterproductive self-representation. Among the various rap groups and artists that have heralded Moore as a vital influence (Big Daddy Kane, Eric B. and Rakim, Snoop Dogg, and members of Niggaz With Attitude [N.W.A.] have all featured him either in recordings or music video), it is the "party" or "booty" rap group, the 2 Live Crew, who have sampled him the most.

Consciously imitating Rudy Ray Moore's business strategy, the 2 Live Crew gained a reputation for the X-rated nature of their material. Their first album, *The 2 Live Crew Is What We Are* (1986), included an extended sample of Moore's "Romeo and Juliet" monologue on "Throw the D," and the album's back cover included the dedication "Thanks to Rudy Ray Moore alias Dolemite." The fact that record stores worked under the threat of a felony obscenity charge if they sold it to minors only helped promote the album as an underground hit. In June 1990, however, the 2 Live Crew became the first music group in U.S. history to be charged with obscenity by the federal court. Controversy surrounded the sexually explicit, pornographic, and misogynist nature of their latest album, *As Nasty as They Wanna Be* (1989), in which Moore was also sampled on the track "Dick Almighty." At the trial Henry Louis Gates Jr. provided expert testimony in their defense, arguing that these rap artists were elaborating on the important African American cultural traditions of playing the dozens and signifying—coded ways of communicating developed out of the need for self-protection in a racist society. Identifying the 2 Live Crew as uniquely obscene in a nation where forms of sexually explicit entertainment proliferate suggested that the group was the focus of a moral panic rooted in stereotypical associations about black masculinity and sexual prowess. Gates contended that there was political purpose to the 2 Live Crew's exaggerations, for "they embrace that stereotype [of blacks having overly large sexual organs and being hypersexed individuals]. They name it and they explode it."[57] As Kimberle Crenshaw elaborates, these decadent party rappers and their "gangsta" brethren become "the very social outlaws that society fears and attempts to proscribe."[58] Moreover, the prosecution's anti-sexist rhetoric actually helped to sanction a deep-seated white racist fear about black male sexuality, reaffirming "the black rapist/white victim dyad."[59]

While this defense attacks the easy syllogism where "degraded" art equates with "moral degeneration," it does not critique the ongoing problem that this kind of challenge to racist mythology depends on the subordination of black women. This important contingency notwithstanding, profiting from stereotype in gangsta style continues to breach racial etiquette in significant ways. As Quinn highlights, the gangsta is both representation of and means to self-determination for a section of society otherwise denied access to normative channels to success. For gangstas, like Moore, creative autonomy, control, and economic independence have come through trafficking in "badness." And as I have argued, this term precisely signifies on the hegemonic even as it may seem to confirm the worst of prejudices. While Moore's way of doing things kept his films underground in their day, a similar structure of cultural production a decade later precipitated the move from the margins to the mainstream. Moore was at the vanguard of what is now a global commerce in black badman imagery circulated primarily in the form of music video.

5 From Goines to Gangsta

Keeping It Reel

The dynamics of Rudy Ray Moore's cultural production parallel those of the African American author Donald Goines. In spite of being touted by his publishers, Holloway House, as "America's #1 Best Selling Black Author," Goines's work did not reach white readers and has gone unrepresented in the canon of African American literature until recently. His was ghetto fiction that suffered exclusion for a host of interrelated issues to do with the politics of taste and race representation. As Greg Goode describes:

> Goines is the foremost example of a literary phenomenon possible no earlier than the 1970s—a successful black author of mass market fiction with a readership which is almost exclusively black.... Goines is a prototype for the author who has achieved popular success and influence but has been almost completely ignored by reviewers, critics, and scholars. His novels have sold well over five million copies and are recommended reading at some New York high schools. The books enjoy strong sales on American military bases abroad.[1]

Much like Iceberg Slim (the pseudonym for Robert Beck), the author who influenced him, Goines's critical obscurity had everything to do with the content and style of his writing. The publication of Iceberg Slim's *Pimp: The Story of My Life* in 1967 set the precedent for a particular kind of niche market, urban- or black-experience fiction. The autobiographical confession of a procurer fighting to retain control of his stable of prostitutes while dealing with drug addiction and prison was framed as literature designed to turn readers away from "the life." The massive popularity of the book among urban African Americans, however, was attributed to the way it connected with the determining conditions and demeaning realities of the black inner city.

Like Iceberg Slim, Goines's uncompromisingly brutal vision of the urban black experience was authenticated by his own criminal biography. He had falsified his age to join the air force, spending time in Japan and Korea, where he became addicted to heroin. Returning to civilian life in Detroit and needing to feed a $100 a day habit led to Goines embarking on a criminal career that included pimping, armed robbery, and bootlegging. It also led to fifteen arrests and seven jail sentences. And it was during the last of these prison terms, inspired by reading Iceberg Slim, that he took to writing as a way out of the life.

Unlike Malcolm X, who had also parlayed a criminal past to grasp reader loyalty, Goines's output did not work toward a politically progressive resolution. Prison and crime do not bring about a positive epiphany. As fan and rap star DMX says of a Goines criminal protagonist:

> For all the terrible things he has done wrong, he doesn't see himself as beyond redemption. But reality hits, and despite the fact that he's coming to terms with some of the wrongs that he's committed, he still gets what he deserves. The message is, "You do dirt; you get dirt."
>
> This is a theme with many Goines characters. No matter what crisis or trouble pushed them into crime, they get it in the end.[2]

Tragically, the same fate was meted out to Goines when gunmen murdered him and his wife in October 1974.[3]

While the lack of full redemption and the nihilistic sense of life as vicious circle may not have been sufficient grounds for the literary establishment (black and white) to ignore Goines, his explicit language and almost pornographic descriptions of sex, drug addiction, and violence probably made him too contentious. Much like blaxploitation cinema, such writing, while popular, seemed to pander to the worst tastes and fed putatively counterproductive images of the community.

Such concerns, however, were not a priority to the publishing company, Holloway House. As an enterprise founded and run by Bentley Morriss and Ralph Weinstock, two white editors and businessmen associated with the soft-porn magazines *Adam* and *Knight*, the explicit and graphic character of Slim's and Goines's writing was to be supported.[4] Moreover, the reticence of any other publishers to take up such writing meant a lack of competition and the consequent ability to keep royalties to a minimum (typically, the *New York Times* refused to print an advertisement for Slim's *Pimp*). This having been said, whatever the contradictions of working for white overseers associated with the less salubrious side of publishing, Morriss did provide a venue for black authors who were otherwise excluded from the chance to publish. And in doing so, Holloway House provided a section of society otherwise indifferent to literature and reading with texts that fueled their interests and in which they could see their own reality represented. As Morriss recalled, following the success of *Pimp*:

> A couple of the editors that we had here went into South Central and went into the Watts Workshop and so on and tried to solicit writers.... We were the only ones out there encouraging young black writers, and we didn't want them to write about the valley of the dolls, and we didn't want them to write about their trips abroad. We wanted their experiences.[5]

The first major recruit on the back of Iceberg Slim was Odie Hawkins, who attended the Watts Workshop and had his book *Ghetto Sketches* published by Holloway House in 1971. Hawkins, although aware of the potentially indentured character of being a Holloway House author, felt the pros outweighed the cons given the discrimination of the wider publishing business:

> I don't want to sound off about publishing houses, especially black publishing houses, but they're very academic and very partial to people who are writing about things in the way they can relate to them. If you put a college professor as the CEO of a black publishing company he's going to look at things from a very middle-class perspective. And that's one the uphill battles some of us have had; they don't want to publish things from what they call "the street." ... I've had experience half a dozen times of talking to a very nice, middle-class black publisher who said, "Well, in order for us to publish your book, you'll have to clean up the language, you'll have to do this, do that." Holloway House never made those conditions.[6]

Along with Hawkins in 1971, Holloway House secured the talents of Goines, who went on to publish a total of sixteen books with the company.

While doing what turned out to be his last jail stint, in the Jackson, Michigan, state prison for larceny in 1969, Goines was given a typewriter by his mother and encouraged by Shirley, his wife, to turn his spoken recollections about the truth of his life into the written word. Sitting with writer's block before the typewriter, a sympathetic inmate gave him a copy of Iceberg Slim's *The Naked Soul of Iceberg Slim* (1969), a collection of autobiographical short stories.[7] Inspired by the model Iceberg Slim provided, Goines started writing a partly autobiographically based novel, *Whoreson*. It told the story of a trick baby, progeny of a black prostitute and unknown white john, who grows up to be a pimp. Although rooted in personal experience, the novel bore a strong resemblance to *Pimp*, testament to the influence of Iceberg Slim in giving Goines the confidence to broach such brutal subject matter.

The book took only four weeks to write. Fellow inmates read the manuscript and were full of praise. Delighted by the positive reception, Goines sent the manuscript to the publishers of *Pimp*.[8] When he was released from Jackson State on December 1, 1970, Goines had a contract in hand from Holloway House, dated October 19, 1970.[9] With the muse upon him and an excited publisher, Goines completed and published another novel, *Dopefiend* (1971), ahead of *Whoreson* (1972). The subject matter was extremely close to Goines, namely, the hustle to maintain a drug habit. Typically there is no redemption, just a wretched confirmation of ruthless dependency, of a world where addicts remain abject before the power of the pusherman.

His third novel, *Black Gangster* (1972), confronted the political legacy of the 1960s, articulating it as ultimately just another con. Melvin "Prince" Walker is released from prison and becomes a successful leader of The Rulers, a gang involved in drug running, prostitution, robbery, sales of illegal alcohol, and extortion, most of which Goines had experienced firsthand. In a move redolent of Chester Himes, Prince Walker devises a front for The Rulers that exploits the genuine desires of the inner-city black community for social and political change. He masks the gang behind an organization called the Freedom Now Liberation Movement (FNLM). The FNLM members are drawn to the rhetoric of revolutionary social change and black pride that Prince espouses. The Rulers, however, channel such legitimate support and financial donations from the sucker public into sustaining their criminal enterprise.

A follow-up novel to *Black Gangster*—*White Man's Justice, Black Man's Grief* (1973)—deals with the way the justice system is endemically racist. It centers on the fate of one Chester Hines who is framed for masterminding a botched heist while in prison (on an already unfair sentence of three to four years for carrying a concealed weapon). Here not only at the level of theme but in the naming of his major protagonist, Goines makes his reverence for Chester Himes as obvious as one can. As Goines biographer, Eddie B. Allen Jr., states, "If it wasn't Donnie's way of offering a literary tribute, it was an uncanny coincidence that he called the man Chester Hines." Allen reminds us of how Goines's and Himes's lives had such similar trajectories and how their recourse to writing uncompromising urban fiction served similar ends.[10]

Jerry H. Bryant argues that Goines's work is best understood as part of the "toast" tradition. As an author of "toast" novels, however, Goines provides very little of the ironic humor, playfulness, and pyrrhic celebratory atmosphere that comes with toasting as a ritual performance (something that Himes and Rudy Ray Moore manage to preserve). The content of Goines's work shares much with the terrain of the toast (pimping and con games), yet the style is coldly realist, supporting a universally bleak and pessimistic outlook. Bryant's eloquent description of Goines's world actually highlights how far the potential of the toast as a creative response to social immiseration has been extinguished:

> When judged from outside the ghetto, Goines's books ... seem to demand some kind of social action. Yet the more convincing conclusion seems even bleaker. Goines's novels are like photographs of a desert: a dry, stony, wide expanse of cracked earth that sprouts no green, its inhabitants engaged in an amoral struggle for the limited food and water, the sun pitiless in its unremitting heat. No social action can transform the desolation of this landscape.
>
> ... The heroes of the ghetto myth seem like demons and furies.... Crime and violence are the media for their bleak fulfillment, and they assure a Hobbesian life: nasty, brutish, and short. Only the sometimes awkward art that forges these details into stories seems to transcend this world.[11]

Yet ghetto-centric as it is, much of the appeal of Goines's work can also be attributed to the way it recycles the American gangster story's uncanny ability to expose the sordid heart of the majority culture too. As William L. Van Deburg outlines in the case of Goines's *Eldorado Red*:

> The outlaw's rugged individualism and their ethic of high living had analogues in the world of legitimate capitalist enterprise....
>
> Like their alleged societal better who resided just across the line separating ill-gotten from hard-earned wealth, black badmen valued sound business practices. For example, numbers bosses, such as Eldorado Red, put in long dangerous hours in order to establish themselves in the trade. Completely self-educated, Red had worked his way up

> from "dime and two-bit plays" to become CEO of a smoothly running organization that took in between $5,000 and $10,000 daily.[12]

While Goines's urban fiction may not have made it across class and color lines, and may not have been found in conventional libraries or major bookstores, it did find its niche audience through alternative sales and lending points. Peter Gilstrap outlines the fact that "though in recent years Holloway material has arrived in chain stores like Barnes and Noble, in the past, you'd likely find the paperbacks for sale at airports, on newsstands, and in liquor stores."[13] And to this list of disseminating venues, as Goode and others have stated, one should add the military base shop and prison library as key sites of lower-class black inner-city readership.[14] It is not surprising, then, that Goines would prove to be a critical influence on hip hop's hard-core generation.

Michael Eric Dyson, for example, notes that gangsta rapper Tupac Shakur was a voracious reader with catholic tastes whose bookshelves included "the riveting corpus of Donald Goines, the Detroit writer who specialized in brutal tales of black street life and who died prematurely and violently."[15] Tupac's reverence for Goines is highlighted in "Tradin' War Stories," in which he raps:

> Criminal ties for centuries, a legend in my own rhymes,
> So niggaz whisper when they mention,
> Machiavelli was my tutor, Donald Goines my father figure,
> Moms sent me to go play with the drug dealers.[16]

The list of rappers who cite Goines is extensive, including two members of the Wu-Tang Clan, Ghostface Killah and RZA. Significantly, Ghostface Killah makes the link between the badman toast, Rudy Ray Moore, and Goines when he raps in "Child's Play":

> Lines from Dolemite,
> A few tips from Goines,
> Birthday,
> Gave her 2 fifty-cent coins.[17]

In "Trippin'," RZA raps that he's "Feeling like a Dopefiend character from Donald Goines," referring to the eponymous novel.[18]

Nas, in "Ecobar '97," plays with one of his gangster personas (Pablo Escobar, the Columbian drug lord), life in the Queensbridge project (QBC), and relates this directly to *Eldorado Red*, a 1974 Goines novel about a crime kingpin:

> With so much drama in QBC,
> Kinda hard being Escobarro,
> Eldorado Red, sippin Dom out the bottle,
> my life is like a Donald Goines novel.[19]

To these one can add Kool G Rap, Andre Nickatina, AZ, Ludicris, MF Grimm, and Grand Puba as rappers influenced by Goines.[20] As the black author and journalist Tracy Grant puts it in an article titled "Why Hip-Hop Heads Love Donald Goines":

> The landscapes and character of Donald Goines's stories are not a far cry from the living reality of many of today's black youth.... Rap music was born out of a reaction to certain social conditions among inner-city kids, who created a new form of expression. The lifestyles among Goines's characters would be called "ghetto fabulous" today.
>
> Goines's greatest strength is his authenticity. Having lived among them and witnessed their lives, he captured every dimension of pimps, dealers, fiends and thieves—their highs and lows, and more importantly, the price they paid for their lifestyles....
>
> Were he alive today, Donald Goines would probably be welcomed at a hip-hop summit.[21]

Kool G Rap, pioneer of "Mafioso Rap," calls himself "the Donald Goines of Rap": "Before Kool G Rap, they weren't talking about selling drugs on the street, murdering; they weren't doing nothing related to the streets. They were talking about making new dances. But with Donald Goines, I took what I was seeing and tried to make it visual like him."[22] Keith Curtis, a veteran pimp and Goines fan, qualifies the author's relationship to hip hop: "While hip-hop as an art form cannot be considered a direct descendent of writers like Goines or Iceberg Slim, they did have a major influence on gangsta rappers. Nas and Royce Da 5'9" both have songs called "Black Girl Lost," which is the title of a Goines book."[23] Curtis also names Tupac and Noreaga as part of the "new generation" who "adapted the long-gone writer as part of their cultural heritage."[24] Recently, DMX, E-40, Ice Cube, Capone, and Fab 5 Freddy all contributed to a tribute documentary film, *Donnie's Story: The Life of Donald Goines* (2004).

The close association of gangsta rappers to Goines's work suggests perhaps that the domain of Goines's representations remains the hardcore hip hop video. Yet there have been moves to turn Goines's work into big screen entertainment. While rappers have exploited Goines's fiction, film options on his work have been slow in their realization. Allen suggests that this may be attributed to Morriss's policy on optioning at Holloway House. In principle, because the chances of realizing an option were so small, it served a small publisher's interest to attenuate things. As Morriss described it in an interview with Allen:

> *Morriss:* "If you know anything about film option—in this town, there's maybe about 30,000 film options a year, and less than one-tenth of one percent ultimately become a film."
>
> *Allen:* "Oh, so that's not such a big deal, in other words?" . . .
>
> *Morriss:* "Well it is to us because they pay option money. . . . They protect it [for their use]. They give you X amount of money. You sign a contract. Then, if they need an extension, they pay additional money and so on. So no, it's pretty good for us."[25]

The capricious character of such publishing agreements aside, it did not help that the first screen adaptation of a Goines novel was a flop. *Crime Partners* (2000) was a poorly adapted version of one of his Kenyatta novels that failed to make the most of the talents of rappers Ice-T, Ja Rule, and Snoop Dogg. While the Kenyatta novels featured elements of ghetto realism, they contained far more fantasy in featuring a black Bond-like action hero as the main protagonist. These novels were originally published under the pseudonym of Al C. Clark—in part to help separate this fiction from Goines's grittier black-experience novels.[26]

Significantly, the first screen adaptation of one of his black urban experience novels, *Never Die Alone* (2004), fared far better at the box office and with critics. Rap star and Goines fan DMX took the lead role of King David and produced the film. In addition to this backing, *Never Die Alone* benefited from promotion by a major distributor, Fox Searchlight Pictures, and direction by Ernest Dickerson, a filmmaker with a strong track record (being the erstwhile cinematographer for Spike Lee and director of films such as *Juice* and *Bulletproof* [1996]). Dan Flory indicates that casting a rap star in the key role brings something new to Goines's book:

> The film seeks to turn the story of King David against itself by showing the other side of hustling life: one of nihilistic emptiness, meaninglessness, and devastation to others. It also seeks to reinforce this flipping of the story by employing a rap artist in the lead role. As a performer who has made a great deal of money exploiting the "bling-bling" image of

> gangstas who live the high life of big money, expensive cars, and material gain from crime, DMX uses his charisma and charm to invest his part with some attractive features and draw viewers into the story.[27]

The complicity of a gangsta rapper influenced by Goines, starring in and producing a feature-length screen adaptation of one of his books, generates a form of mise en abyme, with Goines's life mirrored in King David's, mirrored in DMX's—offering up a space of generative reflection on the inevitability of exploitation. As part of this (ill)logic, DMX, in his foreword to the Goines biography, *Low Road*, intimates that he is backing a film version of *Daddy Cool* as a producer.[28]

The formula, however, of bringing gangsta talent to bear in realizing screen depictions of black inner-city experience is hardly new. Ironically, what may have delayed screen realizations of Goines's work most of all until recently was the hood film cycle of the early 1990s. This cycle not only established conventions associated with hard-core representation but also exhausted them as film fare before those interested in translating Goines (or any other Holloway House author) to the big screen had had the opportunity. In spite of this it remains clear that Holloway House authors have still had a tremendous influence on this aspect of gangsta culture.

THE HOOD FILM CYCLE

In the early 1990s a series of films made by African Americans focusing on the plight of the black inner city provoked mass-media attention and an attendant moral panic. Although small in number and short-lived, this cycle of ghetto-centric films tapped into an increasingly volatile climate of racial discontent fueled most infamously by the televised airing of Los Angeles Police Department (LAPD) officers beating up a black motorist, Rodney King, in 1991—an incident that sparked the Los Angeles rebellion one year later following the acquittal of the policemen involved.[29] Collectively categorized as "hood" films, *Straight Out of Brooklyn* (1991), *Boyz N the Hood* (1991), *New Jack City* (1991), *Juice* (1992), and *Menace II Society* (1993) brought a sense of hard-core realism about the African American inner-city experience that mainstream feature films had failed to represent adequately.

While these films grossed disproportionately large returns at the box office given their low production costs, the terms of such success were controversial. Uncompromisingly violent and oriented around gangsta protagonists, these films struggled to provide a positive message about the fate of America's black urban communities and fomented discord over the responsibility of African American filmmakers. Gang-related violence among audiences at premiere screenings of *New Jack City* and *Boyz N the Hood* and the fact that these films were crossover hits among both black and white youth only exacerbated concern about the social, moral, and political value of this kind of race representation.[30] Uncannily, the furor that surrounded this 1990s film cycle resembled that which greeted the first generation of Hollywood talking gangster films in the early 1930s.[31] However, the links between gangsta and gangster have yet to be given proper treatment.

Understandably, scholars have been drawn to the early 1990s hood cycle because waves of Hollywood black filmmaking are very rare. Debate has focused primarily on the import of the cycle in terms of the development of a controversial and distinctively black (realist) film aesthetic that worked in tandem with the growth of a larger hip hop cultural continuum deeply associated with gangsta rap and music video.[32] Scholars such as S. Craig Watkins and Eithne Quinn have provided key studies of the global trafficking in gangsta representation, in which the hood film is a significant but ephemeral part.[33]

This framing understanding of gangsta as the symbolization of distinctively black entrepreneurial acumen, however, has fed tendencies in film studies to approach the hood cycle as emblematic of a cinema apart. The work of Manthia Diawara and Dan Flory on the generative interrelation between Hollywood film noir and a broader categorization of recent African American crime films (as "noir by noirs") notwithstanding, emphasis in the study of hood films has fallen on the degree to which the cycle is either separate from or risks complicity with Hollywood's constructions of black experience and identity.[34]

Sympathetic as I am to the argument that Hollywood has done more to perpetuate white racist perceptions of black folk than to challenge them, it behooves us to pay far more attention than current axiomatic frameworks allow to the way such films are deeply related and indebted to one of mainstream cinema's most recognizable genres, the gangster film. More specifically, there has been no interrogation of the link between the black-made hood film and the Hollywood gangster film's historically special relationship to the concerns and ambitions of ethnic and racial others—and no evaluation of how the gangsta notion of keeping it real taps into the realist aesthetic of the mainstream gangster formula. When rap and *Boyz N the Hood* star Ice Cube states, "It's the American way, cos I'm the G-A-N-G-S-T-A,"[35] he confirms not simply a local "real" identity as a street-savvy young black man from Compton in Los Angeles but also an association beyond the hood with the generic "mythic" gangster of the national imagination, especially as shaped by Hollywood (from James Cagney to Al Pacino—two gangster stars "reclaimed" as hip hop icons). Connecting gangsta to gangster will open up a more nuanced understanding of what was to be gained by black filmmakers in the early 1990s through crossover allegiance and identification with this particular Hollywood archetype.

The period for the cycle is bookended by two Spike Lee films, *Do the Right Thing* (1989) and *Clockers* (1995).[36] *Do the Right Thing* is significant because its box-office success helped to usher in the era of the hood cycle. The film addressed the problems of racial division in Lee's native Brooklyn, New York, neighborhood of Bedford-Stuyvesant, in the context of the growing racial tension that marked Mayor Ed Koch's 1980s reign. Opening to much media hype, *Do the Right Thing* posed an awkward question about the right direction forward for African American communities in light of the distance that had grown between the civil rights and Black Nationalist (protest) generation of the 1960s and 1970s and the inner-city black youth of late 1980s USA. It also raised concomitant questions about the responsibilities of black film. The violent conclusion—where Lee, playing the role of the film's main protagonist, pizza delivery man Mookie, finally takes action by hurling a trash can through his Italian employer's parlor window—only helped to keep debate alive about what "doing the right thing" constituted.

Do the Right Thing sparked an excited response not just from media journalists but also from a new generation of black filmmakers. Motivated by a desire to capitalize on the inflammatory power of *Do the Right Thing*'s subject matter and by the ambition to improve on this cinematic vision of the black inner city, directors Mario Van Peebles (*New Jack City*), Matty Rich (*Straight Out of Brooklyn*), and John Singleton (*Boyz N the Hood*) seized the moment. Both *New Jack City* and *Straight Out of Brooklyn* were first shown at the Sundance Film Festival in January 1991. The initial critical approval that these films garnered was subsequently harnessed to the sensationalism surrounding the Rodney King incident in March of the same year. Made on an extremely modest budget of $300,000, *Straight Out of Brooklyn* eventually grossed over $2.7 million—a remarkable return for a film that had only very limited distribution and release. Although independently made, *New Jack City* had a larger budget of $6 to $8 million and benefited from major studio distribution deals (Warner Brothers) that enabled it to reach over nine hundred screens nationwide. The film grossed $33 million in its first five weeks alone—eventually making over $47 million. *Boyz N the Hood*, released in July 1991 and set as it was in inner-city Los Angeles (the scene of the King incident), had a similarly incendiary impact at the box office, returning over $56 million, having cost only $6 million. *Boyz N the Hood* also made an impression on Hollywood's critical establishment, which honored its director and screenwriter, Singleton, with two Oscar nominations.[37]

Even if these films sought to produce a harder and less compromising vision of black inner-city realities than Spike Lee's films, there is still much continuity of representation. *New Jack City* and *Boyz N the Hood*, for example, gave more diegetic presence to hard-core rap. Where Lee had given the rap group (the appropriately named) Public Enemy powerful aural significance (featuring their agit-rap "Fight the Power" prominently in the opening credits and on a major protagonist's ghetto blaster), Van Peebles and Singleton gave starring roles to the prominent gangsta rappers Ice-T and Ice Cube, respectively. Such casting decisions were a way of upping the ante in the quest to provide more credible or putatively authentic screen treatments of the black inner city as well as increasing these films' box-office appeal by tapping into the music audience market.

In light of these and other attempts to hone the hood formula in a realist manner, Lee returned to the inner-city scene with *Clockers* (1995). *Clockers* told the tale of a young low-level drug dealer (or clocker), Strike, trapped by the deterministic logic of a wasted life in the Brooklyn projects. Strike's deep fascination with his model train set and its circular track reflects both the problem of being caught in a loop and the desire to be taken elsewhere. Lee's optimistic ending—whereby Strike does eventually exchange the model train for a journey out of New York on the real thing—cannot hide the film's otherwise muted sense of possibility. Lee hoped that *Clockers* would "be the final nail in the coffin" to what he thought had become an overworked and jaded formula.[38]

Thus far I have outlined in very general terms how these films came to constitute a generically distinctive group. This does not mean, however, that their frame of reference and way of generating meaning depended on outright rejection of mainstream conventions or was limited to an exclusively black referent world, filmic or real. Even as *New Jack City*, for example, was understood as the product of an African American filmmaker addressing specifically black urban realities, the tagline for the film and its main protagonist gang, the Cash Money Brothers, ran: "They're a new breed of gangster. The new public enemy. The new family of crime." In other words, this kind of film was sold to the public as the latest version of an established formula—running approximately from the time of the original *Scarface* (1932) to its remake in 1983.

Clearly it made marketing sense to pitch the hood film as belonging to a popular generic heritage, albeit a criminal one. To some, however, the hood cycle demonstrates precisely the degree to which the economic viability of black-made film depends on the perpetuation of counter-productive representations of the black experience. Norman K. Denzin clarifies this point of view:

> A single thesis ... structures my interpretation of this film cycle. These realistic social-problem texts fuelled conservative racist discourse. They helped fearful white Americans blame blacks for the problems of the inner city. They suggested that blacks caused their own problems. The problems of the ghetto were not shared by the larger society.[39]

To Denzin the success of these films was predicated on feeding mass-media stereotypical visions of the black inner city and on sanctioning patriarchal and misogynist understandings of both the problems confronting this urban community and their solution. What Michael Eric Dyson terms the "foreshortened view of gender relations" in hood films has been given considerable coverage in the literature to date.[40] It is not my intention to dispute such criticism. Rather it is to relocate the problem of patriarchal reinforcement as an attribute not simply of flawed black cultural politics but as a defining feature of the gangster genre more generally. Such an understanding might allow us to elaborate more effectively on bell hooks's insight that some of the values hood films seem to support are actually endemic to "white supremacist capitalist ideology."[41] The hood film, in the process of advancing patriarchal ideology within such a violent and confrontational framework, draws attention to the perversity of gendered rules that underwrite not just local but national identity politics.

As the scholars who have provided the most sustained analyses of the hood film to date, Paula J. Massood and Watkins understand that African American filmmaking success is always contingent and comes with costs. However, they do not see this as totally debilitating. To Watkins, exploitation of a putatively counterproductive self-image has always been a prerequisite for black commercial cultural production. As he puts it: "Is the production of black cinema any more or less exploitative than the production of black film in general?"[42] And Massood understands this as a necessary danger:

> The fact that hood films even exist indicates a literal move out of the ghetto for black filmmakers and points to an important movement of African American film onto the commercial screen. Furthermore, in choosing to place in the center of the screen narratives based on or about a disenfranchised part of the African American diaspora, young urban men, filmmakers such as Singleton and the Hugheses deliberately link representation to power by calling into question the images that have been reified by mainstream Hollywood.[43]

Such an argument at least acknowledges that concession to commercial priorities need not be a matter of complete compromise. Yet rhetorically it still positions Hollywood in a definitively negative relationship to presumably more authentic forms of race representation and the possibilities of a genuinely black cinema. As a result, the relationship between hip hop gangsta and Hollywood gangster remains unexplored. The fact that archetypal Hollywood gangsters have also been ethnically marked—from James Cagney's Irishness to Al Pacino's Italian-ness (or Cubanness in the case of his role as Antonio "Scarface" Montana)—has gone without comment in the academic appraisals of the hip hop gangsta's blackness. Equally, special claims made by Massood for the unique way in which the hood cycle mediates urban spatial and temporal dynamics are overstated given the fact that the documentary-realist aesthetic advanced by these films is consciously connected to a Hollywood legacy.[44]

For their part, African American film directors have had no hesitation in drawing on and "sampling" the Hollywood gangster film as a prime source of inspiration. Given this fact, it is not enough to make a case for the 1990s hood cycle as a genre to itself—or as a cycle that belongs to a strictly black visual economy representing ontologically black concerns. To illustrate more concretely how and why this potentially corrupting dialogue with hegemonic conventions made sense to black filmmakers, I shall devote the remainder of this chapter to an examination of *Menace II Society*.

CASE STUDY: REAL TO REEL IN *MENACE II SOCIETY*

As a later entry in the early 1990s hood cycle, *Menace II Society* offers itself up for analysis in terms of genre consolidation. Costing only $3 million to make, the film grossed $27 million at the box office,[45] repeating the pattern of low cost/high return that marked the films that preceded it in the cycle. Equally, *Menace II Society* consolidated familiar hood film themes in telling the violent story of conflicting loyalties among black inner-city youths in Watts, Los Angeles. A bleak tale, it focuses on the plight of two young men, Caine (played by Tyrin Turner) and O-Dog (Larenz Tate), and a young mother, Ronnie (Jada Pinkett Smith), whose husband is doing life in prison. Caine is a pessimistic young drug dealer (a profession inherited from his long dead father) who hangs out with O-Dog, an amoral reckless fellow "gangbanger." Ronnie tries to offset Caine's sense of aimlessness by providing a love interest, moral guidance, and a way out—to Atlanta and a potentially different future away from his gang friends and the self-destructive logic of black-on-black crime. The film concludes fatally with Caine falling victim to a drive-by shooting while trying to protect Ronnie's son. Ironically, the murderous O-Dog survives.

Many aspects of *Menace II Society* reflect the ambitions of its makers, Allen and Albert Hughes (the Hughes Brothers), to produce a real hood film—one that did not fall victim to the sentimentality and upbeat moralistic intentions they thought compromised earlier entries in the cycle.[46] Two key moments in *Menace II Society*, for example, could be understood as overt "riffs" on conventionalized treatments of hood problems in *Do the Right Thing* and *Boyz N the Hood*. The shocking and senseless murder of two Korean grocery store owners by O-Dog, who has taken umbrage to the couple's suspicious gaze and the suggestion that he is a bad son (the husband's statement, "I feel sorry for your mother," is enough to provoke armed retaliation), is in many ways a devastating return to the more humor-laden altercations between Korean owners and black customers that feature in *Do the Right Thing*. In a similar manner *Menace II Society*'s tragic ending, in which Caine is killed and O-Dog survives, inverts the logic of *Boyz N the Hood* (which the Hughes Brothers dissed as "an 'after-school special' with cussin' "),[47] which had its main moral protagonist, Tre (Cuba Gooding Jr.), able to survive and escape the ghetto by going to college with his girlfriend, leaving his gangsta friend Doughboy (Ice Cube) to face an inevitable death.

By 1993 the terms of *Menace II Society*'s success depended on the degree to which it could satisfy audience expectations of an established formula in innovative ways. Yet this film also reveals the way such difference is generated in specific relationship not simply to other black films but to mainstream generic frames for representing "others" as criminal. This works in two ways: first through the deliberate connection to the previous noteworthy moment of black cinematic production in the 1970s, generically termed blaxploitation (also low-budget black crime films that made disproportionate box-office profit); and second through reference to Hollywood's gangster film tradition. These two reference points are not mutually exclusive. Indeed, any reference to blaxploitation necessarily invokes a Hollywood tradition at the same time. Major examples in that cycle, such as *Shaft* (1971), *Superfly* (1972), and *Black Caesar* (1973), reworked tropes and conventions associated with Hollywood gangster and detective films. *Black Caesar*, for example, was clearly a black version of the rise-and-fall gangster narrative established by films such as *Little Caesar* (1930) and *Scarface* and most obviously exploited the contemporaneous success of *The Godfather* (1972) in the early 1970s.

Menace II Society looks backward to the era of blaxploitation in terms of the time of some of its early scenes and the style with which this period is represented. A flashback sequence narrates Caine's upbringing in the early 1970s as the son of a drug pusher (played by Samuel L. Jackson) and junkie mother. Jackson's character is drawn out of the blaxploitation vault of "badass" hustler types, and his main scene includes dialogue about Ron O'Neal (the actor who played Youngblood Priest, the pusherman star of *Superfly*). As Massood notes, this 1970s sequence is filmed in "over-saturated" color, redolent of blaxploitation's visual style.[48] This almost camp homage to the contrivances of blaxploitation exists in tension with the film's larger attempt at bringing a documentary-realist style to screen treatments of the hood.

The Hughes Brothers' background in hard-core hip hop music video (as makers of gangsta rapper Tupac Shakur's earliest videos) and in reality crime television (*America's Most Wanted*)[49] services an on-location or live aesthetic that is also bound up with the film's thematic concern over the hood as object of 24/7 surveillance. The film opens with historical black-and-white film footage of cops beating black protestors during the Watts riots of 1965. Interestingly, this clip has been subject to heavy pixilation, which both blurs the image into something generic and, as an attribute of *digital* interference, invites comparison between then and now (collapsing the past into the present) in terms of how black struggle has been represented in the media. Superimposed over this image is a news bulletin soundtrack of the 1992 rebellion. This mix of aural and visual times also and most obviously invokes the live capture on video of cops beating Rodney King in 1991.

The Hughes Brothers borrow from reality crime television, surveillance photography, news bulletins, documentary footage, and use vérité camera work to try and achieve a sense of "liveness" and urgency, which is also bound to the sense of being "captured" and "framed." The self-conscious juxtaposition of visual styles emphasizes the degree to which the black inner city's criminal reality is always something constructed. It highlights how the *Menace II Society*'s re-release tagline, "This is the truth. This is real," is as much about the reality of problematic media representations as it is about any pro-filmic black social truth. Such formal concerns over the framing of black urban experience are thematically reinforced through the fact that much of the dramatic action flows from the procurement of the closed-circuit television surveillance tape of O-Dog's gratuitous shooting of the grocery store owner.

The policing intent of the store owner's gaze is reinforced by the technology of surveillance television. O-Dog's frustrations with always being watched, and in the process criminalized, lead to him not only firing back but to reappropriating the logic of being the conspicuous object of surveillance. He takes the tape not simply as a way to destroy evidence but precisely as a testament to his prowess as a real gangsta. The tape becomes a mini-movie in which O-Dog can star; his narcissistic desire to see himself as "America's Most Wanted" is achieved through its repeated playback in the company of his homeboy friends.

While this formal concern about the criminal mediation of black identity may seem solipsistic, it actually connects *Menace II Society* to a Hollywood crime tradition. This film-within-a-film conceit is a form of mirror act common to other key hood films where gangstas look at *gangsters* (and look to Hollywood gangsters for inspiration). It echoes the obsessive fascination of *Juice*'s most compelling and violent character, Bishop (played by gangsta rapper Tupac Shakur), with the famous self-immolating conclusion of *White Heat* (1949), where gangster Cody Jarrett (James Cagney) pronounces, "Made it, Ma! Top of the world!," and goes out with a spectacular gasworks explosion. O-Dog's self-actualization as a "real" hoodlum through his filmed ("reel") image as killer also links back to *New Jack City*, a film in which the main gangster protagonist, Nino (Wesley Snipes), styles himself after Tony Montana in the 1983 version of *Scarface*. Moreover, within *Menace II Society*, the Hughes Brothers double this real-to-reel relation in a scene where Caine, recovering from bullet wounds in hospital, is shown watching a cop-killing scene from a film noir police procedural (*film policier*), *He Walked by Night* (1948).

Significantly, the identification here is not with a classic gangster archetype such as Cagney or Pacino (as in *Juice* and *New Jack City*, respectively) but rather with a more anonymous criminal protagonist in a film that embodied a documentary-realist experiment that used the veneer of verisimilitude to advance pro-police and government agency messages. Made at the height of the period of film noir, *He Walked by Night* was part of a cycle of films that reenacted crimes based on actual police cases. Alongside *He Walked by Night*, films such as *T-Men*, *Naked City*, *The Street with No Name*, and *Call Northside 777* (all 1948), constituted forerunners of today's investigative crime television shows, such as *America's Most Wanted* and *CSI*. These films made a feature of on-location shooting and proclaimed to be factual reconstructions of everything as it happened ("only the names have been changed"). *He Walked by Night* was based on a real LAPD case. This film was the genesis of the celebrated television series *Dragnet*. It featured a young Jack Webb (in a minor role as a forensic cop, Lee), who went on to be the star (as the LAPD's top moral crusader, Sergeant Joe "just the facts" Friday), writer, director, and producer of the show's two successful runs, from 1951 to 1959 and from 1967 to 1970.

As filmmakers who honed their skills in making documentary video, the Hughes Brothers' decision to include a clip from *He Walked by Night* as a Los Angeles–based *film policier* makes sense. It situates *Menace II Society* in relationship to a history of mass cinema's mapping of the dangerous city. *He Walked by Night* starts out with a police map of Los Angeles and a stentorian voice-over inviting us into the interior life of the nation's biggest and toughest police beat. And then like other films of its kind, it proceeds to make the city itself the star. Los Angeles is introduced as, among other things, "the target of gangsters." By contrast, *Menace II Society* shifts the procedural perspective on the scene of criminal action, inviting interrogation of the manipulating gaze rooted in the authority of a long-running popular show like *Dragnet*.

Both *He Walked by Night* and *Dragnet* were vehicles designed to valorize the LAPD. *Dragnet* in particular was designed to operate as law-enforcement propaganda, and its content was approved by the LAPD. In this sense the history of Hollywood's factual gaze (or application of verisimilitude) is deeply linked to policing and its legitimation. *Menace II Society* revisits this history in light of the footage that captured officers of the LAPD beating up Rodney King. The Hughes Brothers' visual strategies return the policing gaze, as it were, by looking at things from the perspective of those criminalized as objects of surveillance.

The overt interplay between Hollywood gangster archetypes and hood film protagonists is something shared with gangsta rap. Today's hard-core rappers are self-styled gangstas who have frequently appropriated the monikers and attitude of earlier mobster icons. And this reverence is cinematically engendered. A film such as *Scarface*, for example, with a braggadocio performance from Pacino in the lead role, exerted a signal influence on this part of the hip-hop music scene. As the documentary *Def Jam Presents: Origins of a Hip Hop Classic* (2003)—made to accompany the twentieth-anniversary special edition of the film—reveals, gangsta rappers appropriated the film as their "bible," seeing their own story of making it against the odds reflected most powerfully in Tony Montana's "come up" (rise out of nothing). "I took the Scarface name because that was me," pronounces the eponymous gangsta rapper, while Fat Joe sees him as "the ultimate ghetto superhero."[50] Significantly, Snoop Dogg identifies with Tony not just as someone who "comes from nothing" but as someone who "struggles to even just get his citizenship." According to Sean "P. Diddy" Combs, the fact that the gangster amalgamates the double problem of being both economically and ethnically marginalized is critical to his appeal among black male youth: "Tony, he was like a lot of us, was backed up against the wall. He had to fight to try and make it in the world. That's one of the reasons why minorities relate to it so much, especially black inner-city minorities."

Such testaments reveal the extent to which the Hollywood gangster's aspirations resonate with gangstas because they emanate from the position and articulate their desires in the language of those stuck on the wrong side of the ethno-racial divide. In the process the gangster highlights the hypocrisy of a culture that excludes on the basis of ethnic/racial difference. Moreover, the conspicuous identification of gangsta rappers with capitalist excess (with Tony's mantras such as "Get money, get money, get money" and "I want the world . . . and everything in it") provides an ironic vision not of the ambition of black outsiders but of the hegemonic values they aspire to. As Nas articulates, "We are all savages in pursuit of the American Dream. Rappers relate to that because that's how we come up." Or as Method Man puts it, *Scarface* shows you "the glamour and the glitz but also the downside which is the murder and the mayhem."

Just as *New Jack City*, *Boyz N the Hood*, and *Juice* employed the talents of gangsta rappers, *Menace II Society* gave roles to MC Eiht and MC Pooh (Pooh-Man) as important members of Caine and O-Dog's homeboy community. While the integration of the gangsta rapper's street voice into hood film narratives enhanced the cycle's claim to authenticity, this should not be understood as a definitively black thing. Rather it is the latest version of the realist vernacular argot that has been part of gangster films since the industry was first wired for sound in the early 1930s. The impact of the early 1930s Hollywood gangster rested in large part on the way the actors most associated with the genre—James Cagney, Edward G. Robinson, and Paul Muni—enjoyed biographical proximity to the urban ethnic hoodlum types that brought them to national prominence. As Lower East Side New York progeny themselves, they brought a new and powerful sense of street realism to the roles they played. At the dawn of sound cinema, they spoke with distinctive non-Anglo ethnic accents and were the first to conventionalize and popularize the way screen gangsters speak.[51] Gangstas have inherited the mantle.

Not surprisingly, given the reverence expressed by gangstas for gangsters, the Hughes Brothers admit to being heavily influenced by Martin Scorsese and Brian De Palma, two directors deeply associated with mainstream gangster films. In their early days of experimenting with video, for instance, the Hughes Brothers spent time reenacting scenes from De Palma's *Scarface*—graduating from this to making a public access cable television short, "The Drive By," which garnered them their first agent.[52] This background further emphasizes the degree to which the black-made hood film of the 1990s has a generic history that cuts across the color line, linking its concerns with those of other urban lower-class groups who have been disadvantaged by their non-Anglo ethnic identities in different historical periods.

As the intertitle "Watts 1993" and a subsequent aerial surveillance shot replete with police bulletin soundtrack declare, *Menace II Society*, in the gangster film tradition, locates its dramatic action in the real time and space of an ethnically and racially segregated urban community. This reality shot gives way, however, to conventional scenes drawn not so much "Straight Outta Watts," as it were, but out of the storehouse of gangster film conventions. We are introduced to Caine's gang of African American homeboys, replete with monikers such as "O-Dog," "Doc," and "A-Wax." This is a scene redolent of Rico's (Edward G. Robinson) introduction to Sam Vettori's gang of Italian American mobster types, such as "Bat" Carillo, "Killer" Pepi, "Kid" Bean, and "Scabby" in *Little Caesar*. Thus, although such elements seem to be drawn from the reality of the street, it is also clear that the street stylizes itself after hyperbolic media images. Recourse to generic convention is therefore not to be confused with betraying reality.

Thematically central to the hood film are issues of loyalty. *Menace II Society* recycles a typical fraternal configuration to help play out the contradictory sense of responsibility that is a source of both strength and destruction in many gangster films. The Caine/O-Dog relation reworks the classic convention of the gangster/sidekick duo (Little Caesar/

Joe Massara in *Little Caesar*, Tommy Powers/Matt Doyle in *The Public Enemy*, Tony Camonte/Guino Rinaldo in the original *Scarface*). This Cain and Abel loyalty motif is most obviously doubled in *Menace II Society* through Caine's naming. And like many gangster films, homosocial bonding is revealed to be critical to survival and success among those stuck on the wrong side of the economic and ethnic tracks. Yet the terms of success inevitably depend on rising out of the crowd—on individualist and egotistical action—on becoming notorious. Robert Warshow highlights this as the most compelling aspect of the gangster film:

> No convention of the gangster film is more strongly established than this: it is dangerous to be alone. And yet the very conditions of success make it impossible not to be alone, for success is always the establishment of individual preeminence that must be imposed on others, in whom it automatically arouses hatred.... [T]he gangster's whole life is an effort to assert himself as an individual... and he always dies because he is an individual.[53]

Menace II Society sets up filial organization against the alternative of heterosexual loyalty. The one contradicts the other. In gangster films, romantic "love" interferes with and threatens the coherence of the gang. Rico's need for Joe as a loyal sidekick in *Little Caesar* is undermined by Joe's love of Olga. Similarly, and more intensely, Guino's love of Tony's sister, Cesca, constitutes a major act of betrayal in *Scarface* (a story repeated with equal effect in the 1983 version). In *Menace II Society*, Caine's father figure, Pernell, is serving life in prison. He takes on a fraternal mission to look after Pernell's wife, Ronnie. This act of brotherly loyalty, however, eventually turns into romantic love and betrayal of one responsibility in the name of taking on another.[54]

As we can see, while such themes are particularly pertinent to black reality, they are not unique to it. This even extends to what scholars have identified as a defining feature of the hood film, namely, the dramatization of the gap between 1990s black youth and their parents and grandparents. The lack of respect and communication between generations symbolizes the distance between the ideals of the protest generation and the stark conditions confronting the disenfranchised youth of the Reagan/Bush years. *Menace II Society* features altercations between Caine and his God-fearing grandparents, who embody certain aspects of the Martin Luther King Jr. legacy. Caine's schoolteacher Mr. Butler, a figure whom one might expect to deliver uplifting and pedagogically sound messages to the younger generation, instead provides a dark and candid statement about their future: "Being a black man in America isn't easy. The hunt is on and you're the prey. All I say is ... survive."

Menace II Society continues the discourse on the generation gap in black culture that started with Spike Lee's *Do the Right Thing* and Mookie's trouble trying to understand Da Mayor's instruction to "do the right thing." The fact that Da Mayor is played by Ossie Davis, a prominent 1960s black activist and actor, only amplified the film's more general concern about whether the protest doctrines of King and Malcolm X had any relevance to the late 1980s.[55] Additionally, Davis's association with blaxploitation cinema (as director of *Cotton Comes to Harlem* [1970] and *Gordon's War* [1973]) also begged questions of what kind of cinema was "the right thing." *Boyz N the Hood* places the issue of paternal responsibility at the center of its thematic interest. Tre's dad, Furious Styles (played by Samuel L. Jackson), is full of the rhetoric of Black Nationalism but cuts a lonely figure in an environment of disaffected youths. *Menace II Society* clearly inherits and replays this problem of disenchantment with politically meaningful collective organization and the ideology of race advancement. Black male youth are left with little other than a narcissistic and ambivalent agenda—that of indulging their image as American nightmare (O-Dog is described as "America's nightmare: Young, black and doesn't give a fuck").

If this theme seems to help define the hood film as a distinctive cycle, it also constitutes a new twist on an older gangster trope. In the 1930s, Tommy Powers, Tony Camonte, and Rico all had problems with the older generation. A prime concern then was the distance between immigrant parents and their modernizing and Americanizing progeny. The gangster film played out the violent cost of acculturation. It revealed that the costs of making it as an ethnic outsider involved divorce from the (moral) world of their parents. The hood film of the 1990s does something similar in linking the shrinking relevance of racial uplift and protest rhetoric with the declining moral authority of parents.

The key issue here has been why black filmmakers of the early 1990s chose to codify their concerns in the way they did. At one level the argument is advanced that these films were necessarily criminal, ghettocentric, or gangsta because they attempted to represent the real lived experiences of the postindustrial black inner city. As much as this seems to make sense, it is equally clear that such representation falls foul of feeding stereotypes about the black community being endemically criminal. Ultimately, the discourse of "keeping it real" is as conventional as fantasy. The glaring allusions to a tradition of gangster representation across race lines have been ignored in the bulk of criticism devoted to analyzing the significance of the hood cycle. Such an omission is very problematic given that it feeds patterns of taxonomic ghettoization rather than coming to grips with how and why a cycle so seemingly parochial in its concerns and representational strategies could have been part of the globalization of hip hop culture (had so much media "reach"). And to understand this requires an approach that looks at the history of the way gangsterism on-screen is as much American as it is black. As Robin D. G. Kelley states about hip hop's gangsta:

> The recasting of capitalism as gangsterism is not simply intended to legitimate the illicit economy or de-legitimate the capitalist exploitation. Gangsta rappers discuss capitalism in varying contexts, and to portray them as uniformly or consistently anticapitalist would certainly misrepresent them.... Their ambivalence toward capitalism notwithstanding, gangsta rappers are consistent about tracing criminal behavior and vicious individualism to mainstream American culture. Contrary to the new "culture of poverty" theorists who claim that the lifestyles of the so-called black "underclass" constitute a significant deviation from mainstream values, most gangsta rappers insist that the characters they rap about epitomize what America has been and continues to be.[56]

CONCLUSION: LIFE IMITATES ART

In sum, then, even in a film that set itself up against the supposed contrivances of previous hood films in the name of telling the truth, recourse to convention is inescapable and indeed desirable. The Hollywood gangster film has functioned as a rule book for gangsta behavior and self-styling. Furthermore, gangster emulation constitutes a means to achieving the status of the mythic celluloid mobster heroes on which gangstas model themselves (a case best and most infamously dramatized through the killing and hagiographical afterlife of gangsta rap's biggest icon, Tupac Shakur).[57]

Perhaps the fate of the two West Coast gangsta rappers, MC Eiht and MC Pooh (Pooh-Man), associated with *Menace II Society* illustrates the contradictory power of the gangster simulacrum most appropriately. MC Pooh had provided a significant rap, "Sex, Money & Murder," to *Juice*. The Hughes Brothers gave him an acting break as "Doc," the "playa" with the best "crib" in *Menace II Society*. In the early 1990s, MC Pooh had released a couple of rap albums full of typical gangsta swagger—*Life of a Criminal* gaining him a particularly strong reputation as one of the most explicit West Coast rappers alongside Ant Banks and Too $hort. He has gone on to truly keep it real by doing time in a Modesto penitentiary for a series of armed robberies in Oakland—the result of trying to finance a heroin addiction.[58]

The gangsta way of making real-on-reel investments, however, is not limited to self-destructive outcomes. *Menace II Society*'s most savvy homeboy, A-Wax, was played by a member of the gangsta rap group Compton's Most Wanted, MC Eiht, who also contributed a hood anthem, "Streiht Up Menace," for the end credits. In a different but no less gangsta manner than MC Pooh, MC Eiht has maintained his credibility and entrepreneurial credentials by featuring as a key star of PlayStation's internationally best-selling *Grand Theft Auto* video game. In providing the voice of one of *Grand Theft Auto: San Andreas*'s main gangland characters, Ryder, and contributing to the soundtrack with "Hood Took Me Down," MC Eiht facilitated the crossing over of gangsta into the gaming market.[59] As MC Eiht puts it: "In making it West Coast originated, and by putting gangs and drive-bys in it, activities that normally go on in the West Coast, it makes the game more realistic for people to play.... The game introduces them to a whole new realm, and it will help open the door of hip hop to expand to a whole new era."[60] Significantly, the particular claim to "keeping it real" that comes with this branch of hip hop has made it attractive to those developing 3-D games whose appeal depends on immersion into a believable experience of a virtual reality.

As Eithne Quinn has highlighted, the entrepreneurial guile associated with gangsta culture has depended on a contradictory investment in a villainous self-image. The media hyperbole about the destructive and demeaning aspects of such criminal self-representation has serviced rather than hindered the proliferation of this kind of cultural production. It is not surprising, then, that a significant amount of work on gangsta rap has devoted itself to covering the heated debate and moral panic about the capital (economic and cultural) thug life generates. The gangsta's celebration of material gain at any cost could have been defended as an ironic vision and critique of the American Dream, as the latest version of the American gangster myth refashioned to address the circumstances that led to the Los Angeles rebellion and its aftermath. Countering those who simply saw gangsta rap as confirmation of the inner-city black male's sociopathic nature, however, has been compromised by the full-blown misogyny expressed in hard-core rap. Consternation about this assault on the work ethic and advocacy that crime pays was only amplified through the fusion of gangster and pimp attitudes. The demeaning references to black women as bitches, hos, and skeezers only added credence to the argument that the gangsta was indeed a sociopath. Such an explicit version of the business-as-pleasure principle was met with outrage and an organized campaign to censor this offensive material. As William L. Van Deburg concludes: "Joined by a commitment to egregious incivility, hip-hop hedonists, black mobsters and gangbangers, and prison inmates seemed the perfect prototypical villains. To borrow a popular new millennial metaphor, this unholy band of brothers—and sistas—could be said to constitute a domestic 'axis of evil.' "[61]

The difficulty confronting rap's defenders against its detractors in the case of gangsta culture is represented by the invidious position it places African American feminist scholars. bell hooks, for example, was keen to intervene immediately in debates over gangsta rap's misogyny, as much to offset the white racist commandeering of the black thug as evidence of degeneracy as to reprimand the brothers for promoting a venally sexist vision of the sistas. As she put it in 1994:

> If black men are betraying us through acts of male violence, we save ourselves and the race by resisting. Yet our feminist critiques of black male sexism fail as meaningful political interventions if they seek to demonize black males, and do not recognize that our revolutionary work is to transform white supremacist capitalist patriarchy in the multiple areas of our lives where it is made manifest, whether in gangsta rap, the black church, or in the Clinton administration.[62]

If, as Van Deburg argues, "inherited notions of racial villainy have served to confirm rumor as actuality" and that the "*actual* threat that these 'bad blacks' pose to the body politic has been overstated," it is clear that a particular fantasy continues to hold sway.[63] And this includes so-called scientific approaches to the question of racial discrimination.

In an uncanny reproduction of the problems associated with the academy's first attempt to deal with the reality of white racism in the United States, Kelley identifies a similar predilection in the anthropological, ethnographic, and sociological imagination:

> The culture concept employed by social scientists has severely impoverished contemporary debates over the plight of urban African Americans and contributed to the construction of the ghetto as a reservoir of pathologies and bad cultural values. Much of this literature not only

> conflates behavior with culture, but when social scientists explore "expressive" cultural forms or what has been "popular culture" (such as language, music and style), most reduce it to expressions of pathology, compensatory behavior, or creative "coping" mechanisms to deal with racism and poverty.[64]

If Gunnar Myrdal could only understand the black inner city's fortune economy as evidence of a pathological condition in the 1940s, today's social scientists have failed to overthrow a deep-seated habit of mind. Conflating behavior with culture continues to blind social observers from seeing that hip hop pronouncements about "keeping it real" and "authenticity" are about being true to the long tradition of storytelling, which in turn is not to reduce the import of such vernacular art to just that. Indeed, if the history of controversy and misunderstanding over criminal self-representation in African American popular culture tells us anything, it is that such an art has been essential to making the most out of the least, to using stereotype against the grain to highlight precisely and uncomfortably how a symbolic order is made to service "real" discrimination.

EPILOGUE

Global Gangsta—Life in Death

On March 3, 1991, a nationally broadcast video of police beating up a black man, Rodney King, set the apparent criminality of gangsta rappers (and their associated hard-core music videos) in relief. The vision of LA's finest ganging up against a hapless black man encapsulated the asymmetry involved in chastising black youth for their moral and social irresponsibility. The cops were seen to be demonstrably working on the part of a white racist social order. And their courtroom acquittal a year later, on April 29, 1992, publicly confirmed the allegiances of the system. The not-guilty verdict by an all-white jury provoked the consequent LA rebellion (reductively interpreted as riot), hardening the battle lines between a desperate white racist protection racket and an angry nonwhite community.

As so-called prophets of rage, hard-core reality rappers became the center of media attention for something more than the explicit content of their raps. As interlocutors of street knowledge, Ice-T, Ice Cube, and Chuck D (to name the most conspicuous) were consulted with the earnestness normally associated with political dignitaries and public intellectuals. And on the back of the cultural and political capital accrued during this period, the gangsta culture industry went into overdrive.

Recently Nick Tosches has asked whether the gangsta posing of many contemporary rap groups is any different from that of the black coon acts of the past: "Is an exaggerated pretense of being bad, dangerous, and lawless anything more than a variation on the exaggerated pretense of being benign, comical, and docile.... Are they not in essence ... theatrical coon acts, built on stereotype?"[1] The distance between "the happy darky of minstrelsy" and the "bellicose gangsta of rap" is, Tosches maintains, an illusion.[2] The gangsta confirms the worst of what's implied by a white racist logic that was consolidated in *Birth of a Nation*: that "black" is a benevolent signifier when it connotes the contented state of slavery, and a threatening signifier when associated with freedom.

Certainly the gangsta image as the apogee of criminal self-representation in African American popular culture constitutes an extremely ambivalent black sign in white America. As Tricia Rose has argued, the success of gangsta rap has come with particular costs to hip hop and the image of the black urban community. In an impassioned explication of how mass-media conglomerates have once again constrained the field of African American representation, Rose laments how the commercial investment in the "gangsta-pimp-ho trinity" has suffocated other forms of hip hop (as less commercially viable) and polarized the terms of debate about the value of hip hop. The ruthless targeting of the "tween" market with sexist and racialized fantasies from the mid-1990s has driven hip hop's progressive spirit to the margins. Moreover, the predominance of stylish thug life images in hip hop has fed a "hyperbolic and polarized conversation about hip hop":

> This conversation has become a powerful vehicle for the channeling of broader public discussion about race, class, and the value of black culture's role in society. Debates about hip hop have become a means for defining poor, young black people, and thus for interpreting the context and reasons for their clearly disadvantaged lives.[3]

This having been said, Rose's criticism is not leveled at gangsta rap per se but at the way hip hop has been itself "pimped" to the highest bidder.[4] As she qualifies: "Categorically rejecting songs about sex or violence or materialism is not the answer, although reducing their overall space certainly is."[5]

Rose's critique notwithstanding, I would argue that today's gangstas remain important for the way they provoke anxieties about the white investment in racist stereotypes. Gangsta rappers have deliberately courted adverse publicity within and outside the black community. Pronouncements against the misogynist and homophobic rhetoric of gangsta rap have only encouraged sales. And the particular popularity of this rhetoric among white youth (as gangsta rap's biggest consumers) has only raised the stakes. Clearly gangsta rap is as much about what is at the heart of the dominant culture as it is about the iniquitous conditions that determine black inner-city life.

Just as gangsta was enjoying accelerated commoditization, the murders of two of its biggest names, Tupac Shakur and The Notorious B.I.G. (a.k.a. Biggie Smalls), pointed toward the exhaustion of this part of hip hop culture. Gangsta culture's extreme reliance on authenticity and being real for its credibility with consumers seemed to have reached its illogical endgame. Both Tupac and Biggie Smalls collapsed the distinction between signifier and signified, between mask and self, between performance and so-called reality. A feud between their record labels, Death Row and Bad Boy Records, carried out initially in vitriolic raps, spilled over into other domains and came to a murderous conclusion in which both stars were victims of retaliatory shootings. This epilogue to gangsta culture, however, did not signal its death.

In a typically gangsta way, death constituted an entrepreneurial opportunity as an epilogue industry emerged that paid homage to (and capitalized on) the fallen. In the first instance this was led by one of hip hop's most flamboyant entrepreneurs, Sean Combs (a.k.a. Puff Daddy, Puffy, P. Diddy, and Diddy). Combs had produced Biggie Smalls's *Ready to Die* in 1994. This album was the first for both Biggie and Bad Boy Records. It was critically acclaimed and massively successful, cementing a close relationship between artist and producer. In response to Biggie's death in 1997, Combs made the single "I'll Be Missing You" (based on The Police song "Every Breath You Take") as a tribute to Biggie. This mix of genuine grief and mawkish opportunism went to number one on the charts, an ironic testament to the way the gangsta's skill in collapsing life/art distinctions could triumph over death. Tupac's death has been exploited even more ruthlessly. To date, five successful posthumous albums have been released (*R U Still Down? (Remember Me)* [1997], *Until the End of Time* [2001], *Better Days* [2002], *Loyal to the Game* [2004], and *Pac's Life* [2006]). An Oscar-nominated documentary, *Tupac: Resurrection* (released by Paramount in 2003), featured Tupac himself as the voice-from-the-dead narrator.

In a further shift that typifies the "ill-logics" of gangsta culture, one of the biggest stars in the gangsta firmament is now a white rapper, Eminem, produced by a black Svengali and original member of the first gangsta generation, Dr. Dre. By tempering its social realism and fervent essentialism and adopting a more mannered, self-parodying, and commercially conspicuous style (embodied in "Mack" and "Don" rap), the gangsta industry has only extended its cultural reach. Worldwide, music videos channel exaggerated images of black pimps and dons (mafia emulators) defying the work ethic as "playas" (and as entertainers), turning pleasure into business by exploiting (and exposing) the amoral possibilities latent in a global postindustrial value order that is rooted in racialized and patriarchal norms.

The year 2007 saw the release of *American Gangster*, a big-budget crime epic directed by Ridley Scott and starring Denzel Washington and Russell Crowe. The blockbuster credentials of the director of films such as *Alien* (1979), *Thelma and Louise* (1991), *Gladiator* (2000), and *Black Hawk Down* (2001), alongside two of the biggest male stars in Hollywood, signaled a screen mainstreaming of what has been marked previously as niche market material. *American Gangster*'s working title was "The Return of Superfly," which tells us much about the intertextual and generic source of the film. Although Scott had been approached to make the film in the first instance, he did not initially follow up the opportunity. Instead the job was offered to Antoine Fuqua, an African American filmmaker who had made a mark with *Training Day* (2001), which featured an Oscar-winning performance by Denzel Washington playing a corrupt LAPD narcotics detective. The Fuqua/Washington combination was revived to turn Universal's option on Mark Jacobson's *New York Magazine* story about the real-life 1970s Harlem drug lord Frank Lucas, "The Return of Superfly," into a movie.

The idea of putting together an African American director with the most successful African American actor to make a film about a black gangster was clearly driven by residual notions of authenticity. Fuqua's association with *Training Day*, concerned as it was with the way the Los Angeles inner-city neighborhoods blurred distinctions between law and gangstas, made him a strong candidate for a treatment of a duel between a vigilant cop and skilled boss of organized crime. Additionally, Fuqua's track record as a successful producer of hip hop music videos only added to his street credentials. Most notably, he had made Coolio's "Gangsta Paradise" video, a massive global hit that had also featured on the soundtrack to *Dangerous Minds* (1995), a film about a white female teacher's (played by Michelle Pfeiffer) crusade to educate disenchanted and hostile inner-city Californian African American and Hispanic students. The video for the Compton-born West Coast gangsta rapper Coolio intercut scenes from the film with the rap artist narrating his story to Michelle Pfeiffer in a smoke-filled graffiti-adorned dark corridor. The opening lines mix the clichéd gravitas of Psalms 23:4 with gangsta nihilism, as Coolio raps, "As I walk through the valley of the shadow of death, I take a look at my life, and realize there's nothing left."

Fuqua has criticized the way African American filmmakers get pigeonholed on the basis of race:

> The dumbest question I've ever been asked always starts off like this: "As a black director ... I hate that! It's a dumb question because I don't look at things as a black director, just as a director, so ask me as a director first and we can segue into the colour thing later. That's a dumbass question because you don't ask any other artist that.[6]

He has also lambasted the industry for films such as *Soul Plane* (2004), a bad-taste comedy film about the creation of a hip hop airline that exploited the talents of rap artists such as Method Man and Snoop Dogg: "It's not worth it, it's not about the money, especially when you're dealing with a culture. It should be about elevating the idea of what we are and who we are as a people in the cinema, and that kind of stuff keeps dragging us back."[7]

These seem strangely unreflective comments given Fuqua's involvement with rap artists such as Coolio and his hardly elevating image of African Americans in *Training Day* (which also cast gangsta rap stars Snoop Dogg and Dr. Dre in cameo roles). The enthusiasm Fuqua articulated about taking on "The Return of Superfly"/*American Gangster* suggests a more contradictory relationship to criminal self-representation. In an interview with *Entertainment Weekly* he declared that a movie about a 1970s black gangster offered several opportunities because "America was changing. Everything was happening. War. Assassination. Drugs.... I'm going to exploit all of that. This is it. This is the one I've been building up to. This is the one that will define me."[8] Perhaps Fuqua should have paid heed to his favorite line from the movies, "Just when I thought I was out, they pull me back in," words uttered by the boss of movie gangsters, Michael Corleone (Al Pacino) in *The Godfather: Part III*.[9] It seems that there is no escaping the contradictory impulse to make it through conforming to type and engaging in a form of self-exploitation. Unfortunately, for a host of reasons (mainly to do with escalating costs), Fuqua was fired from the project in October 2004.[10] The project was shelved until 2006, when Ridley Scott took over.[11] And what resulted attempted to transform blaxploitation and hood cinema's niche associations with low-budget exploitation into a prestige vehicle for global consumption.

The deep identifications across the color line with African American criminal self-representation at the beginning of the twenty-first century highlight the way the gangsta has become (like the gangster before him) a vehicle for concerns beyond the ghetto. The seemingly self-marginalizing and local grammar of the gangster/gangsta's ethnically (and criminally) marked performances is essential to his global appeal. Moreover, such local marking has been key to the gangster/gangsta's entry into the (inter)national language not as something that confirms or reifies the existing racializing of the social order, but as something that disturbs the mainstream from within.

Gangsta rap makes a particular claim on what is real. Ironically, the obvious posing and stylized language of gangsta rap point not in the direction of the mask (or even race anymore) but instead toward authenticity. On this rests gangsta rap's success with white youth as a way of being real. As the gangsta's in-your-face attitude declares: "We know who we are. Who are you?" Looked at in this way, the ghetto-centric world of gangsta culture is filled with what's apparently missing in the world that surrounds (and sustains) it. And in the context of a world increasingly characterized by processes of deracination (an attendant force of globalization), the gangsta, in turning deficit into plenitude, continues to meet an ever more desperate desire for something that connotes roots.

This, of course, is an attractive way of accounting for (or salvaging) the seditious potential in what might otherwise be seen as a profoundly dysfunctional form of self-representation on the part of black youth. However, there remain clear differences between the privilege of the white onlooker to appropriate this sign of blackness and the black popular cultural producers whose opportunities remain restricted to making the most of imposed white racist stereotypes. In such a world, many white consumers want to have the symbolic capital of authenticity and identity associated with being a "Nigga" without the inconvenience of the lived reality of being black in a white racist culture. Yet the ongoing cross-racial, cross-class, and transnational identification that is agitated by the gangsta—one that is fostered and encouraged precisely through processes of commoditization and mass-media circulation—is not insignificant. The gangsta as global blackface performance exemplifies what Homi Bhabha in another context describes as "the *productive* ambivalence of the object of colonial discourse—that 'otherness' which is at once an object of desire and derision, an articulation of difference contained in the fantasy of origin and identity."[12] And it is here *within* the field of a globalizing truth regime (through the very mass-media machinery that rationalizes its amoral economy) that African American criminal self-representation continues its "ill-logical" work in exposing the ongoing racialized contingencies of power.

In a world so constrained, so beset by compromises, what constitutes liberation? What can make for a road to freedom or way out? African American popular cultural producers over such a long time span and across various media—such as Rudolph Fisher, Ralph Cooper, Chester Himes, Julian Mayfield, Rudy Ray Moore, Tupac, and Biggie—have had to work in an environment where their choices have been severely delimited by the complicity of exploitative industrial and commercial interests with race prejudice. To varying degrees all of these writers, filmmakers, and musicians engage with violence and actual death as a means to countering the social death that remains the legacy of slavery for black folk. This common interest is exemplified by Fisher's conjure man, Frimbo, who must risk his own death to discover his murderer, Cooper's policy gangster, who would rather die in order to be free; Himes's and Mayfield's almost absurdist views of Harlem as a place of the living dead; Moore's jocular confrontations with the afterlife; and Tupac's and Biggie's conflation of rap and violent death.

Thus, as much as such criminal self-representation risks fueling the vicious circle of blaming the victim Rose so trenchantly identifies in the case of gangsta rap, it also establishes how the threat of death determines the ground for struggle and the terms of freedom and autonomy. Building on Jean Baudrillard's declaration that "no revolutionary strategy can begin without the slave putting his own life at stake,"[13] Abdul JanMohamed maintains that "the slave's road to freedom lies not through a commitment to work but through the renegotiation of the death contract that has bound him in the very process of forming him as a subject."[14] Although difficult to frame in progressive terms, criminal self-representation has continually engaged with the violent and coercive force of racial subordination. Criminal self-representation negates the power of those who threaten death, restoring the agency of death to those once subordinated. Such a process of negation may seem the basis for only pyrrhic victories, but it still constitutes a ground for liberation from one's subjection as a socially dead person and provides one way to unfetter the present from a past determined by the master. While it is understandable that such emancipative political potential has been overlooked in debates about the value of criminal self-representation in African American popular culture, I hope to have helped illuminate how this life in death configuration, and the violence on which it depends for its realization, is so much more than self-defeating.

Notes

INTRODUCTION

1. Mississippi John Hurt, "Stack O'Lee," *Mississippi John Hurt Avalon Blues: The Complete 1928 Okeh Recordings* (Columbia/Legacy, 1996).

2. Cecil Brown, *Stagolee Shot Billy* (Cambridge, MA: Harvard University Press, 2003), 154.

3. Roger D. Abrahams, *Deep Down in the Jungle: Negro Narrative Folklore from the Streets of Philadelphia* (Chicago: Aldine, 1970), 132. This version is taken from John A. Lomax and Allan Lomax, *American Ballads and Folk Songs* (New York: Macmillan, 1934), 99, a seminal collection based on the Lomax's recordings of such material during the early twentieth century.

4. Manthia Diawara, "Noir by Noirs: Towards a New Realism in Black Cinema," *African American Review* (Winter 1993), at http://findarticles.com/p/articles/mi_m2838/is_n4_v27/ai_15342198/?tag=content;col1.

5. "Chocolate City," from the eponymous 1975 Parliament album on the Casablanca label, produced by George Clinton. Although CC was parlance for DC, given the high black demographic in the nation's capital, Clinton's implication was that this could be the basis for a move on the rest of America.

6. Abrahams, *Deep Down in the Jungle*; Alan Dundes, ed., *Mother Wit from the Laughing Barrel: Readings in the Interpretation of Afro-American Folklore* (Jackson: University Press of Mississippi, 1990); Lawrence Levine, *Black Culture and Black Consciousness: Afro-American Folk Thought from Slavery to Freedom* (New York: Oxford University Press, 1977); Bruce Jackson, *Get Your Ass in the Water and Swim Like Me: Narrative Poetry from Black Oral Tradition* (Cambridge, MA: Harvard University Press, 1974); John W. Roberts, *From Trickster to Badman: The Black Folk Hero in Slavery and Freedom* (Philadelphia: University of Pennsylvania Press, 1990).

7. Jerry H. Bryant, *Born in a Mighty Bad Land: The Violent Man in African American Folklore and Fiction* (Bloomington: Indiana University Press, 2003).

8. Abdul JanMohamed, *The Death-Bound-Subject: Richard Wright's Archaeology of Death* (Durham, NC: Duke University Press, 2005).

9. Houston Baker, *Blues, Ideology, and Afro-American Literature: A Vernacular Theory* (Chicago: University of Chicago Press, 1984), S. Craig Watkins, *Representing: Hip Hop Culture and the Production of Black Cinema* (Chicago: University of Chicago Press, 1998).

10. Robin D. G. Kelley, *Race Rebels: Culture, Politics, and the Black Working Class* (New York: Free Press, 1994), William L. Van Deburg, *Black Camelot: African-American Culture Heroes in Their Times, 1960–1980* (Chicago: University of Chicago Press, 1997).

11. William L. Van Deburg, *Hoodlums: Black Villains and Social Bandits in American Life* (Chicago: University of Chicago Press, 2004).

12. George P. Rawick, *From Sundown to Sunup: The Making of the Black Community* (Westport, CT: Greenwood Publishing, 1972).

13. Levine, *Black Culture and Black Consciousness*, 401.

14. Todd Boyd, *Am I Black Enough for You? Popular Culture from the 'Hood and Beyond* (Bloomington: Indiana University Press, 1997), 9.

15. Derrick Bell, *Faces at the Bottom of the Well: The Permanence of Racism* (New York: Basic Books, 1992); Homi Bhabha, *The Location of Culture* (New York: Routledge, 1994); Richard Dyer, *White* (New York: Routledge, 1997); Paul Gilroy, *Black Atlantic: Modernity and Double Consciousness* (Cambridge, MA: Harvard University Press, 1993); David Theo Goldberg, *The Racial State* (Oxford: Blackwell, 2002); George Lipsitz, *The Possessive Investment in Whiteness: How White People Profit from Identity Politics* (Philadelphia: Temple University Press, 1998); Charles W. Mills, *The Racial Contract* (Ithaca, NY: Cornell University Press, 1999); David Roediger, *The Wages of Whiteness: Race and the Making of the American Working Class* (London: Verso, 1991).

16. Hazel V. Carby, *Cultures in Babylon: Black Britain and African America* (London: Verso, 1999); bell hooks, *Outlaw Culture: Resisting Representations* (New York: Routledge, 1994); Michelle Wallace, *Black Macho and the Myth of the Superwoman* (London: Verso, 1990).

17. Victor Anderson, *Beyond Ontological Blackness: An Essay on African American Religious and Cultural Criticism* (New York: Continuum, 1999); Michael Eric Dyson, *Reflecting Black: African American Cultural Criticism* (Minneapolis: University of Minnesota Press, 1993); Kenneth Mostern, *Autobiography and Black Identity Politics: Racialization in Twentieth-Century America* (Cambridge: Cambridge University Press, 1999); Ross Posnock, *Color and Culture: Black Writers and the Making of the Modern Intellectual* (Cambridge, MA: Harvard university Press, 1998); Mark Reid, *PostNegritude Visual and Literary Culture* (Albany: State University of New York Press, 1997).

18. Susan Gubar, *Racechanges: White Skin, Black Face in American Culture* (New York: Oxford University Press, 1997); W. T. Lhamon Jr., *Raising Cain: Blackface Performance from Jim Crow to Hip Hop* (Cambridge, MA: Harvard University Press, 1998); Eric Lott, *Love and Theft: Blackface Minstrelsy and the American Working Class* (New York: Oxford University Press, 1993); Michael Rogin, *Blackface, White Noise: Jewish Immigrants in the Hollywood Melting Pot* (Berkeley: University of California Press, 1998).

19. Frantz Fanon, *Black Skin, White Masks* (London: Pluto, 1986).

20. Bhabha, *The Location of Culture*, 96.

21. JanMohamed, *The Death-Bound-Subject*, 298.

22. Brown, *Stagolee Shot Billy*, 3.

23. Gunnar Myrdal, *An American Dilemma: The Negro Problem and American Democracy*, vol. 2 (New Brunswick, NJ: Transaction Publishers, 1996), 928.

24. Jonathan Munby, *Public Enemies, Public Heroes: Screening the Gangster from* Little Caesar *to* Touch of Evil (Chicago: University of Chicago Press, 1999).

25. Stuart Hall, "What Is This 'Black' in Black Popular Culture," in *Black Popular Culture: A Project by Michele Wallace*, ed. Gina Dent (Seattle: Bay Press, 1992); James Snead, *White Screens, Black Images: Hollywood from the Dark Side* (New York: Routledge, 1994).

26. Langston Hughes, *The Big Sea: An Autobiography* (New York: Alfred Knopf, 1940).

27. Mostern, *Autobiography and Black Identity Politics*, 145.

28. Baker, *Blues, Ideology, and Afro-American Literature*; JanMohamed, *The Death-Bound-Subject*.

29. Chester Himes, *Blind Man with a Pistol* (New York: Vintage Books, 1989), 5.

30. Greil Marcus, *Mystery Train: Images of America in Rock 'n' Roll Music*, 4th ed. (New York: Plume, 1997), 68–78.

31. Nick Tosches, *Where Dead Voices Gather* (Boston: Little, Brown, 2001), 281.

32. Ice Cube, "AmeriKKKa's Most Wanted," from the eponymous album (1990).

33. Tricia Rose, *The Hip Hop Wars: What We Talk About When We Talk About Hip Hop—And Why It Matters* (New York: Basic Books, 2008).

34. Michael Eric Dyson, *Between God and Gangsta Rap: Bearing Witness to Black Culture* (New York: Oxford University Press, 1996), 186.

CHAPTER ONE

1. Claude McKay, *Harlem: Negro Metropolis* (New York: Dutton, 1940), 101.

2. *New York Herald Tribune*, October 16, 1927, unpaginated clipping, New York Public Library, Schomburg Center for Research in Black Culture.

3. LeRoi Jones, *Blues People* (New York: Morrow Quill, 1963), 96.

4. W. E. B. Du Bois, review of *Nigger Heaven*, by Carl Van Vechten, *Crisis* 33 (December 1926): 81.

5. W. E. B. Du Bois, "Two Novels," *Crisis* 35 (June 1928): 202.

6. George Schuyler, "The Negro Art Hokum," *The Nation*, June 16, 1926, reprinted in Henry Louis Gates Jr. and Nellie McKay, eds., *The Norton Anthology of African American Literature* (New York: Norton, 1997), 1171.

7. Ibid., 1173.

8. Ibid., 1174.

9. Langston Hughes, "The Negro Artist and the Racial Mountain," *The Nation*, (June 23, 1926), reprinted in Gates and McKay, eds., *The Norton Anthology of African American Literature*, 1271.

10. Henry Louis Gates Jr., "Harlem on Our Minds," in *Rhapsodies in Black: Art of the Harlem Renaissance*, ed. Richard J. Powell and David A. Bailey (Berkeley: University of California Press, 1997), 166.

11. Maria Balshaw, *Looking for Harlem: Urban Aesthetics in African-American Literature* (London: Pluto Press, 2000), 31.

12. John McCluskey Jr., ed., *The City of Refuge: The Collected Short Stories of Rudolph Fisher* (Columbia: University of Missouri Press, 1987). *The Conjure Man Dies* was reissued first in 1971 by Arno Press and then in 1992 by the University of Michigan Press, which also reissued *The Walls of Jericho* in 1994. Other than McCluskey, Balshaw, *Looking*

for Harlem, and Stephen F. Soitos, *The Blues Detective: A Study of African American Detective Fiction* (Amherst: University of Massachusetts Press, 1996), have been at the forefront in reintroducing Fisher as a significant Harlem Renaissance contributor.

13. Soitos, *The Blues Detective*, 95.

14. Ibid., 95, quoting from Arna Bontemps, *The Harlem Renaissance Remembered* (New York: Dodd, Mead, 1994), 45.

15. Balshaw, *Looking for Harlem*, 31. To Himes and Reed, one could add Walter Mosley to this legacy.

16. Rudolph Fisher, *The Conjure Man Dies* (1932; London: The X Press, 1995), 93. Hereafter cited in text.

17. It is significant that Chester Himes, the next great African American detective writer, would resuscitate the idea of sperm elixir in *Blind Man with Pistol* (1969); see chapter 3.

18. McKay, *Harlem: Negro Metropolis*, 75. Hereafter cited in text.

19. David Levering Lewis identifies Holstein as one of six figures crucial to nurturing the Harlem Renaissance. See *When Harlem Was in Vogue* (New York: Penguin Books, 1997), 121, 129–30, 220.

20. Lewis, *When Harlem Was in Vogue*, 220.

21. McKay, *Harlem: Negro Metropolis*, 105.

22. Ibid.

23. For a full history of the white mob's invasion of Harlem's policy racket, see Walter A. Bell, "Black Gangs of Harlem, 1920–1939," at http://www.trutv.com/library/crime/gangsters_outlaws/gang/harlem_gangs/7.html. *Hoodlum* (1997), a film directed by Bill Duke, starring Laurence Fishburne as Bumpy Johnson, Tim Roth as Dutch Schultz, Andy Garcia as Lucky Luciano, and Cicely Tyson as Stephanie St. Clair, also covers this period.

24. McKay, *Harlem: Negro Metropolis*, 113.

25. McKay dedicated *Harlem: Negro Metropolis* to Johnson as "friend and wise counsellor"—a clear nod to the tradition that he was working with and against.

26. Nathan Huggins, *Harlem Renaissance* (New York: Oxford University Press, 1971), 215.

27. Gilbert Osofsky, *Harlem, the Making of a Ghetto: Negro New York, 1890–1930* (1966; Chicago: Ivan R, Dee, 1996), 212.

28. St. Clair Drake and Horace R. Cayton, *Black Metropolis: A Study of Negro Life in a Northern City* (Chicago: University of Chicago Press, 1945), Richard Wright's introduction to the first edition, xxix.

29. Gunnar Myrdal, *An American Dilemma: The Negro Problem and American Democracy*, vol. 2 (New Brunswick, NJ: Transactions, 1996), 928–29.

30. Ibid., 873. For a full critique of Myrdal's view of religion and his more general discussion of the pathology of black communal life, see Stephan Thernstrom and Abigail Thernstrom, *America in Black and White: One Nation, Indivisible* (New York: Simon and Schuster, 1997) and Roderick Ferguson, "Nightmares of the Heteronormative," *Cultural Values* 4, no. 4 (2000): 419–44.

31. Ibid., 928.

32. Ferguson, "Nightmares of the Heteronormative," 425.

33. Ibid., 432.

34. Arthur Huff Fauset, *Black Gods of the Metropolis: Negro Religious Cults of the Urban North* (Philadelphia: University of Pennsylvania Press, 2001), 427–28.

35. Drake and Cayton, *Black Metropolis*, 493–94.

36. Ibid., 486.

37. Ibid., 474.

38. George J. McCall, "Symbiosis: The Case of Hoodoo and the Numbers Racket," *Social Problems*, 10 (Spring 1963): 361–71, reprinted in Alan Dundes, ed., *Mother Wit from the Laughing Barrel: Readings in the Interpretation of Black Folklore* (Englewood Cliffs, NJ: Prentice Hall, 1973), 419–27.

39. Rufus Schatzberg, *African American Organized Crime: A Social History* (New York: Garland, 1996; and New Brunswick, NJ: Rutgers University Press, 1997).

40. Paul Oliver, *Blues Fell This Morning: Meaning in the Blues* (London: Cassell, 1960; 2nd ed., Cambridge: Cambridge University Press, 1990).

41. William Barlow, *Looking Up at Down: The Emergence of Blues Culture* (Philadelphia: Temple University Press, 1989), 263; Paul Garon, *The Devil's Son-in-Law: The Story of Peetie Wheatstraw and His Songs* (Chicago: Charles H. Kerr, 2003), 3–11, 78–81.

42. Barlow, *Looking Up at Down*, 263.

43. "Peetie Wheatstraw Stomp," *Peetie Wheatstraw: Complete Works, Volume 4*, Document DOCD-5244 (2000; original recording, 1937).

44. "Gangster Blues," *Peetie Wheatstraw (1930–1941)*, RST Records, CD 3541-2 (1988; original recording, 1940).

45. Barlow, *Looking Up at Down*, 265.

46. Elijah Wald, *Escaping the Delta: Robert Johnson and the Invention of the Blues* (New York: Harper Paperbacks, 2005), 41.

47. Paul Garon suggests that Wheatstraw's absence from the canon can be attributed to the way postwar blues revivalists favored guitar players to pianists, and Gennett to Decca recordings (Decca being Wheatstraw's primary label). Garon, *The Devil's Son-in-Law*, 109.

48. "Interview: Elijah Wald on Escaping the Delta," Afropop Worldwide (2004), at http://www.afropop.org/multi/interview/ID/66/Elijah+Wald+on+Escaping+the+Delta. Accessed September 28, 2009.

49. "Numbers Blues," *Peetie Wheatstraw: Complete Works, Volume 2*, Document DOCD-5242 (2000; original recording, 1934).

50. "Playing Policy Blues," *Blind Blake: The Complete Works, Volume 4*, Document DOCD-5027 (1991; original recording, 1930).

51. See Paul Oliver, *Blues Fell This Morning*, chapter 5, "The Jinx Is on Me," 117–37, for the most sustained treatment of how numbers featured in blues music; and "Aunt Sally Policy Dream Book" by Catherine Yronwode for details on how Blind Blake manipulates the meaning of numbers, at http://www.luckymojo.com/auntsallys.html, accessed September 29, 2009.

52. "Policy Dream Blues," *Bumble Bee Slim (Amos Easton), 1934–1937*, Wolf Records, B.o.B 6 CD (1994; original recording, 1935).

53. "Bring Me Flowers While I'm Living," *Peetie Wheatstraw (1930–1941)*, RST Records, CD 3541-2 (1988; original recording, 1941).

54. Garon, *The Devil's Son-in-Law*, 106–9.

CHAPTER TWO

1. Michael Eric Dyson, *Reflecting Black: African American Cultural Criticism* (Minneapolis: University of Minnesota Press, 1993); Michael Eric Dyson, *Between God and Gangsta Rap* (Oxford: Oxford University Press, 1996); Robin D. G. Kelley, *Race Rebels: Culture, Politics, and the Black Working Class* (New York: Free Press, 1994); Robin D. G. Kelley, *Yo' Mama's Disfunktional: Fighting the Culture Wars in Urban America* (Boston: Beacon Press, 1997); Eithne Quinn, "'Who's the Mack?' The Performativity and Politics of the Pimp Figure in Gangsta Rap," *Journal of American Studies* 34, no. 1 (2000): 115–36; Eithne Quinn, "'Pimpin' Ain't Easy': Work, Play, and 'Lifestylization' of the Black Pimp Figure in Early 1970s America," in *Media, Culture, and the Modern African American Freedom Struggle*, ed. Brian Ward (Gainesville: University Press of Florida, 2001), 211–32; Eithne Quinn, *Nuthin' but a "G" Thang: The Culture and Commerce of Gangsta Rap* (New York: Columbia University Press, 2004); William L. Van Deburg, *Hoodlums: Black Villains and Social Bandits in American Life* (Chicago: University of Chicago Press, 2004).

2. Other terms for these films existed—such as "all-Negro" and "all-Colored"—but "race film" best captures the burden these films bore as agents of racial uplift or improvement. For a fine exploration of the term's origins, appropriateness, and problems, see Jane M. Gaines, *Fire and Desire: Mixed-Race Movies in the Silent Era* (Chicago: University of Chicago Press, 2001). In the early 1990s Mark A. Reid raised some initial speculations about the connections between the 1960s/1970s black gangster types (in both film and literature) and the 1930s/1940s black-cast gangster film. See Mark A. Reid, "The Black Gangster Film," *Journal of Social Philosophy* 24, no. 3 (1993): 143–54.

3. Paula J. Massood, *Black City Cinema: African American Urban Experiences in Film* (Philadelphia: Temple University Press, 2003), 8.

4. J. Ronald Green, *Straight Lick: The Cinema of Oscar Micheaux* (Bloomington: Indiana University Press, 2000) offers the most exhaustive coverage of Micheaux's films—and sets these as the dates that bookend his moviemaking career, from *The Homesteader* to *The Betrayal* (see 239–42). See also Patrick McGilligan, *Oscar Micheaux—The Great and Only: The Life of America's First Black Filmmaker* (New York: HarperCollins, 2007); Gaines, *Fire and Desire*; and the entry on Micheaux in Michael R. Pitts, *Poverty Row Studios, 1929–1940* (Jefferson, NC: McFarland, 1997), 261–63.

5. For more on the antitrust features of this system and the challenge to its legitimacy see Ernest Borneman, "United States versus Hollywood: The Case Study of an Anti-Trust Suit," in *The American Film Industry*, ed. Tino Balio (Madison: University of Wisconsin Press, 1976), 332–45.

6. For more on the contingencies of independent film production and distribution see Balio, *The American Film Industry*, 107–9; and Pitts, *Poverty Row Studios*, vii–viii, 261–63.

7. From the Baltimore *African American*, "Open Letter to Oscar Micheaux" in 1933, cited by Gaines, *Fire and Desire*, 125 and Daniel Leab, *From Sambo to Superspade: The Black Experience in Motion Pictures* (Boston: Houghton Mifflin, 1975), 191.

8. Thomas Cripps, *Slow Fade to Black: The Negro in American Film, 1900–1942* (Oxford: Oxford University Press, 1977), 323.

9. Mark A. Reid, "Pioneer Black Filmmaker: The Achievement of Oscar Micheaux," *Black Film Review* 4, no. 2 (1988): 7.

10. Henry T. Sampson, *Blacks in Black and White: A Source Book on Black Films*, 2nd ed. (Metuchen, NJ: Scarecrow Press, 1995), 12.

11. Cripps, *Slow Fade to Black*, 330–31.

12. Gaines, *Fire and Desire*, 108–9.

13. Ibid., 125–26. Gaines draws on Charlene Regester's argument that Micheaux's work needs rereading in terms of two phases, 1918–29 and 1930–48, silent and sound. See Regester, "The Misreading and Rereading of African American Filmmaker Oscar Micheaux: A Critical Review of Micheaux Scholarship," *Film History* 7 (1995): 426–49.

14. Cedric J. Robinson, *Forgeries of Memory and Meaning: Blacks and the Regimes of Race in American Theater and Film before World War II* (Chapel Hill, NC: University of North Carolina Press, 2007), 367.

15. Stuart Hall, "What Is This 'Black' in Black Popular Culture?" in *Black Popular Culture*, ed. Gina Dent (Seattle: Bay Press, 1992), 21–33; James Snead, *White Screens/Black Images: Hollywood from the Dark Side* (London: Routledge, 1994), especially 121–29; and Gaines, *Fire and Desire*.

16. See Donald Bogle, *Toms, Coons, Mulattoes, Mammies, and Bucks: An Interpretive History of Blacks in American Films* (New York: Continuum, 2001); Cripps, *Slow Fade to Black*; Ed Guerrero, *Framing Blackness: The African American Image in Film* (Philadelphia: Temple University Press, 1993); Snead, *White Screens/Black Images*; and Michael Rogin, *Blackface, White Noise: Jewish Immigrants in the Hollywood Melting Pot* (Berkeley: University of California Press, 1996) for further elaboration on the development of Hollywood's Old South black typology and racial masquerade in the wake of *Birth of a Nation*.

17. See Gaines, *Fire and Desire*, chap. 5, 161–84, for more on the history of the film's hostile reception, disappearance in the United States, and rediscovery abroad.

18. Ruth Vasey, *The World According to Hollywood, 1918–1939* (Exeter: University of Exeter Press, 1997).

19. *Dark Manhattan* PCA file, Martha Herrick Library, Academy of Motion Picture Arts and Sciences (hereafter cited as MHL-AMPAS).

20. *Moon over Harlem* PCA file, MHL-AMPAS.

21. Snead, *White Screens/Black Images* (especially in chapters 4 and 6) provides a fine discussion of the coding of blackness in terms of white lack in plantation films.

22. "The Negro on the Screen," *New York Age*, July 23, 1932, unpaginated clipping from the New York Public Library's Schomburg Center for Research in Black Culture (hereafter cited as Schomburg Center).

23. *The Exile*, *Ten Minutes to Live*, *The Girl from Chicago*, *Underworld*, *Swing!*, and *Lying Lips* were all viewed at Library of Congress Motion Picture and Television Reading Room, Washington, DC, Black Films: Paper Print Collection. *Murder in Harlem* viewed on VHS.

24. Cripps, *Slow Fade to Black*, 323.

25. *Kansas City Call*, July 15, 1932; article reprinted in Sampson, *Blacks in Black and White*, 432.

26. *Philadelphia Independent*, April 24, 1938. Review reprinted in Larry Richards, *African American Films through 1959: A Comprehensive Illustrated Filmography* (Jefferson, NC: McFarland, 1998), 171.

27. *Temptation* PCA File, MHL-AMPAS.

28. McGilligan, *Oscar Micheaux—The Great and Only*, 289.

29. Ibid., 267–68.

30. Sadly, of these films only *Dark Manhattan* (Library of Congress Black Film Col-

lection and Turner Classic Movies), *The Duke Is Tops*, and *Gang War* (both on DVD) seem to be extant. Synopses and other information on the other films are drawn from press clippings and Kenneth W. Munden, exec. ed., *The American Film Institute Catalog of Motion Pictures Produced in the United States* (New York: Bowker, 1971–).

31. Ralph Cooper with Steve Dougherty, *Amateur Night at the Apollo: Ralph Cooper Presents Five Decades of Great Entertainment* (New York: HarperCollins, 1990), 53.

32. Cooper, *Amateur Night at the Apollo*, 55.

33. Ibid., 103.

34. Ibid., 44.

35. Ibid., 120.

36. Cripps, *Slow Fade to Black*, 323. See also McGilligan, *Oscar Micheaux—The Great and Only*, 249 and 257–58, for the ambivalent attitude toward Schiffman as both champion and exploiter of African American theatrical talent.

37. McGilligan, *Oscar Micheaux—The Great and Only*, 270–71.

38. Ibid., 128.

39. Dan Burley, *New York Amsterdam News*, August 19, 1939, unpaginated clipping, Schomburg Center.

40. *Philadelphia Tribune*, February 25, 1937, unpaginated clipping, Schomburg Center.

41. *Philadelphia Tribune*, September 30, 1937, unpaginated clipping on microfilm, Schomburg Center.

42. Robinson, *Forgeries of Memory and Meaning*, 364.

43. Cooper, *Amateur Night at the Apollo*, 124.

44. Ibid., 125.

45. See Jonathan Munby, *Public Enemies, Public Heroes: Screening the Gangster from* Little Caesar *to* Touch of Evil (Chicago: University of Chicago Press, 1999) for a full account of the gangster's volatile meanings for "hyphenated" Americans fighting an embattled WASP hegemony in the aftermath of the Wall Street Crash.

46. Robinson, *Forgeries of Memory and Meaning*, 367.

47. See Cooper, *Amateur Night at the Apollo*.

48. Mel Watkins, "Francine Everett, Striking Star of All-Black Movies, Is Dead," *New York Times*, June 20, 1999. The obituary states that Billy Rowe was journalist for the *Pittsburgh Courier* and the *Amsterdam News*. At http://www.nytimes.com/1999/06/20/nyregion/francine-everett-striking-star-of-all-black-movies-is-dead.html.

49. All films viewed at Library of Congress, Motion Picture Division.

50. Peter Bogdanovich, "Edgar G. Ulmer: An Interview," *Film Culture* 58–60 (1974): 222. See also Jonathan Munby, "*Heimat* Hollywood: Billy Wilder, Otto Preminger, Edgar Ulmer, and the Criminal Cinema of the Austrian-Jewish Diaspora," in *From World War to Waldheim: Culture and Politics in Austria and the United States*, ed. David F. Good and Ruth Wodak (New York: Berghahn Books, 1999), 154.

51. Prior to directing *Moon over Harlem*, Ulmer's sojourn in New York involved working on a series of Yiddish films, most notably *Grune Felde* (*Green Fields*) (1937), a film based on Peretz Hirschbein's play dealing with the dissolution of Jewish customs as the community urbanized and which he codirected with Jacob Ben-Ami, prominent in New York's Yiddish theater; *The Singing Blacksmith* (1938), a musical version of David Pinski's play *Yankl der Schmid*; and *The Light Ahead* (*Di Klyatsche*) (1939), a film about East European Jewry's dreams of living beyond the confines of the shetl. Ulmer was

also involved in making films for the Ukrainian American community, *Natalka Poltavka* (1937; based on the eponymous nineteenth-century Ukrainian nationalist play and opera, revived by the Soviets in 1936) and *Cossacks in Exile* (1939). Both were filmed in the Ukrainian language. See Munby, "*Heimat* Hollywood," 147–48.

52. Todd McCarthy and Charles Flynn, eds., *Kings of the Bs: Working within the Hollywood System* (New York: E. P. Dutton, 1975), 409. See also Munby, "*Heimat* Hollywood," 148.

53. Cripps lists *Murder on Lenox Avenue* (1941) as the only other black gangster film of the period that dealt in a nuanced way with issues of class division and in-group violence. *Slow Fade to Black*, 334–35.

54. Shirley Castle Ulmer, "Interview and Introduction to *Moon over Harlem*," in *Edgar G. Ulmer: Archive* (2005), DVD collection by the Edgar G. Ulmer Preservation Corporation and All Day Entertainment.

55. Aside from composing music for an array of talking race films, Donald Heywood had been associated with a range of black-cast Broadway productions, including *Africana* (1927), *Hot Rhythm* (1930), *Blackberries of 1932* (1932), and *Black Rhythm* (1936). See the Internet Broadway Database, at http://www.ibdb.com/person.php?id=13662. According to Shirley Castle Ulmer, Heywood was a very close friend of Ulmer's, which may explain in part why Ulmer was attracted to this project. See Shirley Castle Ulmer, "Interview and Introduction to *Moon over Harlem*," in *Edgar G. Ulmer: Archive*.

56. Watkins, "Francine Everett, Striking Star of All-Black Movies, Is Dead."

57. PBS documentary, *Soundies: A Musical History* (2007).

58. Ibid.

59. Cripps, *Slow Fade to Black*, chap. 13, "The Politics of Art," 349–89.

60. Typical of Hollywood's caution when it came to broaching the volatile issue of civil rights, the industry delimited things to such an extent that only one African American, Sidney Poitier, seemed to be entrusted with the responsibility of representing racial conflict throughout the 1950s and 1960s.

CHAPTER THREE

1. Chester Himes, *The Quality of Hurt* (London: Michael Joseph, 1973), dust jacket comments.

2. Larry Neal, "Beware the Tar Baby," *New York Times*, August 3, 1969, cited in Ed Guerrero, *Framing Blackness: The African American Image in Film* (Philadelphia: Temple University Press, 1993), 74. Figures for Poitier's earnings, Guerrero, *Framing Blackness*, 75. Against the grain of such hostility, Guerrero provides a more measured analysis of the contradictory terms of Poitier's screen success and the limits of improved black representation on the big screen in the 1950s and 1960s. Poitier's journey to stardom started in 1950, with *No Way Out*, a gritty film noir, which was followed by starring or costarring roles in notable films such as *Blackboard Jungle* (1955), *Edge of the City* (1957), *The Defiant Ones* (1958), and *Porgy and Bess* (1959). The 1960s saw Poitier earn a best actor Oscar for *Lilies in the Field* (1963) and become Hollywood's top box-office attraction in 1967 following the successes of *To Sir, with Love*, *In the Heat of the Night*, and *Guess Who's Coming to Dinner*.

3. Poitier himself turned away from the kinds of roles and stories that had made him a household name—attempting to reinvent himself in a more radical and more pithy vein with films such as *The Lost Man* (1969), in which he stars as a black revolutionary out

to finance his group's agenda by stealing from "The Man's" bank, and two further and harder incarnations of his role as NYPD cop Virgil Tibbs (*They Call Me MISTER Tibbs!* [1970] and *The Organization* [1971]). He also starred in and directed *Buck and the Preacher* (1972, a comic Western with Harry Belafonte about freed slaves outwitting bounty hunters in post–Civil War America) and *Uptown Saturday Night* (1974, a lighthearted comedy crime film with Bill Cosby), both of which indicated Poitier's desire to appear more "hip" to black audiences, especially in the context of the rise of blaxploitation cinema.

4. Richard Wright, "Blueprint for Negro Writing," *New Challenge* 11 (December 1937): 53–65, an essay since reprinted in many major anthologies of African American literature, including perhaps most seminally, in Addison Gayle Jr., ed., *The Black Aesthetic* (Garden City, NY: Doubleday, 1971), 315–26.

5. For an analysis of the reciprocal relationship between Wright's literary theory and the Chicago School of urban sociology, see Carla Capetti, "Sociology of an Existence: Richard Wright and the Chicago School," *MELUS* 12, no. 2 (1985): 25–43. Wright went on to produce his own version of a sociological tract with *Twelve Million Black Voices* in 1941.

6. See Bill Mullen, "Marking Race/Marketing Race: African American Short Fiction and the Politics of Genre, 1933–1946," in *Ethnicity and the American Short Story*, ed. Julie Brown (New York: Garland, 1997), 33; *Norton Anthology of African American Literature* (New York: W. W. Norton, 1997).

7. *Norton Anthology of African American Literature*, 1468.

8. Kevin K. Gaines, *American Africans in Ghana: Black Expatriates and the Civil Rights Era* (Chapel Hill: University of North Carolina Press, 2006), especially the chapter on Mayfield, "Escape to Ghana: Julian Mayfield and the Radical 'Afros,'" 136–78. Gaines offers us the first sustained analysis of Mayfield's significance as a radical expatriate—invaluable as this is, treatment of Mayfield's domestic significance is necessarily limited given the focus of the book.

9. Unless otherwise noted, biographical information on Mayfield is garnered from the Schomburg Center for Research in Black Culture's "Biographical Sketch" available via the New York Public Library Digital Library Collections, which is based on the Mayfield Papers holdings, at http://digilib.nypl.org/dynaweb/ead/scm/scmayfld/@Generic_BookTextView/171;pt=137. Accessed June 14, 2009. The "Biographical Sketch" maintains that he joined the CPUSA in the late 1940s (based on claims made by Mayfield in his unpublished autobiography). Gaines states that Mayfield never joined the party, but highlights how he was openly affiliated with leftist organizations (most notably the Committee for the Negro in the Arts [CNA]) and was friends of CPUSA members throughout the 1950s. Gaines, *American Africans in Ghana*, 146.

10. While John Hope Franklin makes this claim (*From Slavery to Freedom*, vol. 2, *A History of African Americans*, 7th ed. [New York: McGraw-Hill, 1994], 470–76), one can see that post–World War II America experienced an exacerbation of long-established patterns of urban segregation built around racial discrimination. In 1945 St. Clair Drake and Horace R. Cayton invoked the terms *ghetto* and *Bronzeville* to describe the segregated character of Chicago's inner city in their groundbreaking work *Black Metropolis: A Study of Negro Life in a Northern City* (Chicago: University of Chicago Press, 1945), and Gilbert Osofsky located the way "Negro" and "slum" became conjoined in the period of 1890 to 1930 in his *Harlem: The Making of a Ghetto* (New York: Harper and Row, 1963).

11. See A. Robert Lee, *Designs of Blackness* (London: Pluto Press, 1998), 102–3.

12. See Richard Wright, "Blueprint for Negro Writing" and "How Bigger Was Born," in *Norton Anthology of African American Literature*, 1320–21; and Lee, *Designs of Blackness*, chapter 6, 90–106.

13. Peniel E. Joseph, "Rethinking the Crisis of the Negro Intellectual: Harold Cruse, Black Nationalism, and the Black Power Movement," in *Harold Cruse's Crisis of the Negro Intellectual Reconsidered*, ed. Jerry Watts (London: Routledge, 2004), 243 (chapter: 241–62); see also Kevin K. Gaines, "The Crisis of Historical Memory: Harold Cruse, Julian Mayfield, and African American Expatriates in Nkrumah's Ghana, 1957–1966," in Watts, *Harold Cruse's Crisis of the Negro Intellectual Reconsidered*, 183–202.

14. Julian Mayfield, "Challenge to Negro Leadership: The Case of Robert Williams," *Commentary* (April 1961), reprinted in *Reporting Civil Rights Part One: American Journalism 1941–1963* (New York: Library of America, 2003), 550–64.

15. "Into the Mainstream and Oblivion" was based on a paper delivered at the American Society of African Culture's (AMSAC) 1959 conference on "American Negro Writers," whose proceedings were published as *The American Negro and His Roots* (New York: AMSAC, 1959) (see Gaines, *American Africans in Ghana*, 137 and 302). The article was reprinted in Addison Gayle Jr., ed., *Black Expression: Essays by and about Black Americans in the Creative Arts* (New York: Weybright and Talley, 1969), 271–75; "You Touch My Black Aesthetic and I'll Touch Yours," in Gayle, *The Black Aesthetic*, 23–30.

16. See Malcolm X, *The Autobiography of Malcolm X* (New York: Grove Press, 1966), 352–53.

17. Bobby Seale, "Jailhouse Interview with Francisco Newton" (1970), cited in Greil Marcus, *Mystery Train: Images of America in Rock 'n' Roll Music* (London: Plume, 1997), 65.

18. Kenneth Mostern, *Autobiography and Black Identity Politics: Racialization in Twentieth-Century America* (Cambridge: Cambridge University Press, 1999), 145.

19. Nikhil Pal Singh, *Black Is a Country: Race and the Unfinished Struggle for Democracy* (Cambridge, MA: Harvard University Press, 2004), 194.

20. Ibid., 202.

21. Ibid., 203.

22. As the next chapter suggests, Goines could be seen as the inheritor of Himes's mantle in the1970s. Alongside Beck (a.k.a. "Iceberg Slim"), Goines, a writer for Los Angeles's Holloway House publishers (which specialized in African American writers), became the favorite reading of young African American inner-city kids who would come to forge the more hard-core edge of hip hop—especially West Coast gangsta rappers such as Ice-T and the members of NWA, including Ice Cube, who took their "ice" monikers from Beck. It is useful to think of Beck and Goines as writers of blaxploitation literature, linking the uncompromising vision of Malcolm X and Chester Himes to those who would forge gangsta culture in the late 1980s.

23. Malcolm X, *The Autobiography of Malcolm X*, 353.

24. Michael Fabre and Robert E. Skinner, eds., *Conversations with Chester Himes* (Jackson: University Press of Mississippi, 1995), 14.

25. Ibid., 141.

26. Ibid., 25.

27. Ibid., 62.

28. Ibid.

29. Frantz Fanon, *Black Skin, White Masks* (London: Pluto, 1986), 156. Himes claimed that Fanon wrote an unpublished treatise on his understanding of violence (Fabre and Skinner, *Conversations*, 78).

30. Alice Cherki, *Frantz Fanon: A Portrait*, trans. Nadia Benabid (Ithaca, NY: Cornell University Press, 2006), 125.

31. Mayfield, "Into the Mainstream and Oblivion," 273.

32. Ibid., 272.

33. Donald Bogle, *Toms, Coons, Mulattoes, Mammies, and Bucks: An Interpretive History of Blacks in American Film* (New York: Continuum, 2001), 182.

34. Mayfield, "You Touch My Black Aesthetic and I'll Touch Yours," 30.

35. Himes, *The Quality of Hurt*, 152–57.

36. Ibid., 323.

37. Chester Himes, *If He Hollers, Let Him Go* (New York: Thunder's Mouth Press, 1995), 88.

38. Ibid., 88–89.

39. Chester Himes, *Lonely Crusade* (New York: Thunder's Mouth Press, 1986), 28.

40. Schomburg Center online "Biographical Sketch."

41. Poitier was unable to meet his Broadway commitment, having been given his first major film role by Twentieth Century Fox in *No Way Out* (1950). Although *Cry the Beloved Country* was published just before the implementation of apartheid as a political system in South Africa, it addressed and protested against the key social structures that formed its basis. The novel was published in the same year as the institutionalization of apartheid, 1948.

42. Phillip M. Richards, foreword to Julian Mayfield, *The Hit; and, The Long Night* (Boston: Northeastern University Press, 1989), vii. All references to either *The Hit* or *The Long Night* refer to this edition.

43. Mayfield, *The Hit*, 81. Hereafter cited in text.

44. *The Hit* was based on Mayfield's earlier play, *417*, which was produced off-Broadway in 1950 and published in *Contemporary Reader* in January 1955. See Schomburg Center, online "Biographical Sketch."

45. Mayfield, *The Hit*, 68–69. Hereafter cited in text.

46. See Maya Deren, *Divine Horsemen: The Living Gods of Haiti* (Kingston, NY: McPherson, 1983), 119–30, 275; Laënnec Hurbon, *Voodoo: Truth and Fantasy* (London: Thames and Hudson, 1995), 70, 143.

47. Deren emphasizes that some of the words for the Agwé incantation are drawn from an untraceable language known only to voodoo priests—she conjectures that the word "cina" may have been derived from Arawak Indian, meaning "our father." Deren, *Divine Horsemen*, 275.

48. Mayfield, *The Long Night*, 116.

49. Mayfield's fascination with Haiti and the legacy of Toussaint Louverture prefigured his commitment to a postcolonial and internationalist notion of black independence politics and his work in the Caribbean for the Forbes Burnham regime in Guyana—one of the subjects of the next chapter.

50. Interestingly, Black Papa is a figure redolent of another tricksterlike cart pusher, namely, Peter Wheatstraw in Ralph Ellison's *Invisible Man* (1952). Peetie Wheatstraw is

a name referring to a famous folkloric badman who married Satan's daughter—hence his moniker as "The Devil's Son-in-Law." The contradictory interface of the folkloric and modernity is highlighted here by the fact that Ellison's jive-talking and blues-singing Peetie pushes a cart full of jettisoned architectural blueprints aimlessly around Harlem streets. In a further twist, Peetie Wheatstraw refers both backward to the badman blues artist (of the previous chapter) and forward to the adopted badman persona of blaxploitation artist, Rudy Ray Moore (one focus of the next chapter).

51. Mayfield, *The Hit*, 100.

52. Mayfield, *The Long Night*, 32. Hereafter cited in text.

53. Chester Himes, *A Rage in Harlem* (New York: Vintage Books, 1991) 93. *A Rage in Harlem* was first published as *For Love of Imabelle* in 1957.

54. Fabre and Skinner, *Conversations with Chester Himes*, 10.

55. Ibid., 102.

56. Ibid., 129.

57. Ibid., 26–27.

58. Addison Gayle Jr., *The Way of the New World: The Black Novel in America* (Garden City, NY: Anchor Press/Doubleday, 1975), 159.

59. Gayle, *The Way of the New World*, 159.

60. Fabre and Skinner, *Conversations with Chester Himes*, 28.

61. Chester Himes, *My Life of Absurdity: The Autobiography of Chester Himes, Volume II* (New York: Thunder's Mouth Press, 1976), 181.

62. Ibid., 181.

63. Ibid., 181–82.

64. Fabre and Skinner, *Conversations with Chester Himes*, 49. When asked in an interview about his experience of the Harlem Renaissance, Rudolph "Bud" Fisher is the first author that comes to Himes's mind—and the inclusion of Fisher in the list of greats who used to meet at the Theresa Hotel in Harlem's heyday in *Blind Man with a Pistol* (20) corroborates the impression that Himes had knowledge and high regard for Fisher's writing.

65. Originally, Himes had called his story "The Five Cornered Square," a story about someone so square he had five corners. Himes was told that in French the slang expression for such a person was *La reine des pommes*, the queen of apples. This is how the book got its French title. Himes, *My Life of Absurdity*, 120–121.

66. Himes, *A Rage in Harlem*, 28.

67. Ibid., 77.

68. Ibid., 51.

69. Ibid., 51.

70. Fabre and Skinner, *Conversations with Chester Himes*, 127.

71. Himes, *My Life of Absurdity*, 178.

72. Himes, *A Rage in Harlem*, 47.

73. Ibid., 88.

74. Ibid., 105.

75. Jerry H. Bryant, *Born in a Mighty Bad Land: The Violent Man in African American Folklore and Fiction* (Bloomington: Indiana University Press, 2003), 114.

76. Fabre and Skinner, *Conversations with Chester Himes*, 87.

77. Ibid., 27.

78. Chester Himes, *Blind Man with a Pistol* (New York: Vintage Books, 1989), 153–54. The novel was first published in 1969. Hereafter cited in text.

79. Ibid., 25. The Marcus/Birgit relation revisits Himes's own troubled experience of being a black man in European exile involved in interracial relationships plagued by misunderstandings. It also revisits one of the central themes of his first and most successful social protest novel, *If He Hollers Let Him Go.*

80. Himes, *Blind Man with a Pistol*, 28. Hereafter cited in text.

81. Fabre and Skinner, *Conversations with Chester Himes*, 135.

82. Ibid., 93–94, 106.

83. Ibid., 102.

84. Himes, *Blind Man with a Pistol*, 98–100.

85. Ibid., 140.

86. Victor Anderson, *Beyond Ontological Blackness: An Essay on African American Religious and Cultural Criticism* (New York: Continuum, 1999), 13.

87. Ibid., 120.

88. Abdul JanMohamed, *The Death-Bound-Subject: Richard Wright's Archaeology of Death* (Durham, NC: Duke University Press, 2005), 277.

89. Ibid., 291.

90. Houston Baker Jr., *Blues, Ideology, and Afro-American Literature: A Vernacular Theory* (Chicago: University of Chicago Press, 1984), 139–72.

CHAPTER FOUR

1. Julian Mayfield, "Challenge to Negro Leadership: The Case of Robert Williams," *Commentary* (April 1961), reprinted in *Reporting Civil Rights Part One: American Journalism 1941–1963* (New York: Library of America, 2003), 564.

2. Julian Mayfield, *The Grand Parade* (1961; London: Panther Books, 1964), 306.

3. Kevin K. Gaines, *American Africans in Ghana: Black Expatriates and the Civil Rights Era* (Chapel Hill: University of North Carolina Press, 2006), 146.

4. Mayfield, "Challenge to Negro Leadership," 564.

5. For extensive detail on this incident and the import of Williams, listen to *Robert F. Williams: Self-Defense, Self-Respect, and Self-Determination as Told By Mabel Williams*, audio documentary by The Freedom Archives (2005); and read Timothy B. Tyson, "Robert F. Williams: Black Power and the Roots of the African American Freedom Struggle," *Journal of American History* 85, no. 1 (1998): 540–70; and Gaines, *American Africans in Ghana*, 144–46.

6. Gaines, *American Africans in Ghana*, 146.

7. Ibid., 136–78. Gaines provides a detailed consideration of Mayfield's significance as an activist in exile in chapter 5, "Escape to Ghana: Julian Mayfield and the Radical 'Afros.'"

8. While for the purposes of this book I go no further in covering Mayfield's political and intellectual travels, it should be noted that he took up the expatriate ideal again in Guyana and went on to work and write at many distinguished U.S. universities.

9. Although the film suggests that King's funeral took place four days after his death, the actual ceremony took place five days later, on April 9.

10. Marking Clarence's deviance as queer can be read as symptomatically homopho-

bic, but the film's more general critique of the intolerantly macho "normative" world of black revolutionary force undermines such a reading. And the sympathetic treatment of Clarence, as a man without a home in either the company of revolutionary brothers or the white world, deliberately conjoins Tank's predicament with his own.

11. Vincent Canby, review of *Up Tight!, New York Times,* December 19, 1968, at http://movies.nytimes.com/movie/review?res=9F03E3DF1430E034BC4152DFB4678383679EDE; Roger Ebert, review of *Up Tight!, Chicago Sun-Times*, February 19, 1969, at http://rogerebert.suntimes.com/apps/pbcs.dll/article?AID=/19690219/REVIEWS/902190301/1023.

12. Paula Massood, *Black City Cinema: African American Urban Experiences in Film* (Philadelphia: Temple University Press, 2003), 80.

13. Cecile Starr, "Boris Kaufman," *International Dictionary of Film and Filmmakers* (Gale, 2001), online reference; also available at "filmreference.com," http://www.filmreference.com/Writers-and-Production-Artists-Ja-Kr/Kaufman-Boris.html.

14. While the film has disappeared into relative obscurity—still unreleased on VHS or DVD—Booker T. and the MGs' soundtrack album, *Up Tight* (Stax Records, 1970) has enjoyed a different fate.

15. See Vincent Canby, review of *The Long Night*, *New York Times*, April 11, 1976, at http://movies.nytimes.com/movie/review?res=9900E2D91231E034BC4952DFB266838D669EDE.

16. New York Public Library, Schomburg Center for Research in Black Culture, "Biographical Sketch" of Julian Mayfield—available online via the New York Public Library Digital Library Collections, at http://digilib.nypl.org/dynaweb/ead/scm/scmayfld/@Generic_BookTextView/171;pt=137. Accessed June 14, 2009.

17. Manning Marable, *Race, Reform, and Rebellion: The Second Reconstruction in Black America, 1945–1990*, rev. 2nd ed. (Jackson: University Press of Mississippi, 1991), 94–96.

18. Greil Marcus, *Mystery Train: Images of America in Rock 'n' Roll Music*, 4th ed. (London: Plume, 1997), 72.

19. Ibid., 78; and Jim Irvin, *Mojo Magazine*, October 1998, sleeve notes for *There's a Riot Going On*, 1998 re-release of the 1971 album.

20. Rickey Vincent, *Funk: The Music, the People, and the Rhythm of the One* (New York: St. Martin's Griffin, 1996), 247.

21. Massood, *Black City Cinema*, 80.

22. Ibid., 92.

23. Vincent Canby, review of *Cotton Comes to Harlem*, *New York Times*, June 11, 1970, at http://movies.nytimes.com/movie/review?res=9C0CEFD61439E63BBC4952DFB066838B669EDE.

24. "Civil Rights Groups Attack Black Films," *Jet*, September 14, 1972, 50.

25. *Ebony,* December 1972, 62.

26. *Jet*, 50.

27. *Ebony*, 62.

28. *Jet*, 50.

29. Ibid., 56.

30. Darius James, *That's Blaxploitation: Roots of the Baadasssss 'Tude (Rated X by an All-Whyte Jury)* (New York: St Martin's Griffin, 1995), 156.

31. *Ebony*, 60.

32. S. Craig Watkins, *Representing: Hip Hop Culture and the Production of Black Cinema* (Chicago: University of Chicago Press, 1998), 93–96.

33. Donald Bogle, *Toms, Coons, Mulattoes, Mammies, & Bucks: An Interpretive History of Blacks in American Films*, 4th ed. (New York: Continuum, 2001), 241.

34. Ed Guerrero, *Framing Blackness: The African American Image in Film* (Philadelphia: Temple University Press, 1993), 93.

35. Peter Stanfield, "Walking the Streets: Black Gangsters and the 'Abandoned City' in the 1970s Blaxploitation Cycle," in *Mob Cultures: Hidden Histories of the American Gangster Film*, ed. Lee Grieveson, Esther Sonnet, and Peter Stanfield (New Brunswick, NJ: Rutgers University Press, 2005), 286–87.

36. Ibid., 295.

37. Massood, *Black City Cinema*, 80.

38. George Lipsitz, *American Studies in a Moment of Danger* (Minneapolis: University of Minnesota Press, 2001), 198.

39. Mikel Koven, *Blaxploitation Films* (Harpenden, UK: Pocket Essentials, 2001), 63–64.

40. Ibid., 64.

41. James, *That's Blaxploitation*, 128.

42. Eithne Quinn, *Nuthin' but a "G" Thang: The Culture and Commerce of Gangsta Rap* (New York: Columbia University Press, 2005).

43. R. D. Abrahams, *Deep Down in the Jungle: Negro Narrative Folklore from the Streets of Philadelphia*, 2nd ed. (Chicago: Aldine, 1970); Alan Dundes, *Mother Wit from the Laughing Barrel: Readings in the Interpretation of Afro-American Folklore* (Englewood Cliffs, NJ: Prentice Hall, 1973); Bruce Jackson, *Get Your Ass in the Water and Swim Like Me: Narrative Poetry from Black Oral Tradition* (Cambridge, MA: Harvard University Press, 1974); D. Wepman, R. B. Newman, and M. B. Binderman, *The Life: The Lore and Folk Poetry of the Black Hustler* (Los Angeles: Holloway House, 1976).

44. John W. Roberts, *From Trickster to Badman: The Black Folk Hero in Slavery and Freedom* (Philadelphia: University of Pennsylvania Press, 1989), 182.

45. Ibid., 202–3.

46. David L. Shabazz and Julian L. D. Shabazz, *Dolemite: The Story of Rudy Ray Moore* (Clinton, SC: Awesome Records, 1996), 20.

47. M. J. Murray, "'Thank You For Lettin Me Be Myself': The Story of Rudy Ray Moore aka Dolemite," Rudy Ray Moore Official Web site, Biography, at http://www.shockingimages.com/dolemite/biography.php (accessed July 3, 2006).

48. Rudy Ray Moore Official Web site, Albums: *Eat Out More Often*, at http://www.shockingimages.com/dolemite/albums/eatout.php (accessed July 3, 2006).

49. Murray, "Thank You For Lettin Me Be Myself." See also liner notes to Moore's album, *Hully Gully Fever*, Norton Records, 2000.

50. James, *That's Blaxploitation*, 129.

51. Shabazz and Shabazz, *Dolemite*, 20.

52. James, *That's Blaxploitation*, 128.

53. Henry Louis Gates Jr., *The Signifying Monkey: A Theory of African-American Literary Criticism* (New York: Oxford University Press, 1989), xxiv.

54. Stuart Hall, "What Is This 'Black' in Black Popular Culture?," in *Black Popular Culture: A Project by Michele Wallace*, ed. Gina Dent (Seattle: Bay Press, 1992), 27–28.

55. Shabazz and Shabazz, *Dolemite*, 15.

56. Ibid., 39.

57. L. Parker, "Rap Lyrics Likened to Literature; Witness in 2 Live Crew Trial Cites Art, Parody, Precedents," *Washington Post*, October 20, 1990, D1, cited by Kimberle Crenshaw, "The 2 Live Crew Controversy," in *Feminism and Pornography*, ed. Drucilla Cornell (Oxford: Oxford University Press, 2000), 232.

58. Crenshaw, "The 2 Live Crew Controversy," 222.

59. Ibid., 224.

CHAPTER FIVE

1. Greg Goode, "Donald Goines," *Dictionary of Literary Biography 33: Afro-American Fiction Writers after 1955* (Columbia, SC: Bruccoli-Clark, 1984), 99.

2. DMX, foreword to *Low Road: The Life and Legacy of Donald Goines*, by Eddie B. Allen Jr. (2004; New York: St. Martin's Griffin, 2008), ix–x.

3. See Eddie Stone, *Donald Writes No More: A Biography of Donald Goines* (Los Angeles: Holloway House, 1974) and Allen, *Low Road* on the speculation that Goines's murder was the result of a fallout with his drug connection or the result of his writing threatening to expose real criminals to authorities.

4. Peter Gilstrap, "The House That Blacks Built," *New Times Los Angeles*, October 15–21, 1998, at http://www.newtimesla.com/1998/101598/feature1-2.html.

5. Ibid.

6. Ibid., at http://www.newtimesla.com/1998/101598/feature1-3.html.

7. Stone, *Donald Writes No More*, 136–39.

8. Ibid., 139–41.

9. Ibid., 157; Allen, *Low Road*, 114.

10. Allen, *Low Road*, 152–53.

11. Jerry H. Bryant, *Born in a Mighty Bad Land: The Violent Man in African American Folklore and Fiction* (Bloomington: Indiana University Press, 2003), 140–41.

12. William L. Van Deburg, *Black Camelot: African-American Culture Heroes in Their Times, 1960–1980* (Chicago: University of Chicago Press, 1997), 140.

13. Gilstrap, "The House That Blacks Built," at http://www.newtimesla.com/1998/101598/feature1-2.html.

14. Goode, "Donald Goines," 99.

15. Michael Eric Dyson, *Holler If You Hear Me: Searching for Tupac Shakur* (London: Plexus, 2001), 96.

16. Tupac Shakur, "Tradin' War Stories," on *All Eyez On Me* (1996).

17. Ghostface Killah, "Child's Play," on *Supreme Clientele* (1998).

18. RZA, "Trippin'," *Gravediggas 6 Feet Deep* (1994).

19. Nas, "Escobar '97," on *Men in Black Soundtrack* (1997).

20. See Wikipedia entry on Goines for a list of rap artists who cite Goines, at http://en.wikipedia.org/wiki/Donald_Goines#Influence.

21. Tracy Grant, "Why Hip-Hop Heads Love Donald Goines—African American Author—Brief Article—Critical Essay," *Black Issues Book Review* (September 2001), at http://findarticles.com/p/articles/mi_m0HST/is_5_3/ai_78226542/?tag=content;col1.

22. Kool G Rap cited in Keith Curtis, *Pimpin Ain't Easy: An Education on the Life* (Lakewood, OH: Condos on the Moon Publishing, 2006), 33.

23. Curtis, *Pimpin Ain't Easy*, 33.

24. Ibid., 32.

25. Allen, *Low Road*, 194.

26. Ibid., 160.

27. Dan Flory, *Philosophy, Black Film, Film Noir* (University Park: University of Pennsylvania Press, 2008), 280.

28. Allen, *Low Road*, x.

29. While this cycle did not constitute the bulk of African American filmmaking during the 1990s, it attracted the most media debate, which only fed audience interest at the box office and encouraged formulaic repetition and generic consolidation.

30. The release of *New Jack City* in March 1991 (the month of the Rodney King incident), was greeted by violence, and *Boyz N the Hood*'s premiere in July of the same year sparked violent reactions at theaters nationwide, leading to two dead and thirty wounded (Ed Guerrero, *Framing Blackness: The African American Image in Film* [Philadelphia: Temple University Press, 1993], 183). It should be noted that concern about the moral value of the hood cycle was part of a more general attack on the hard-core violent or sexually explicit elements of hip hop at the time, especially gangsta rap.

31. See Jonathan Munby, *Public Enemies, Public Heroes: Screening the Gangster from* Little Caesar *to* Touch of Evil (Chicago: University of Chicago Press, 1999).

32. See Donald Bogle, *Toms, Coons, Mulattoes, Mammies, & Bucks: An Interpretive History of Blacks in American Films*, 4th ed. (New York: Continuum, 2001); Patricia Hill Collins, *Black Feminist Thought: Knowledge, Consciousness, and the Politics of Empowerment* (New York: Routledge, 1991); Manthia Diawara, ed., *Black American Cinema* (New York: Routledge, 1993); Michael Eric Dyson, *Reflecting Black: African-American Cultural Criticism* (Minneapolis: University of Minnesota Press, 1993); Guerrero, *Framing Blackness*; bell hooks, *Outlaw Culture: Resisting Representations* (New York: Routledge, 1994) and *Reel to Real: Race, Sex and Class at the Movies* (New York: Routledge, 1996); Paula J. Massood, *Black City Cinema: African American Urban Experiences in Film* (Philadelphia: Temple University Press, 2003); S. Craig Watkins, *Representing: Hip Hop Culture and the Production of Black Cinema* (Chicago: University of Chicago Press, 1998).

33. Watkins, *Representing*; Eithne Quinn, *Nuthin' but a "G" Thang: The Culture and Commerce of Gangsta Rap* (New York: Columbia University Press, 2005).

34. See: Manthia Diawara, "*Noir* by *Noirs*: Toward a New Realism in Black Cinema," in *Shades of Noir: A Reader*, ed. Joan Copcek (London: Verso, 1993,) 261–78; and Dan Flory, "Black on White: *Film Noir* and the Epistemology of Race in Recent African American Cinema," *Journal of Social Philosophy* 31, no. 1 (2000): 82–116.

35. From "Amerikkka's Most Wanted" on the eponymous album, 1990.

36. One could also say the cycle's end was signaled by the outpouring of films in the mid-1990s that parodied the hood formula, such as *Don't Be a Menace to South Central While Drinking Your Juice in the Hood* (1996), a film whose title testifies comically to the exhausted nature of the hood film formula by 1996.

37. Figures drawn from Watkins, *Representing*, 190–91, and the Internet Movie Database (IMDb).

38. Massood, *Black City Cinema*, 189, citing Jonathan Bernstein, "Spike Lee," *The Face*, December 1997, 202.

39. Norman K. Denzin, *Reading Race* (London: Sage, 2002), 112.

40. Dyson, *Reflecting Black*, 95; see also hooks, *Outlaw Culture* and *Real to Reel*, and Watkins, *Representing*, for sustained analysis of the patriarchal tenets of the cycle.

41. hooks, *Outlaw Culture*, 116.

42. Watkins, *Representing*, 172.

43. Massood, *Black City* Cinema, 173.

44. Ibid., 7, and chap. 5, 45–174.

45. IMDb, "Business Data for *Menace II Society*," at http://www.imdb.com/title/tt0107554/business, July 30, 2006.

46. Amy Taubin, "Girlz N the Hood," *Sight and Sound* 3, no. 8 (1993).

47. Susan Wloszczyna, "The Brothers Hughes," *USA Today*, October 18, 2001, at http://www.usatoday.com/life/movies/2001-10-18-hughes-brothers.htm.

48. Massood, *Black City Cinema*, 164.

49. Hughes biography by Aubry Anne D'Arminio, *All Movie Guide*, at http://www.allmovie.com.

50. Many of the rappers interviewed typically adopt gangster monikers. In addition to Scarface, the Def Jam stable of gangsta rappers in the documentary include Capone, Big Boi, and Ghostface Killah.

51. See Munby, *Public Enemies, Public Heroes*, for a full treatment of the gangster's ethnic voice.

52. Massood, *Black City Cinema*, 147, citing Henry Louis Gates Jr., "Blood Brothers: Albert and Allen Hughes in the Belly of the Hollywood Beast," *Transition* 63 (1994): 171. See also D'Arminio, *All Movie Guide* and Wloszczyna, "The Brothers Hughes," who reports Hughes Brothers' influences as Steven Spielberg, Martin Scorsese, Brian De Palma's *Scarface*, Francis Ford Coppola's *Apocalypse Now* (1979), Sergio Leone, Oliver Stone, and vintage gangster melodramas.

53. Robert Warshow, *The Immediate Experience: Movies, Comics, Theatre, and Other Aspects of Popular Culture* (New York: Atheneum, 1970), 132–33.

54. This theme is common to most hood films where women are figured as dangerous to gang loyalty.

55. The stuttering character, Smiley, carries around photos of King and Malcolm, which he tries to peddle and fails to explain in what constitute awkward narrative interjections.

56. Robin D. G. Kelley, *Race Rebels: Culture, Politics, and the Black Working Class* (New York: Free Press, 1994), 200–201.

57. Tupac Shakur was gunned down in Las Vegas in September 1996, in the midst of a bitter feud between his West Coast record label, Death Row, and its East Coast gangsta rival, Bad Boy. See Randall Sullivan, *LAbyrinth* (Edinburgh: Canongate, 2002), for a full account of the fatal terms of living up to the gangsta image.

58. *Hip Hop News* FNV Newsletter, "Oakland's Pooh Man Arrested for Bank Robbery," August 2, 1999, at http://daveyd.com/fnvaug2html.

59. Top40-charts.com, "FBI Nabs MC Eiht for Grand Theft Auto," November 18, 2004, at http://top40-charts.com/news.php?nid=11235.

60. Ibid.

61. William L. Van Deburg, *Hoodlum: Black Villains and Social Bandits in American Life*

(Chicago: University of Chicago Press, 2004), 213. See pages 196–214 for coverage of the way the criminal street attributes of gangsta rap were rendered as "moral contagion" in the press and leaders of antirap campaigns in the mid-1990s.

62. hooks, *Outlaw Culture*, 123.

63. Van Deburg, *Hoodlums*, 213–14.

64. Robin D. G. Kelley, *Yo' Mama's Disfunktional: Fighting the Culture Wars in Urban America* (Boston: Beacon Press, 1997), 16–17.

EPILOGUE

1. Nick Tosches, *Where Dead Voices Gather* (Boston: Little, Brown, 2001)

2. Ibid., 281.

3. Tricia Rose, *The Hip Hop Wars: What We Talk About When We Talk About Hip Hop—And Why It Matters* (New York: Basic Books, 2008), 5.

4. Ibid., 9.

5. Ibid., 245.

6. Adrian Hennigan, "Getting Direct with Directors ... Interview No. 18: Antoine Fuqua," BBC, 2004, at http://www.bbc.co.uk/films/callingtheshots/antoine_fuqua.shtml.

7. Ibid.

8. Rebecca Asher-Walsh and Jeff Jensen, "'Gangster' Wrap," *Entertainment Weekly*, October 22, 2004, at http://www.ew.com/ew/article/0,,724273_2,00.html.

9. Hennigan "Getting Direct with Directors."

10. Asher-Walsh and Jensen, "'Gangster' Wrap."

11. Michael Fleming, "'Gangster' Redux," *Variety*, February 13, 2006, at http://www.variety.com/article/VR1117938111.html?categoryid=10&cs=1.

12. Homi Bhabha, *The Location of Culture* (London: Routledge, 1994), 96.

13. Jean Baudrillard, *Symbolic Exchange and Death* (London: Sage, 1993), 40.

14. Abdul JanMohamed, *The Death-Bound-Subject: Richard Wright's Archaeology of Death* (Durham, NC: Duke University Press, 2005), 270.

Index